Robert William Barbour

Letters, Poems And Pensees

Collected For Private Circulation

Robert William Barbour

Letters, Poems And Pensees
Collected For Private Circulation

ISBN/EAN: 9783744653367

Printed in Europe, USA, Canada, Australia, Japan

Cover: Foto ©Thomas Meinert / pixelio.de

More available books at **www.hansebooks.com**

ROBERT W. BARBOUR:

LETTERS, POEMS, AND PENSÉES.

COLLECTED FOR PRIVATE CIRCULATION.

πατρίδα ἐπιζητοῦσι.

Printed at the University Press by
ROBERT MACLEHOSE, WEST NILE STREET
GLASGOW.
1893.

PREFACE.

SCARCELY anything in this book was written for publication. Indeed it is less a book than an album—an album in which some old fellow-students have wished to preserve for their own sakes a few things which remained to them in the handwriting of their friend. The Poems included here are partly taken from an early volume which Mr. Barbour published when leaving College, but many of them are new. The Pensées have been extracted from sources purely informal, and, like the Letters, are printed exactly as they were written.

Published for those who knew him, no detailed biography has been added. But that no attempt even at portraiture is prefixed to these Letters has perhaps the deeper explanation that no hand among us was equal to the task of tracing it. The outward circumstances, indeed, of Robert Barbour's life can be simply told, and in the " Memorial Chronology " they will be found in outline. At the end also are preserved a few delineations of feature which those who knew him less will

be glad to have recalled. But these personal impressions—
for which we have almost reluctantly found room among
his own writings—can never record what he was to us, or
express the quality of his influence. The total effect, also,
of his career upon his country and his church is so bound
up with what he was, that to attempt to summarise it in
records of work done or schemes achieved would be wholly
vain. What Robert Barbour did for his generation was
simply what he *was*. His great work was unconscious. It
lay less in planning reforms, though he had the mind to
conceive them ; or in furthering philanthropies, though he
had the power to carry them out; or in proclaiming ideas,
though his gift of eloquence might have won him a world-
wide hearing. It lay rather in making impressions, impressions upon individual minds and souls, impressions of
saintliness and other-worldliness, of unselfishness, meekness,
and single-eyedness, impressions as of one who habitually
walked with God, and lived only to serve. A genius who
was also a little child, a scholar with an almost elemental
faith, a man of position who made himself of no reputation, one who with a nature and disposition limited, to
start with, in some directions, yet by the grace of
Christ grew so into sympathy and beauty and fulness
of love and life that he made an instantaneous spiritual

mark upon everyone who even casually crossed his path,—this mainly, and increasingly as the years went on, was our friend. It is clear that no printed page can ever reflect, still less perpetuate, an influence such as this. One fact alone, a circumstance that has almost awed us in editing these letters, we must here record—that in going over the large number from which the selection is made, not one has been found among them containing an ungentle word or judgment of any human being: not one which could not be printed as it stands without injuring the feelings or the reputation of the least among the long list of contemporaries to whom he refers.

In addition to the personal object held in view in making this collection, a still more sacred purpose has lain not far in the background. Mr. Barbour has left four children. The heritage they have lost they can never know. But if these pages can preserve for them a few echoes of their father's voice, and convey to them even some faint suggestions of the inner life he lived, and which he would have them follow, the gathering together of these casual words needs no apology.

HENRY DRUMMOND.

CONTENTS.

Memorial Chronology.

Contents.   xi

Letters.

Biographical Notices.

MEMORIAL CHRONOLOGY.

I.

ROBERT WILLIAM BARBOUR was born November 29, 1854. A.D. 1854. Æ.T.
He was the first child of the family after his parents lost
their two boys, Frederick and George, in a railway accident
near Manchester, as narrated in Mrs. Barbour's book, *The
Way Home.* His sister Margaret, now Mrs. Simpson, was in
the accident, but made a marvellous escape. His brother
Hugh, now Dr. Freeland Barbour, and his sister Jane, now
Mrs. Whyte, were younger than he. His father survived
till 1887, and his mother outlived her son a few months.
There were many uncles, aunts, and other relatives living
in different parts of England and Scotland, whom he visited
from time to time. But Springland, Perth, the abode of
his grandmother, Mrs. Stewart Sandeman, whose life was
written by his mother, always was the chief resort till her
death in 1883.

A.D.   Æ.T.   His father and mother influenced him strongly from first to last—the father by his dignity, method and exactness, the mother by her enthusiasm and literary tastes. The atmosphere in which he grew up was intensely religious.

During his boyhood and youth he had two homes—Bonskeid in summer and Edinburgh in winter. To both he was singularly attached—the one becoming the centre of his personal feelings, the other of his public and patriotic sentiments, which were exceptionally strong.

His education was carried on by tutors. For a short time he attended Edinburgh Collegiate School, in Charlotte Square.

As a boy he was shy, difficult and introspective—the very reverse of what he became in later life. For years he poured himself out in private diaries, written in prose and verse, and there are whole volumes of these boyish productions.

1869.   15.   The principal event of his boyhood was the winter spent by the family in the South of France—at Cannes, Nice, Mentone and Pau—in 1869-70. Here he began to be drawn out of himself. In the hotels where the party stayed he formed acquaintance with people of different nationalities. The beauty of the Mediterranean and the Riviera made the deepest impression on him, and he drank in the novel aspects of life at every pore. Always afterwards this period hung in his memory as a dream of romance, and he revisited its scenes in subsequent years with enthusiasm. Here he learned French and Italian. Mrs. Fowler and her daughter Charlotte, who ten years afterwards became his wife, were living that winter in the same hotel at Cannes.

II.

After returning from France Robert, along with his brother Hugh, began his course as a student by entering the University of Edinburgh in November, 1870, where he continued for five years. This proved for him a period of immense labour, excitement and happiness. He distinguished himself in all the classes, except the mathematical, for which he had no aptitude, and he won some eight or ten medals. Not only had he the power of steady, continuous work, but he could, at a crisis, put on a spurt which carried everything before it. He finished his course by graduating with first-class honours both in Classics and Philosophy—at that time a very rare performance in Edinburgh—and gaining the Rhind Fellowship in Mental Philosophy.

He would have followed a common enough course if at this stage he had passed to an English University; but he preferred, with great deliberateness, to commence at once the study of Theology with a view to the ministry of the Free Church, and for this purpose entered the New College, Edinburgh, in November, 1875. Here the course lasted other four years, and at the exit examination in 1879 he took the highest place, gaining the first Cunningham Fellowship.

The brevity of the Scotch academic session, which lasts only from November to April, allows students who may be so disposed to take a summer session at a German University; and between his first and second sessions he availed himself of this opportunity by taking the summer session at the University of Tübingen. This opened to him the treasures of German theological literature, though his stay was too short to give him a real mastery of the language. In the holidays he made excursions in the Black Forest, and on the way home he took a wide circuit by Vienna, Dresden and Berlin, going down the Danube as far as Belgrade—that part of Europe being at the time aflame with the Bulgarian atrocities, which stirred his deepest emotions. He had made a brief tour in Italy with Professor Simpson in 1872, and he visited the Paris Exhibition in 1878.

Crowded with work as his college years were, he yet A.D. ÆT.
found time for other interests. He threw himself into the
social life both of the University and the New College,
and distinguished himself as a speaker, especially in the
Theological Society. He had many friends, the classes to
which he belonged containing men of great brilliance and
singularly high tone, to whom he attached himself. Thus
he learned still more to live in others, and divested himself of the somewhat morbid tendencies of his boyhood.

During this period also he took a sympathetic part in
two religious movements. The one was the first visit of
Mr. Moody to Scotland in 1874. In the summer of that
year he, along with a friend and fellow-student (now the
Rev. Frank Gordon, of Vienna), accompanied Rev. Dr.
Burns, of Kirkliston, and Rev. Dr. Wilson, of the Barclay
Church, Edinburgh, on a visit to America, and in many
cities of the United States and Canada helped to tell of
the revival of religion in Britain. Copious notes of this
tour from his pen appeared in a periodical entitled *Times
of Blessing*. The other movement, in which he took a still
more active part, was a series of remarkable religious services
for children carried on in Edinburgh by Mr. Spiers in 1877.

Before his College course closed he published anony-
mously a volume of poems entitled *Jeroveam's Wife*. 1879. 24.
b

A.D.   Æ.T.   III.

1879.   24.   In the Scottish Church, when a student has completed his theological course, he is licensed to preach by his Presbytery, and thereby becomes eligible to be called by any vacant congregation to be their minister. At this stage he is termed a probationer, and frequently spends a year or more as assistant to an ordained minister. Of course the time of waiting varies in different cases. Robert left College in 1879, and was not settled in a charge of his own till near the end of 1881.

In May, 1879, he attended, at Springfield—the country house, near Cupar, of Provost Swan, of Kirkcaldy—a meeting of a club, formed a year before by a number of companions, most of whom were rather in advance of him, for the purpose of prolonging the friendships of College into subsequent life. For some fantastic reason this club was denominated the Gaiety, and it has met every year since for a week in May, the place of reunion changing from year to year. He was nearly always present, both giving and receiving abundantly; and these friendships ripened as time went on. The other members have been Rev. James Brown, Professor Drummond, Rev. John F. Ewing, Rev. Frank Gordon, Rev. D. M. Ross, Rev. Alex. Skene, Professor

G. A. Smith, Rev. Dr. Stalker, Provost Swan, Rev. John A.D.   ÆT.
Watson.

September 25, 1879, he was married at Corsham, Wilts, 1879.   24.
to Charlotte R. Fowler, daughter of Sir Robert Fowler,
who was twice Lord Mayor of London. By his marriage
he was brought into acquaintance with a wide circle of
relatives, in experience and church connection different from
him ; but this was only another opportunity of widening
his own sympathy and experience, as he had by this time
acquired complete openness for all forms of goodness, though
he remained intensely devoted to the interests of his own
church and country.

The marriage tour was an extended one—to South Africa,
and it lasted about a year. In Natal he met with Bishop
Colenso, and became interested in the native problem.
They stayed long at Lovedale, where he taught for a time
in the Institution ; and he formed a warm attachment to
Dr. and Mrs. Stewart. The scenery of some of the more
romantic parts of the country, and the habits and customs
of the natives suggested to his mind numerous remarkable
coincidences with the *Iliad*, which he and Mrs. Barbour
were studying on the journey ; and he embodied these
impressions in a pamphlet entitled, *Homer on the Katberg*.

When they returned to Scotland in the autumn of 1880,

A.D.   Æt. various suggestions were pressed on him as to his future work. He was urgently requested, for example, to become minister of a new charge at North Queensferry. But he decided to seek some experience first in an assistantship; and, before the year ended, they settled in the town of Brechin, where he continued for several months as assistant under the genial superintendence of the Rev. John Fraser.

IV.

1881.   26.   Having been called by the congregation of Cults, he was ordained there October 13, 1881.

Cults is the second station out of Aberdeen on the Deeside Railway. It is near enough the city to allow its minister to feel the influence of the commercial and academic centre and to take part in its public life; yet it is quite a country place, situated on the edge of the valley of the Dee, up which the Braemar mountains are visible in the distance. The congregation consists partly of villa people, whose business is in Aberdeen, and partly of the rural population; and it is of considerable size, with possibilities of extension.

He was full of enthusiasm for the work, and threw

himself into it with ardour. His sermons absorbed the greatest portion of his time and strength; but he also visited assiduously; and he put into operation every kind of appliance for the good of the people which the Christian zeal of our age has been able to devise. He devoted himself especially to the young, and took immense pains with the farm servants—a class whose condition never afterwards ceased to exercise his mind. His influence was felt in many ways in Aberdeen, where there soon sprang up a singular reverence and affection for him. In 1882 Mr. Moody, who was evangelizing in the city, went out to Cults and held an impressive service. While, however, he thus spent himself for his congregation and for every class in it, perhaps his most characteristic work was done for individuals. Whenever he met with any case of special necessity—such as a poor person in illness, or a drunkard verging towards *delirium tremens*, or a student in need of means—his whole being was for the time occupied; he would visit the house incessantly; carry anything with his own hands; and not let go till his end was accomplished. If these cases could be collected, the record of them would form one of the most unique pages in the history of the modern ministry; but they are sacredly kept in the memory of those whom he

A.D.   ÆT. benefited till the day which will bring all hidden things to light.

His friends at a distance were always waiting for some literary product of his thought and learning; but for this he was too busy at home. Yet, in 1882, he produced an essay of an elaborate character on *John Knox*, which was published in a series entitled *The Evangelical Succession;* and this was perhaps his best effort in prose. He had previously published a magazine article on the Theology of Beck, under whom he studied at Tübingen. He immensely enjoyed a visit to Bishop Lightfoot in 1882; and interest in Luther's life took him to the Luther places in Central Germany, in the summer of 1883.

Most who saw him for the first time in those years, with his tall figure, pale face, bright and eager eye, thought that he had not strength for anything like the amount of work he was imposing on himself. But his friends had faith in his muscular vigour, which had long been wont to prove equal to immense efforts. At length, however, it began to be manifest that the sword was too keen for the scabbard. This was hastened by domestic affliction, which told on his sensitive nature with shattering

1884.   29. effect. In the beginning of 1884 Mrs. Barbour was laid down with severe and prolonged illness; and in the

midst of this anxiety their second child, Robin, somewhat ^{A.D.}　ÆT.
suddenly died.　That winter it was necessary to proceed
to the South of France; and, after a summer and autumn
at home, a portion of the following winter was spent in
Egypt.　It was feared that similar long absences might
still be necessary in the future.　Besides, his own health
was suffering from the strain.　With great reluctance he
had at length to face the idea of quitting Cults.　At first
he thought of a change to a charge in some milder spot;
and there was talk for some time of a transference to the
English Presbyterian Church at Bournemouth.　But ulti-
mately it was decided to be necessary to abandon, at least
for a time, the active duties of the ministry; and he re-
signed his charge in November, 1886, after having held ^{1886.　32.}
it for five years.

V.

After the resignation he proceeded with Mrs. Barbour
to Corsica, where they were surprised by the news of his
father's death.　Thence they went to Sicily and the South
of France.　In the spring of 1889 they were again in Italy.
In both 1887 and 1889 he paid brief visits to Ireland, being
keenly interested in the Irish question.　After his father's

death he resided at Bonskeid, till in November, 1889, he acquired the neighbouring property of Fincastle, with a good house, in which he established himself, while his mother occupied Bonskeid. Of his children the eldest, Freeland, was born February 15, 1882 ; Robin, whose death has been already mentioned, November 15, 1883 ; Maida, July 3, 1885 ; Margaret, August 12, 1887 ; Gwendolen, February 21, 1890.

Though he was now living in retirement, his interest in the world and in the kingdom of God continued unabated ; and opportunities of usefulness of various kinds soon presented themselves without his seeking. He preached frequently in the Glen of Fincastle, where his family have maintained service in a private chapel for a lengthened period ; and his many ministerial friends throughout the country were always eager to avail themselves of his help. The reading and answering of letters, which poured in on him from every side, asking for pecuniary assistance for individuals and causes, occupied much of his time ; for he made the distribution of a very large proportion of his means for good objects a part of the business of life. He was asked to enter parliament, a constituency which could have been easily won being offered him ; and some of his friends believed that this was the work for which he was peculiarly fitted; but he was resolute in refusing, on the ground that, if strength were given him again, it was already covenanted to the ministry of the gospel. He accepted, however, the presidency of the Scottish Branch of the Anti-Opium League, and he both spoke and wrote strongly on this and the kindred subject of Temperance. His father had for many years acted as President for Scotland to the China Mission of the English Presbyterian Church, and, at his death, Robert took over this position. His door was always open to provide a resort for missionaries home on furlough; and one of his projected schemes was a visit to the stations of this mission in China. He did not live to carry his design into effect; but since his death it has been accomplished by his brother.

In 1888 Professor Lindsay was sent out to India on a special commission by the Foreign Missions Committee of the Free Church, and someone had to be appointed to fill his place in Glasgow College during his absence. The Senatus asked Robert to undertake this duty, and he 1888. 34. agreed. He brought his family to Glasgow, to the great joy of his friends there, and rented a furnished house for the winter. He read the Professor's lectures, at the same time, however, studying the subject—Church History—

A.D.   ÆT. with care as he went on, and making the work living by adding much of his own. He enjoyed it, and the students spoke enthusiastically of the spiritual influence which he exerted in the College.

In the summers of 1889 and 1890 there were gatherings at Bonskeid of students, representing the various religious and missionary societies in most of the Universities of England and Scotland, and here also he was thoroughly in his element, enjoying the spectacle of many fresh minds in friendly collision with each other, and of men with different traditions and creeds brought together to talk harmoniously about the religious and social interests common to all Christians.

1890.   35. Next year a juncture arose in the United Presbyterian Divinity Hall in Edinburgh, through the death of one of the professors, similar to that in which he had lent his aid in Glasgow, and he was invited by Principal Cairns and the College Committee to conduct the class during the winter, 1890-91. To this he readily consented, both because he liked such work and because an act of courtesy to a sister church might forward the interests of union. He was preparing to fulfil this engagement, and in October took his family to Edinburgh, where a temporary home was secured. But the work was destined never to com-

mence. In August he had caught a cold, which settled A.D.   ÆT.
down on his lungs. He strove hard to get rid of it,
especially as the College session drew nigh. But it clung
to him, and the commencement of his lectures had to be
deferred to Christmas. Long before this date arrived,
however, it had become manifest that he was in the
grasp of dangerous disease. Week after week, amidst hope
and fear, in spite of everything being done that medical
skill and domestic love could contrive, the illness pursued
its inevitable course. In February he travelled to Mentone,
and thence in May to Aix-les-Bains, where, on May 27, 1891. 36.
he passed into eternal peace.

Besides Mrs. Barbour, Dr. and Mrs. Whyte and Professor Drummond were present at the close. They brought
home the beloved dust, and he was laid in the lonely
burying-ground, amidst the weeping birches, in the West
Wood at Bonskeid, side by side with his child Robin and
his father; and there, a few months later, his mother
was also buried.

As this brief record has been written for the eyes of
those who knew him and do not require any description
of his character, it has been confined, as far as possible,

to the bare facts of his outward life. Yet it is not easy to lay down the pen without at least a word of thankful recognition for what he was made by the grace of God.

As has been already indicated, his character underwent, in the course of years, a decided development, and it grew and clarified until the end. Perhaps the completeness of this transformation was the most remarkable element in his history. From being close and unsociable, he grew to be the very soul of frankness, enthusiasm and unselfishness. Though he never lost a certain grand air on appropriate occasions, he learned to stoop to the weakest and the least.

It will, for example, be remembered by all his friends with what reverent affection he was regarded by the servants in every household in which he was familiar. A good deal has been said above about his intellectual eminence; and as a student he had his own share of ambition. But in his later life he hid the gifts of learning out of sight; and many who approached him or heard him preach had no idea of the resources concealed beneath the simplicity of his manner and the earnestness of his words.

It was the love of man entering into him which made him forget himself. The philanthropic and missionary instincts of the age took complete possession of him, not running to seed in words, but embodying themselves in acts. Misery of every kind touched him to the quick, and his feelings blazed up, even to excess, in the presence of selfishness and wrong. A visit from him to the house of any of his friends was like the coming of sunshine; and, when they went to his, they were ashamed of the kindness with which he overwhelmed them.

But there was a still more transforming passion at work. On very rare occasions he mentioned to those most intimate with him a day at Springland, in his boyhood, when between him and Christ there took place something about which he could give no very connected account, but which marked a crisis and a beginning. From this seed there grew that which at length overspread his entire existence. During his later years all who knew him remarked his Christ-likeness. Even in these years, indeed, he often displayed a rollicking buoyancy of spirits; and he had always been fond of fun. Yet there was withal something tense, pure and absorbed, which made a unique impression. Even those thrown casually into his company felt that they had met something such as they had not seen before; and an interview of a few hours with him sometimes made a mark on a young soul to endure for a lifetime. It was the indescribable influence of holiness. Many throughout his native land had come to think of Robert Barbour as one apart, who, if he were spared, might intervene in our affairs with a power and an effect all his own. My own strongest wish was that he might sometime pour all the resources of his mind into a great poem, instinct with Christian feeling and conviction, which would take rank with the classics of our literature. There were so many possibilities! for he had hardly begun to put forth the powers that lay in him. It has pleased the Eternal Wisdom to resume all into Himself, leaving the world so much emptier for us. But we know that everything will unfold there and fulfil its purpose under far happier conditions; and we thank Him for granting us to enjoy this gift so long.

JAMES STALKER.

PENSÉES.

PENSEES.

FRIENDS electrify each other; there is a dulling down when they part.

Avignon, April, 1885.

A TENDER heart with wounds is better than woodenness without.

Oct. 30, 1885.

THE Lord's goodness surrounds us at every moment. I walk through it almost with difficulty, as through thick grass and flowers.

May 22, 1879.

CHILDREN have the effect on your spirit that morning air has on your body. There is no exhaustion in them; they are charged with life and health and sunshine.

Moyallon, July 23, 1889.

A

THERE is something very strange to me in a child's voice. It is like a sound from a better life and a better land, so simple and pure.

Edinburgh, Oct. 26, 1882.

CHILDREN do more for us in our hours of joy than we know; Browning teaches, in Jochanan Hakkadosh, I think, how much they may do in an hour of sorrow.

Nov. 27, 1889.

THEY used to say that old blood could be made young by pouring young blood in. I think they meant that children, either natural or spiritual, were the grand restorers.

Cults, May 30, 1884.

THE possession of a child of one's own opens up the possibility of an entirely new world of experience, and therefore of an entirely fresh revelation of the First Author and Supreme Object of all experience. I think I have told you before what my first thought was when I caught sight of a little living, moving, grumbling thing, mouthing its fingers and rubbing its fists in its eyes, on the floor before the fire. It was as if the Father in heaven had fairly (if it is not irreverent to say so) shaken hands— offered me His hand—and said, Thou art forgiven.

Mentone, Saturday, December 13. 1884.

I THINK I would get cured of the disease of unsatisfied desire if I saw a few souls won to Christ through me.

Cults, May 30, 1884.

ONE yearns to unite the deepest revelry of soul in spiritual things, with the clearest mind to report upon them to others —and especially to men in need.

Cults, May 30, 1884.

I AM trying to watch and pray hour by hour, but it is no easier to learn to do that than it was 1800 years ago. The second hour is as difficult as the first; and I have learned to fear that the third may be the hardest of all; and one just wakens to find the Master is on foot once more, and needs watching with no longer.

Cults, May 14, 1884.

THE artist is known by his omissions as much as by what he includes.

Ajaccio, Jan. 22, 1887.

"WE shall meet where death shall not dissever." I have just read these words at the head of one of Knox's letters. He has a way of writing something of that sort at the top of the page—a prayer or a promise—and, like everything he does, it is as full of beauty as meaning. His life is only another revelation of how rich their lives are made who are truly God's people—how thought-full and sympathetic and suggestive. One learns on every page how real goodness deepens a man's humanity every way.

April 18, 1882.

THE ornament of a meek and quiet spirit is like the dust from flowers in bloom. It insinuates and instils. The meek man is not without opinions, or a stranger to enterprise. He does not live in an untroubled sphere, but he has no desire to see his opinion imposed on any. Children find out the meek, for meekness is the childhood of the soul. Haughty men are never young, the meek never grow old. Most of us have known some. The young are warmed by them, the middle-aged soothed, and the old supported.

Meek hearts live for ever. They are the stock of an immortal tree. They inherit lives that live after them, they are spiritual children. David says, "God is meek": Christ says, "I am meek." The Holy Spirit's emblem is a dove. The dove comes when you do not stir it. Ask gently in silent prayer. He came thus to Christ and will to you when kneeling and broken down. Thou, who art Thyself meek and lowly, take pity and create in us Thy meekness.

Pitlochrie, Aug. 1889.

IT is pleasant in beginnings (household, no less than those of a higher kind) that you can for a time at least refuse everything that is not beautiful or that has not a beautiful association. Nothing enriches a life like rich surroundings; and we have scarcely a book, picture, or piece of furniture which does not call up the affection, or at least the *idea*, of a friend. Everything we have is either a memory or a memento of someone dear to us; so that, when the friends themselves have visited us, certain parts of the house stand out for a little afterwards like the traces of phosphorescence in the dark.

Cults, Nov. 29, 1881.

GRACE or favour (in the Old Testament) means the immense honour (and sometimes even outward beauty) which God's goodness confers on a man. It refers to the unspeakable ennoblement of the whole of human nature

by its contact with God. So it may come to mean (as
in Psa. xc.) the sort of "beauty" or "glory" (in the New
Testament) which passes upon Christians from the presence
of their Master, clothing them with radiance, winningness
and power.

May 26, 1879.

NOW the sun is strong, and I get my strength for arm
and limb from him ; but for *its* strength my heart travels
to God and to home; for he who is near Christ is near
the hearthfire.

Dec. 5, 1883.

THE rarest Christian graces—you can almost see them
springing up day by day ; as you fancy you hear the
grass grow in hot climates after rain, marked with the
high healthy colour and the dew of youth. Tears are
too large for the little eyes. There (in that little believer)
is one of the fruits of the Spirit, one of the first, finest,
and most inimitable of them all—care for another soul ;
and all of a night's growth.

The work begins to exert an indescribable fascination
over the worker ; infinite openings suggest themselves as

the conversation goes on ; he is guided to the right word by a sure instinct ; there springs up in him unconsciously that deft and delicate touch which in other things we call "tact"; he learns to give the little ones less pain, to be faithful and to be gentle ; he finds not two things, but only different ways of one. Meantime his own faith has helps unheard of ; the realities of Eternity take living shape and form; he gains confirmation of his own experience in that which is passing under his eyes ; he sees the thing going on "outside of himself," independently of anything he may say or do ; it is *there*, a great power, a supernatural influence. Another is there, who worketh like the wind, which bloweth where it listeth. He feels as those three disciples must have felt whom Christ took in with Him alone into the sick-room and the chamber of death, not to say anything or do anything or even lend a helping hand, but simply to keep as still as possible and not interrupt Him at His wonder-working, as it went on in their very presence.

ONE thing is evident in Mr. ——. He has a perfect passion for children : the world for him is made up of little ones. On the street he sees nothing else. Indeed,

had he been in heaven, we firmly believe he would tell
us he had not noticed any old people there. . . Such
singing it is—just talking in song. The little lines might
be unharnessed out of their rhymes and stand as texts
or bits of an address by themselves.

Feb. 1878.

WE are having bright warm days again after last week's
rain, four inches of which fell in a day or two. . . About
the hymns—it would be well, I think, to introduce as many
as possible which the boys actually sung, or, if not, at
least about the things they are interested in. Do not let
it be all "goody-goody," a great mistake in children's services, and let there be as little about "death" and "grief"
and "pain" and "mist on the mountains" as you can
—the former of which frightens children—except those
who are being made ready for it, who need no "ministries
of song." The "grief and pain" and "earthly-friends-may-
leave-and-fail-us" business, though true enough, never touched
me one bit—though, perhaps, the children of the poor know
more about it. The children in the Emigrant Home in
Lauriston, I remember, always chose "hard trials and
tribulations," or something of that sort, when they had

their choice. So there should be something put in for juvenile martyrs, perhaps, only not much.

Then there ought to be some things with *really good music*. Luther always would have that. It is a faculty— a child's fine ear—that we evangelicals cannot too early capture for God. Then there are a number of fine things in our new hymn - book, which should not be lost sight of. Last, there are the "Jubilees" and "Spiers'" Collection.

Mentone, Feb. 6, 1885.

ONLY hearts that do not live in themselves know what life is. Nur Herzen die aüsser sich leben haben Erlebnisse.

North Berwick, July 16, 1890.

IT is good for us to know that some whose studies lead them into strange places, and into utterances about parts of God's revelation so unlike what we have been accustomed to and may think ourselves still bound by reason as well as tradition to believe, are at heart rooted and grounded in the very faith and love from which we draw our lives. Every day I live I hear, louder

and more loud, that saying of our Lord : " JUDGE NOT
THAT YE BE NOT JUDGED." What a word that is for
disciples.

North Berwick, July 7, 1890.

HOW different —— was in his colleague days. I remember him massive, and powerful, and conscience-striking as
now, holding your intellect, winning your reverence. But
what a difference! *Then* he was like a half-trained lion
going along in harness with another lion — older, and
mightier, and thoroughly trained—giving a lurch, shaking
his shoulders, and "raxing out" the reins and other harness
occasionally, as if there was something more in him, but
then relapsing again into the becoming, eighteen-forty-
three regulation stride, to keep step with the old lion ;
but never, almost never at least, fairly breaking out and
loose, and going all fours into the air, harness and chariot
along with him, in the way that some Biblical animals,
Ezekiel's and John's, *e.g.*, are morally bound to do.

Biarritz, Nov. 15, 1884.

HIS lectures on poetry are the best part of that [the
Rhetoric course]—just because he never wrote a verse :

he is a dumb poet, and can keep time, as many of the dumb creation will do, when there is music going on.

The Katberg, March 8, 1880.

I CAN conceive of no more perfect or quaint object on a study table than the little brown bookie [a reproduction of an old Latin copy of À Kempis] which delights one every time he lifts his eye. I am sorry I have got so little hitherto from it inwardly, chiefly, I suppose, because the quiet from which it came and to which it points has been so little sought or gained in my life. It always seems to me that the À Kempis-Keble order of living leans too much to the mere *self-denying* side of Christianity, making it indifferent what sphere you fill or whereunto you attain ; whereas our Lord says indeed, " Lose your life," but " Lose it only to gain it " ; not " Lose it here and gain it hereafter," but " Lose it here and gain it here " : Get from me that life for which I seized you— that self which *can do all things* through Him that giveth it power. However, that is of opinion.

Yet even the *title* of the little book contains for me, and I suppose for all of us, a truth excelling all attainment. " To copy Christ," that seems to be Christianity

as none has hitherto been Christian. If we could sing
the "προωρώμην τὸν Κύριον ἐνώπιόν μου διαπαντός," perhaps
we should come nearer the close of the canticle: "ὅτι ἐκ
δεξιῶν μου ἐστὶν ἵνα μὴ σαλευθῶ." That unwavering, that
equal walk we ask for ourselves and you.

Cults, Nov. 29, 1881.

I MAY err, but I do not know if you are aware what a
breath of the Mediterranean is. It has blown through
my life these twelve years now, and I feel it as fresh
while I write as the first morning I threw open my
window at Cannes in December, 1869. It is just twelve
years, to a day or two, since we went there. It is just
the season to go, and you can run right through without
a break. Why, your own Newman could tell you about
it; he got his hymn in the harbour at Marseilles. Write
and ask your father confessor, if you distrust a lay brother
whether it is right to go. The chance may not return,
and trust me there are more inspirations to be had there
for home work than you might judge from returned
ministers' lectures on hotel life, antiquarian jokes, and
general drivel.

Edinburgh, Nov. 27, 1882.

I HAVE seldom felt before how possible it is to get pure health and pleasure just in a moment by complete isolation. We were living at the end of the world. Nothing went by; scarcely anything even reached us; no letters, papers, visitors. It was like being on board ship without being on the sea. Your letter came very fitly at the end of it. I had time to take it in as an extra sip of honey, with the heather, and the sunset, and the hills.

It takes leisure to make cream gather on one's life, and when you are in a constant commotion it requires a very deep-seated joy indeed to bring up riches to the surface every day. But two experiences do suffice, I find, to bring it—the love of God and the love of wedded souls. . . . To the heart which loves God and loves another, a daily freshness and growing youth is ever given.

Brechin, July 27, 1881.

ABOVE all things, use post-cards — ten of them to every one letter you write. If I could have given you this advice on the back of one, believe me you would have had it. You don't know how much more people respect you when you give them post-cards! Now do it.

Brechin, Feb. 5, 1883.

I SHOULD say, read M'Crie's "Life of Knox," or M'Crie's (the younger) "Sketches of Scottish Church History," or Chalmers' Life, or Guthrie's; or Green's "Short History," or Stanley's "Jewish Church," or his "Life of Arnold," or "Memorials of a Quiet Life," or Trevelyan's "Macaulay," or Farrar's "Paul." Perhaps the last or first two would be best; only get one, get it done. Before you begin each evening's reading, get your reader to question you upon last day's lesson. That is worth two readings. History is the very best kind of reading. It connects, collects, and cools one's mind. It gives you illustrations, examples that light up your own life and the life of the present day. Religious history is perhaps the best for us; but there is no good history of Scotch or English religion. If you take secular, Froude's, which is re-appearing just now, might be good. Have you read Livingstone's? If not, you might get that for Sabbath. It is the most Christ-like life I have ever heard of, except Paul's.

Brechin, June 22, 1881.

I HAVE been much in spirit to-day at Newman's burial. How little his later associates seem to have found in him! I can hardly credit the reports of their sermons, they are so utterly inane. It confirms the opinion I have always held, that his creative period lay almost wholly within the years before he joined the Church of Rome.

Hutton's eulogium was not unworthy of the writer. But how false any unqualified admiration sounds from the lips of a Christian man. Saint-worship is a far sadder thing than hero-worship, inasmuch as the saint-worshipper's ideal is so much higher than the hero-worshipper's. "Call no man your father upon earth," has been going in my ears these last days. "Call no man your Master or your Lord." The Speaker knew how very hard it was not to do that; so He said it over to us these three times. He said something harder and more wonderful still — to sense harder, more wonderful to faith. "It is expedient for you that I, even I, go away."

Yes, dear Absenter of Thyself, it is true! For what follows?

Ah, *père* Newman, if we could only learn of the Third Person in the Blessed Trinity, each by ourselves, and all together in the Church Catholic, *to worship the Holy Ghost;* even as we learned of Him, by thee, to worship the unbegotten Son!

I am not a theologian, nor the son of a theologian, but I am beginning to be able to adore the Spirit equally with the Father and with the Son. It is a wonderful and a blessed thing to do that. We must not speak much of it; but we must try to do it, and do it more.

Royal Hotel, Edinburgh, Aug. 19, 1890.

AFTER sending away my letter at 4, I sat reading " Luther" (Köstlin's Leben)—the part about the Wittenberg troubles and his return in 1522. More and more the one source and secret of his power, many-sided as it was, comes before me — his knowledge of and trust in God's Word. And for him God's Word always meant the Good News ; it was the personal message of pardon which it had brought to him that made him prize the Bible so deeply. It was the discredit, too, which the "prophets" tended to bring on God's truth which first stirred his soul against them. If we could only get and cherish this living interest in Scripture, as the record of redemption, how it would stimulate us to activity and soothe us in trouble.

Bonskeid, Aug. 30, 1883.

IT is for God's children John wrote that golden line, " The blood of Jesus Christ His Son cleanseth us from all sin." To confess that is to be forgiven. To walk in the light, and to bring everything before Him into the light, that is to have the only perfect communion with each other; that is to be cleansed from all sin. May we get the secret of forgiveness, and know to give it to others.

Edinburgh, Oct. 27, 1883.

ABUSES are like weeds: they need only toleration to spread and grow. Reforms are tender plants: they flourish only on stubborn effort, on broken clods of patient toil, on showers of secret tears, on the irresistible sunlight of the Almighty's smile.

May 16th, 1890.

I SUPPOSE that, or something like it, was the faith, or rather mental substitute for faith, he (Byron) went on living on, or trying to live — what is commonly called Pantheism, but which I think is a mere negative — all that is left when one casts away, or loses, or rather has never possessed, the excellency of the knowledge of a personal God in Christ. I have seen many who have lost all hope because they have lost that faith. That seems to be the reason why so many have no light on

B

what lies beyond this life ; which only comes with the sure grasp — sure and certain, though shaking — of the Father's hand here and now. And it is the craving of the heart after immortality, at least after a hope for others in the hereafter, if not at first for themselves, which has led many back to the belief in a personal God.

But how one ought to be living, if all he believes— or any of it — is true ! Even with a little separate gold strand of one's own in the great rope which goes for us through the veil, how little and how seldom the heart is sensibly tugged thither, how little and how seldom it hears the tiniest cracking of a thread or root (for they are roots too, and they grow if they are not cut, and even when they are) which holds him to earth, and sense, and time.

Biarritz, Nov. 13, 1882.

WHAT is the Bible, but a collection of letters from our great Friend. You know what a friend's letter is. With what eagerness you open it ; with what care you scan every line of it. How it delights you to find himself in his letter, to point to this and this, and say "so like him." How you read it, and re-read it, and keep it in the safest, most sacred place.

IF you have any plan already, any rule or course of reading, *keep to it.* But in any case, *have a Bible of your own, and have one Bible;* bring the one you use in your room to church and meeting. Do not leave your Bible behind either at church or at home, if you can help it. I have seldom seen an outstanding Christian man who did not prefer his own Bible to any other.

Do you ask, How much ought one to read at a time? A chapter is the ordinary, and it is a safe, advice. But I should rather say, Read on until you reach a verse where, if it be night-time, you can lay your head right down as on a pillow; or where, if it be morning, you can plant your foot as upon a rock; and stop there. Wait till you come to a word which will bear the day's burden—its sin, sorrow, struggle, duty, joy, and there let your whole weight lean.

IF Bible-reading be like getting your friend's letter, then prayer is like a visit from your friend. If I know my friend and I are soon to meet, how glad I am to think of the moments we shall spend together. How I try to make the most of them. I go over in my mind all that has happened since we last met. I note what I have to tell him; I put down the questions I wish to ask him. There are books I have been reading or am going to read; people I have been seeing or am hoping to see; things I have been doing or am trying to do. Now, is there any preparation of that kind before we pray? Might we not at least think an instant or two before we kneel, and go over what we have to say. *Aug. 8, 1882.*

SING to Christ when you sing. Think of Him, and He will be in the psalm. That is the way to forget others; speak out every word to Him. How it helps the minister to preach when everybody tries to sing. Again, *Pray to Christ* when you pray. Let me ask how you accompany the minister when he prays. If you can, you ought to follow every word in thought, under your breath. It is not difficult if you try; it becomes a habit like everything else. If you cannot do that, then let your whole heart go with the sense of what the minister says. If not, at least add an Amen in your heart when the prayer comes near you. When absent friends are prayed for, look up in fancy at the face of your absent friend, or breathe his name.

HOW differently a minister prays when he feels that the whole heart of the congregation is going forth with him as one man. Prize especially the moments of silent prayer after the benediction; prolong them; do not restrain prayer; put the sermon into a petition. At no time should the heart be better prepared than just then.

August 8, 1882.

IF you are not sure about anything, *shun* it. There is no true cleaving without shrinking. Every Christian has a shrinking side to his life; there are some things he utterly loathes, is heartily and wholesomely afraid of, cannot think of without a shudder. There is no fear but that this will come if you keep near Christ.

August 8, 1882.

A DRIVE up the dear old roads—dearer they get every time I go along them—they seem more real, more *the* real; it is I who am the shadow, who change.

Bonskeid, Feb. 22, 1889.

HOW good it is to hail pilgrims on the great journey even for an hour by the way: the sound of their 'tramp, tramp' quickens one's own tread and makes one take in his knap-sack-strap one hole further.

Park Circus, July 18, 1889.

I THINK less and less of the outward marks and turnings
in life: we can hardly read the record at all until the ink
is very pale. Perhaps even then it would be better if we
left that—the reading of it—to the Editor, and only opened
hopefully and wrote resolutely upon the next page.

Edinburgh, Aug. 23, 1890.

THE riots in England were reported. They will make the
cause of progress much harder; but those who go in for
being bearers of burdens must lay their account with un-
looked-for additions to the load. If only these commotions
might be the means of startling Christian men into life and
activity, as they did the Haldanes and others a century
ago. There is but one reform worth working for. Would
we might see more of it accomplished, and encourage each
other to look for its sure coming.

Egypt, Feb. 14, 1886.

THE sight of him [Dr. Stewart of Lovedale] always touches
me—and never more than this time. He is so true, and
so noble, and so lonely, as all the truest and noblest souls
it seems, must ever be.

Glasgow, 1888.

THERE seems something to be learned here [Lovedale] that one did not and could not know elsewhere; something of the wants of men, and of the work of our Lord, and of the noble sacrifice and devotion of His servants. Yet it is the same things we see here as at home; everything goes to tell us that it is one service the wide world over, and that it matters very little in which part of it one is engaged.

1880.

IF we be in Christ, then we are in a new world, and all things must be becoming new to us. Now tell me, was there more light on God's world when you woke up this morning than there was a year ago? Or were the daily duties easier and delightfuller to-day than they were last week? Then you are in Christ.

FOR to those in Christ all things are not only new, but they are growing continually newer. In the old world, and with the old man, it is just the other way. Things are always getting older, until life gets to be an unsufferable burden, a dreary round, a wretched repetition, and we see backs bent with nothing but pure sorrow, and heads white with none other sickness than vexation of spirit, and men brought to the grave because life was too wearisome, and time too intolerable, and existence too aimless and stale, to be supported any longer. But in the new world, and with the new man, the whole is reversed; and the new cry ever waxes more frequent and more loud, " Look, and look again, how the old is passing, how the new is coming, how things are getting new." Every day more of the old is weeded out, more of the new is coming in. Life is "fresher and freer" and fuller of promise. There are new discoveries of the Father's love, new revelations of Christ's grace, new experiences of the Spirit's comfort. Life becomes interesting, and entertaining, and significant, and splendid, and grand beyond belief. What views of life Christ's world contains ; what heavens of expansion overarch it ; what an earth of solid stability supports it ; what hills of attainment are reared upon it ; what distances of outlook are discernible from it. Yourself, Christ, God—what thoughts about them all, you could never have conceived before ; History, Time, Eternity —what feelings they stir in you, you never could have felt before; Purpose, Progress, Achievement—what mighty motions of the will they produce.

Murthly, June 7, 1891.

OH for love to be as gracious to another as one is to oneself! to put the same favourable interpretation upon their acts to make the same liberal allowance for opinions; to choose among many the more generous motives; to be as gentle of the living as of the dead—as kind toward the present as the absent; as jealous of to-day as one is wistful about yesterday.

WHEREVER love has been, there joy will surely be. Do the act, and the feeling will come. Love anything, anyone, and joy will follow. You never loved but it brought you happiness. The happiest hour in your life is the hour when you loved most.

SOME have the great grace given them of late years to go in and out, lie down and rise up, always staff in hand, like apostles on pilgrimage—always with loins girt, never with more in the purse than will carry them one stage on; never with more in their wardrobe than the daily wear. Like Wesley, if they are suddenly taken, they have left no engagements unfulfilled, they have no letters to answer or matters to arrange. The children they leave cannot but talk about them, as if they had just been seen off on some happy excursion. No farewells to say, no tears to be shed; nothing but to go after them in a day or two.

Cults, Jan. 27, 1884.

NOT so much to sudden and bold strokes does the marble owe its utmost perfectness; no, but to the silent, oft-repeated passages of the chisel over the stone, little more than audible in their occurrence, almost imperceptible in their separate result; it is these that leave the statue a marvel and a desire. "Let us run with patience."   Cults, Feb. 19, 1882.

THE supreme impulse of all in a man's life comes sometimes with the simple resolve just at last to let something go.
                    Cults, Feb. 19, 1882.

PERHAPS there are comforts and compensations that one who has not suffered knows nothing of—like the lamps that nobody sees till the tunnel comes.

NOBLE examples are not enough to live upon: it needs the same grace which produced them to make their impress durable.   Palermo, Feb. 19, 1887.

HERE again I am in the old place—not too changed, thank God, but that I can still feel something of the old man. One does change, I find, more than one thought he could when he had only been through one or two periods of life ; but not so much as to shake his confidence in that centre of all certainties—the soul ; which means one's own soul, for that is the only soul one knows. And yet, there again I must distinguish, for the only self worth having and worth keeping, or worth hoping to have more of, is the second self—the new man—and that seems strangely slow in coming or in growing. Do you know I think sometimes—and the more I try to think of it the more it appears to me certain —that the beginnings of that second life lie very far back— farther than one can at times see. Perhaps the new birth admits of that—nay, means it. Only along with that, one holds ever more tightly to the truth of an entire change—of a complete new creation ; at least I see painful cause to draw the line for myself ever sharper and sharper between the new and the old. Beau Séjour, Cannes, Jan. 3, 1885.

AND underneath us everywhere, deeper than the darkness of Death and the emptiness of the grave, are those everlasting arms. . . The dead make no weight in His arms; they do not toss, and fret, and give Him trouble as we do. Their deaths are precious; for then He gets them all to Himself, feels the full weight of them, and they lie still in His arms.

July 7, 1879.

GOD be praised for the prospect of a life which shall terminate this painful strait betwixt the earlier joys which were so good and the latter joys which would be perfect if one did not feel sometimes as if they were pushing the earlier out of reach. Such a feud has the heart with the memory. God speed the hour when Time shall have struck its last misleading and defrauding chime, and we shall have our best at once and for ever.

Cults, May 10, 1885.

HEAVEN—The land where there are no two hemispheres, but only one infinite circle of united love.

Ajaccio, Jan. 22, 1887.

EARLIER POEMS.

HARMONIES.*

Sounds from the organ in the under-room !
  Slowly the broad bass throbs up through the air,
  Reft of the melody.   But from some strange where
Is it heart or fancy shapes in the helpful gloom
  Harmonious treble? making full and fair
These deep notes, else like nothing unless doom.
So, often, sauntering by the flying spume,
  I have put in high child-music, scarce aware,
Timid with joy, to join the cataract's chords
  With something human ; often sung low note
  To the lofty star-tune, till the artless throat
Went hoarse with unmeant melody.   So the Lord's
  Wand beckons, we here beat out our life's bass,
  While He builds up the treble in His own high place.

[* Dear Frank,
  Can you make anything of the enclosed ?   The thing
seems to want the " obstetric art of utterance." The thought

was something after this fashion. Often when very little,
I used (either from sense of imperfection or far-away-ness in
nature) to try in a matter-of-fact sort of way if I could not
sing a literal part, in harmony with the sounds of the outer
world—say, bass to the shrill wind, or treble to the deep
river.   Which thing I even yet, metaphorically of course,
do attempt.   Now, to-night, hearing in my little room two
storeys up, the organ droning in the dining-room, but only
the bass (the treble being lost through distance and from
being of a finer sort), and finding myself able, either from
imagination, or memory, or deeper feeling in the deep darkness, to supply a richer, fuller, more significant chord from
the bass which was otherwise meaningless, except perhaps
in the weirdness of its droning ; having this experience, I
say, the old one (which was similar) came floating in upon
me in a thousand forms, and I sought to link the two in
a sonnet, with a further analogy from God's standing as
Leader of all our music, rod in hand, and giving us a (seem-
ingly) senseless, imperfect, nay, fearsome bass to play, the
finer parts of which are being worked out by Him above
(to be revealed some day).

I have failed ; as you will scarcely need to be told after
reading.   Which nevertheless I request you to do several
times aloud to yourself (and not at one time) before you

begin to *think*, far less *speak*, of it ; so that the rhythm, if there be any, may have some chance of entering you.

ROBERT W. BARBOUR.

P.S.—To save you a gratuitous stumbling-block at the close of the seventh line, the last word is an Elizabethan from the Italian *fiume*, stream). Such are the straits of *rime* (as the rabbit remarked as it brushed the dust from its fur pelisse after a tumble on the slippery hoar-frost).]

c

COMPENSATIONS.*

THERE'S a leaf gone, look, and a leaf,
   And another, the grey ground staining!
To count the rest, O grief,
   So few are found remaining.
But the distance breaks between,
   High hill-top and deep dingle;
The rents in the pretty screen
   Leave the far-view fair and single.

There's a friend gone, aye, and a friend,
   And another! The poor Past's richer
To tread upon. Ripe boughs bend,
   Break—fruit fills the brim of the pitcher.
But a hand shakes, see, behind,
   Same hand set. Our loss heightened
Means His love heavier. Kind
   Were His heart, if His handstroke lightened?

There's a year gone, yes, and a year,
    And another, sad count I'm keeping,
No gain in memory clear,
    No loss in forgetfulness sleeping.
But the break in the days bodes this:
    There's an end here beside a beginning—
Vanish, dark Past, O bliss
    That allows a new essay with sinning!

11 George Square, Edinburgh,
Tuesday Afternoon, Nov. 30, 1875.

[* DEAR FRANK,

In accordance with your usual habit of accusing me by means of quotation-marks from my own epistles, I might justify myself for seeming to break what was promised to-day. I heard something then about "some of Newman's Sermons"; now, on reaching home, I find—well, your kindness knows what.

However I can charitably enough account for it by the well-known psychological fact, that in some men, when they become emotional, feeling entirely overcomes reason, and to this extent they may, for the time, be reasonably regarded as totally irrational.

Nothing just now can express my state of mind, simply because I don't understand it—don't understand this 29th

Nov., '75, and the doubt about *it* threatens to make the past pretty dark as well. I can't see why I have been let live until now ; or, indeed, what I have been doing living at all these so many years. The question comes with terrible irony, τί ζητεῖτε, to what purpose art thou here ? But, thank God, "*quod nunc nescio, olim sciam.*" You have at least been happy as well as good (and what sure instinct like goodness ?) in your choice of books. In seeing them there is that additional pleasure which one feels when one's friends are kindly treated (even more than when oneself). For books are my real friends ; and, after dear human faces, only less dear. Any thoughtfulness shown about them brings thus a strange double sort of delight to me.

Outside of this single circumstance, you will find all I have been able yet to feel about my birthday in these rude verses, beaten out when I was waiting for the dawn on Monday morning, watching the wind busy with its last barbarities in the trees before the house. Your interest will interpret them, I hope.—Yours sincerely ever,

R. W. BARBOUR.]

'ΕΣ' ΑΕΙ.*

O STARS, that will rise and shine
For other eyes than mine,
When these are rapt with the radiance of light divine;
O stars, will ye tell of me true,
As I have spoken of you,
Will ye shine far brighter than stars unsung could do?

O night, who hast trusted me
Such secrets deep and free,
As told ye had spoken with others, ere I with thee;
Wilt pass from mind as sight,
Because it is written: No night?
Will thy face lean forth from some gladsomer gleam of light?

O hills, that will catch the glow
When I'm in the Long-ago,
Will ye break yourselves open for other hearts to know?

Will one in the After say,
When the sunset's too fair for the day :
He is singing this scene on the hills that are far away?

                                    Bonskeid, Tuesday Night.

[* DEAR FRANK,

  I leave to-morrow at 2.20. One message : If a favourable answer about Reading-room comes before close of week, village should be assaulted with the news. You will see Sorley is Ferguson Scholar.

  The lines on the reverse contain all I have ever felt or thought about my life in the country. If you have time or heart to study them, you will find, I think, three ideas, without which I could not live here :—*(a)* Intense kinship with those who have had communion with nature from the first, especially Christ ; *(b)* thereby a sort of welcomeness in the thought of a coming world with its possible interpretations of things dark at present ; and yet *(c)* an unutterable desire to hold at once both this and that, whence all the trouble and trial that is in the earth—that eternal "strait betwixt two" ; which is better, I know no more than Paul.

  Keep the thing to yourself; if it helps, you may be able to tell me how to make any little point more musical ; if it confuses—" *ad leones.*" This is the first clean copying, and what has seemed hitherto to move with some slight melody in the brain, looks as if it had lost all the music upon paper.—Yours sincerely ever,

R. W. BARBOUR.

P.S.—If any date should stand at the close, perhaps the week after our return from the States first saw the rhymes tacked on ; but, as I say, the matter is old as the marrow of my rheumatic bones.]

REMEMBERING ARNOT.*

I saw the sunset, as it wandered west,
Mingling the very mists with light, flee forth
And strike the tops of heaven. A cloud, lit up,
One moment grasped the glory, whose grand fall
Stole half its snowy shelter. Into gloom
The world went from me. I was left alone.
Straight in the thinning winter of that cloud
A star stood smiling, as it were its child,
And lo, a storm of stars sent laughter back!

Christ seems to set with each departing saint;
But in the morning He is here again,
And will be with us still; new radiance wraps
His latest triumph, His last trophy taken,
Last captive taken home.
The skies are stricken with His chariot wheels;
The heavens His horsemen hold. Why breaks the west
With sudden burst of glory at the death,

Save that some new world wakes in welcome? Why
Such crowding of all colours in the daylight,
As they are borne away, but that beyond
Beams something better, some eternal thing?

'Twas but a beam of brightness left the earth;
'Tis only earth can seem a little less.
Heaven shrinks not ; oh, her stars are all the more !
The wider grows that world, the friendlier
And closer far to this. Such passages
Are no more severance, but attraction,
And bring the heavenlies almost within hail.
O thou, to whom the shadows were so much,
How dost thou bear the substance? If that earth
Were signful so, and set about with lights
That had their meaning from a source unseen,
See'st now Heaven's shadows hanging towards earth,
Since earth can cast no curtain over heaven?
O'erlean these steep celestial summits, look down,—
See what great glooms they let upon us go,
What shapes are shone into us by their serene
And super-eminent glory,—see how the symbol
Prophesies, ay, and will produce the soul.

Still dimmer. These are tears ! Can it be true?—
Thou weepest? Nay, the shade becomes a mist—
That city's shade—and seems to weep with me.
Tears that the far reflection is so faint,
Tears that the image trembles so ; sad tears
That thou art,—nay, *thou* weep'st not ; nor will I.
Who weeps with heaven at her gates?—weeps when the ranks
Roll out a long rejoicing?—weeps to see
The chorus of a comrade crowned?

                         Yet, like the friend
Of some great general borne from battle-field
Victorious—whom his king comes forth to claim
Guest at his court for ever—his poor friend
Turns in the tumult of the drums aside,
And seeks a corner from the crowd, and still,
Pride poured on bitterness and love on pride,
His sobbing dulls the distance of the drums,—
So must I weep, in outrage of the sound,
Sight, thrill, wherewith eye, ear, and heart abound.

He will be with us still. And it is He
Who is the substance ; so be life a shade.
What finer mystery than to fall from Him !
Thus learn we the high lesson of this life

Gone from us, and the secret of its going,
Which saith :—*All things are but the shadow cast
By the great Master, Christ, across the world,
Himself the sole, the grand Reality.*

June 4, 1875.

Bonskeid, 1875.

[* DEAR FRANK,

Being, in such matters, one of my small public, I do not make myself common by sending the enclosed to you.

The thing is old, written of another, with an added brine-bubble dashed in to crystal round Arnot's name.

For I felt his death in no feeble fashion. Yet scarcely his more than any other departure; all loss catching up my breath with the same sort of angina cordis—is there such an expression or intermission of heart-beat—aye, and heart-everything as well, till at length the faintness fades off into a sicklier craving, that unspoken, inexpugnable ἀθανασίας πόθος. Verily, immortality exhausts its believers beyond belief. Indian goddess Vrama never charmed her votaries into such ἐκστασία (literally 'exist from one's skin'). To dream of it is palpable evisceration.

However, it is no use dying before one's time; moreover, by general persuasion, we are already, as it is, immortal. Nay, more, are not other men immortal as well as we are? And why shall we not eat, drink, and sleep on the back of it as our brothers seem to find it profitable to do. Let us eat and drink, for we live for ever.

This is considering your future very likely. For one fears such leaps after the future may arise most chiefly from decided defect in the little patch of eternity, which alone is priceless, and price*ful* to us at present.

And yet—and yet, would to God we were in the Book of the Revelation. I suppose Arnot is there now — he and others we have known. Hope is harder, much harder, to me than faith; who yet, like John, seem to live in it. Only when the two strike and stream off into each other do I understand either. And we call the golden drop— Love.

R. W. B.]

JEROVEAM'S WIFE.

I laid the draught upon his lips once more
With no leave-taking; moved the palm-leaf twice,
Till he half-smiled; then left it to the maid—
A little Memphian maid my lord saw, loved
And gave to me when we were married first—
With strict injunction, putting my wish for him
In words to her, thinking he nothing knew.
    But, as I stooped to raise the tapestry,
A sudden pause, or paroxysm, came,
And in it a wild look and cry for me.
I dared not stop; he turned him to the wall
And slumbered. But, as I hurried down beneath,
That cry was nearer to me than my breath
And seemed to catch it. Would I might have stayed,
For it was near the noonday, and, at night,
Said the physician, 'twould be salvation . . . or . . .
I dared not say it; my boy fought hard for life.
    But where the gallery strikes the outer stair,
I met my lord: and: "Art thou then prepared?

Why tarriest?" . . . I made no answer; he moved on
Toward the sickroom, musing many things.

 Then altering even these my nurse's weeds
For coarser clothing : such seemed natural then;
Nor would I help the prophet in the least—
Who knows what thoughts he harbours towards our house?
Or hold a peg for him to hang on doom :
Beneath a heavy sackcloth veil I hid
Three cakes of mine marked with the Egyptian seal,
A jar of honey sucked out on the heaths
Of Mount Gerizim, with those clusters fine
That purple half the hills, whereof he sings,
Our Tirzah poet, in the first of spring :

 Come, get up early to the vineyards; see
 If the vine flourishes; if the vine-blossom
 Shakes itself open.

    At the door there came
Nadab, the elder, huge and swart of skin,
From early hunting; on his shoulders hung
A leopard's hide from Cush; Javan, the hound,
Clamoured about his heels. I cried him Peace
For his sick brother; then, with the strange joy
Of a last deed done for a dear one, hurried on.

 'Twas noonday now; and five hours lay before
'Twixt this and Shiloh; but my eager feet

Would be at Shiloh ere the sun was down,
To know the best and worst about my boy.
So from the palace by a winding path,
Unseen and unsalamed, I gained the vale.
Tirzah, the Lovely, Tirzah, lay behind,
Well named—the letters of its name make Love—
But I ne'er looked, lest that same lattice, green
With plants well-watered, for the wind to blow
Over and in upon his face, should loose
My knees and make my hands hang. I moved the veil
And set the jar upon my shoulder, and so
Balanced the quicker heart-beat with stiff arm.
The other held the cakes and raised a fold
My skirt for the rough watercourse turned way.
　　But where the valley straitens and the brook
Comes round the spur from Shechem, I *must* turn :
For distance made one look not dangerous :
And from the shadow gaze back to the sun.

　　O Tirzah, lovely Tirzah, on the hill
Written out run the letters of thy name,
The long strokes lying, the short standing up,
Whereon the windows dot their dagesh-points,
Like those strange characters the Hebrews use.
　　O Tirzah—such he called me by the Nile,

Sware on the calf, mixing his gods and mine;
And such should be our dwelling when we came
Across the desert, a second Solomon,
A second daughter of Pharaoh; whence that song
His Northern poet wrote to shame the loves
Of Judah : Fair as Tirzah, proverb turned
For all that's lovely—twenty years ago.

Oh what a dream was then ; the very thought
Shines like the chastened sunlight ere a storm ;
Of his land, Israel, reconciled with mine,
Of priests at worship with a world at play.

Oh that new desert wandering, which was to yoke
Egypt to Canaan, in no exodus,
But common concourse of the sundered lands—
Egypt-to-Canaan being but half the song,
Canaan-to-Egypt coming as refrain.

He hindered nothing, let me name my babe
First-born—not like that Jewish birth of blood—
Nadab, that's : Willing; freewill-offering he,
The altar was that kingdom which should be.
And in his face, tinged from the Ethiop East,
I spelt out all the answer of our hopes.

So we came northwards through the sands of Zin,
But all the brooks were full; the valleys bloomed
Oasis round about us; Sinai's head
Had neither clouds nor thunder; only the peak
Of Pisgah, fabled for its prospect far,
Was wrapped in gloomy vapours as we passed.

And he would mark the places, making note
Of all that God had done for Israel—
Israel at length a kingdom, he the king—
Guiding their journey; and going further back,
Of that same Joseph who made Egypt his,
Whose family, holding headship, now besought
Him for their head; and I, I mingled myths
Of Isis and Osiris kept at On,
Stringing the two together for the child,
Until my lord was minded variously,
Now leaning here, now there : at length he too
Thought Moses Amun, Joseph Horos, and so
Found Egypt's memories, Canaan's hopes the same.

So came we where king Solomon's boy-babe
Fretted and fumed at Israel, and Israel took
My lord Jerôvĕám and made him king;
And we twain dwelt at Tirzah.

D

                              Our first work—
The city's self once built and beautified—
Was: How confirm the people's serious heart
In their revolt?   How drive regrets away?
So were our dreams made real.   For at Dan,
The little, northern, old, oft-peopled town,
Where traders come; and Bethel, the other end,
Of ancient memories too, and far inland,
A place the people going southward pass
Last on the way to Salem; there we set,
Strange to their temple, but not strange to them,
The gods they found it in their heart to make
Even in the bellowings of the Mount Divine,
The gods which led them from the land of Ham,
Two golden calves, to which the people prest—
Fewer frequented Zion, so 'twas said—
To native worship gathering natural rite,
Until they made a nation.   Never plague
Fell on the celebrants.   Nay, these rugged souls
Felt Jahveh nearer in the fruitful form,
The land's old deities their fathers loved,
Than ever at Salem in an empty fane.
Round these there grew a priesthood, he, my lord,
Mingling in all and using the twin-rite,
Fallen to disuse, of high priest and of king.

Only the prophet's office stood aloof,
And one adventurer out of Judah came—
So ours too cross the border carrying Woe—
And railed against the altar; going home
A lion tare him and his lies in twain,
And he was buried by the outraged shrine.

At length round altar and priests a people grew,
Weaned from old worship, true to us and ours;
For when the land was settled, came a child,
A little Israelite, to my lord and me,
And to the land which longed for such an one,
All fair and ruddy to look on, features sharp
And calling Canaan up at every turn,
And telling me, more than words, what David was
And Samuel and Solomon and the rest
On whom grace settled from their earliest years.
He seemed no babe of ours, but of the land.
And I, who leant to the people's persuasion more
And heard them call him—for they clung to him—
Son of their God, I let him keep the name:
Jahveh-my-father, such Abijah means,
No other parentage beseeming him.

So Nadab, who ne'er won the people's heart,
Grew ever more from Israel, loving sport

And easy grandeur, all that Egypt means.
And Egypt seemed to stretch out hands to him;
For King Susákim and his childless bride,
Young Thekemina, my sweet sister, these
Would have their sister's child to share their throne.
And all these years Abijah gained the heart
Of all the people, and the people said
In him was found some good thing of the Lord,
Their God of Israel; therefore he should reign
After Jerôvĕám, my lord, the king.

With such long thoughts was the hill country clomb,
And on the edge of evening Shiloh came,
All the old proverb beating in my breast,
Uttered in Egypt: They shall not want a king
While men still come to Shiloh. Was it ours,
Or was it Judah's? There the village lay
Between the kingdoms, leaning neither way;
And there had Samuel judged, and there the Ark—
That empty effort at idolatry—
Had rested, handing down a holiness
For many days. Therefore the prophet chose
This spot, left lonely 'twixt two capitals,
To be his dwelling. For he neither clave
To Judah, having crowned my lord, the king,

Nor yet inclined toward Jerôvĕám,
But lived a distant and a midway life
Between the nations. Yet my lord, the king,
Had him at heart in reverence, and even now
In trouble bade me go disguised to him,
And know what thing was coming on my boy.

So, thus disfigured, to the door I came,
Musing how best to buoy a sinking heart
With speeches blown out full. But on the steps,
So busy was I mustering my thoughts,
I could not guard my goings; and in the dim,
Half-lighted chambers of his cloistered mind
Some traitor echo must my feet have made,
Faltering between the stateliness of a queen,
The anxiety of a mother. For he cried,
His whole face flashing up the deepened gloom,
Struck from a world beyond the world, and said:
Come in, come in, wife of Jerôvĕám:
Why feignest thou thyself to be another?
For I am sent to thee with heavy tidings.
Even as a messenger met by one dispatched
From him to whom he goes, who turns him back
Answered or e'er he asks, so turned my heart,
Meeting the news it thought itself to bring.

There opened on me not the prophet's cell
Or that pale face pronouncing words of doom;
But all the future, yawning horribly,
Leapt from the cleft heart of my former sin.
Then through the dizziness flitted a wild look,
The fevered look of him I left at home,
And parcht lips calling: Mother. I could have swooned;
But those harsh words of prophecy held me up.
I bowed against them, and they bore my weight,
I flung me on them, but they would not yield;
So, steadying me by the doorpost, I heard on:

Go tell Jerôvĕám: Thus saith the Lord
The God of Israel: Forasmuch as I
Exalted thee from among all the people
And made thee prince over my people, Israel,
And rent the kingdom from the house of David
And gave it thee:
And yet thou hast not been as My servant David,
Who kept My statutes and who followed them
With all his heart, to do right in Mine eyes;
But hast done evil over all before thee:
For thou hast gone and made thee other gods
And molten images to provoke to anger
And hast cast Me behind thy back:
See, I bring evil on Jerôvĕám's house......

I heard no more; only a muttering
Like the dull thunders of some far-off doom
Tipped with these lightnings: The Lord hath spoken it.

The universal Woe was spoken forth,
And I stood speechless, fearful to find out
How my boy's fortunes were bound up therein.

But while I waited for a bolt to strike
And held my quivering heart up under it,
There fell like gentle drops that hurt and heal
And heal and hurt: Thou therefore arise and go,
    Get thee to thine own house, and, when thy feet
    Enter into the city, the child shall die;
    And all Israel shall mourn and bury him,
    And of Jerôvĕám he only hath such an end,
    Because in him there is found some good thing
    Toward the Lord, the God of Israel,
    In the house of Jerôvĕám.
                    I heard the sound
Of rain beat on a lattice and wind that blew
Over and in upon his face, and he,
Glad with the wafting of the watered plants,
Turned over toward them and smiled .... and slept.

He told me, sad at heart, my lord, the king,
How, when I reached the city's gates again,
There came a breath and blew in on his cheeks—
For it *had* thundered, as I dreamt, and rained,
And all the lattice was refreshed with rain—
And he had turned toward it . . . smiled . . . and slept—
And as I entered still he slept . . . and smiled.

SWALLOW-FLIGHT.

Swallow, fly high, the hour is nigh,
We shall be wedded, my love and I,
Wing away up, and tell the sun,
He shall not hurry, till all is done.

Swallow, fly high, flash through the sky,
Meshlike and mazy your passages ply,
Swoop not to earth to take one strand
To your web from out of this weary land.

Swallow, fly high, the best ye try
Hope will better it by and by;
Heaven's not too high for hope to covet,
Earth's too low when heaven's above it.

THE SOURCE OF SONG.

"WHAT does it take to sing, my Love?
What does it take to sing?"
"The first fine day in spring, my Love."
"The first fine day in spring?
But such a little thing, my Love?"
"Just such a little thing,
A day in spring."

"What does it take to sing, my Love?
What does it take to sing?"
"An arm like yours to cling, my Love."
"An arm like mine to cling?
But if it burden bring, my Love?"
"Yes, though it burden bring,
An arm to cling."

"What does it take to sing, my Love?
What does it take to sing?"

"The feeling of a king, my Love."
"The feeling of a king?
But I am not a queen, my Love!"
"Oh be what you have been,—
My Love's a queen!"

MORNING.

LOVELY is the morning when it breaketh,
Lovely is the morning when it goes,
Lovely is the morning when it taketh
Colour from the opening rose.

Lovely is the morning when it lieth
Pale upon the lap of noon,
Lovely is the morning when it dieth,
Lovely—but too soon.

TWILIGHTS.

JUST when the night is casting
  Her curtain over me,
A sense of the everlasting
  A moment comes.   I see
Strange light in the westering sunward,
  And hasten it with a hymn;
When I turn my eyes again downward,
  My book is dim.

Just when the soul is weary
  With watching of herself,
And even the desk is dreary,
  And dreary is the shelf,
A calm, clear call comes to me
  From the Blessed and the Beyond—
Bright fire-burst, oh how gloomy,
  Free fancy, oh how bond.

Just when the darkness presses,
　I do not care to own,
And I cling to these strange caresses
　To make me not all alone,
When the silver-streaks grow slender,
　And the pencil's shadow long,
I make the moment tender
　With a song.

THE LINNET.

To my first sorrowing there came
A linnet chirping in the leaves,
That yearly laid delightful claim
To covert 'neath the eaves.

She sang as they can only sing
Whom common troubles draw to men,
And sympathy woke up a string
I never knew till then.

"Thy love is gone, and gone the flowers,
The flowers will come again in spring,
And when are past the wintry hours,
Thy love will hither wing.

"No happy trysting waits for me,
The cruel arrow pierced my mate,
He never will return to see
How leal I watch, and late.

"There in the forest by the brook,
   The ground is red, the feathers lie,
Ah woe is me! the dying look,
   The faint, expiring sigh."

I rose and let the linnet in,
   She hopped upon my beating wrist,
She poised her on a finger thin,
   I bent me down and kissed.

She looked up in my brimming eyes,
   She twittered to my quivering lip,
And half she let a warble rise,
   And half she let it slip.

And half I filled it up for her,
   We sang together lover and bird;
We saw not, with our eyes ablur,
   We saw not, but we heard.

And in between the notes there stole
   A something sweet, a something smooth,
It could not make a sick heart whole,
   But still it seemed to soothe,

And leave for pain a pleasing want,
A willingness to wait and see;
And this was all the linnet's chant,
And this she did for me.

VOCATION.

Oh who would sing another's song,
  Such beauty round him strewn?
I've danced to others' notes too long,
  Now let me chant my own.

I've felt their words rise naturally,
  When walking through the wood,
Its voice seemed half an alien cry,
  Now be it understood.

Great spirits, thanks, who led me to
  Sweet Nature at her best;
And yet I've felt a strain run through
  Not hitherto exprest.

A something dropt from every tree
  The deepest thing it held,

More subtle sweet than ever bee
  By her close press compelled;

More fresh and new than ever breeze
  Wafted to life in spring—
Something that moved behind all these
  Bird's heart-beat 'neath his wing.

Instinctively I used to long
  To take it free and fair,
For 'tis the stuff that shapeth song,
  And others got it there.

I called it mine, because it moved
  Toward me from the tree;
It seemed myself, because I loved,
  And it seemed loving me.

SPRING.

EVERY evening light's a little longer,
  Summer pushes night-time further North ;
Every day the thrush's note is stronger,
  Floods the lark a fuller music forth.

All the world's at one to banish winter,
  All the world is wishing well to spring,
April's in, the dainty daisy-tinter,
  May's alive, ere birds her beauty sing.

Every evening less for books and study,
  All the school is out of doors again.
Strength goes up the sinew, cheeks grow ruddy,
  Joy's not withered yet from sons of men.

HAUNTED.

THERE'S a place on the path as you come along,
    The wind comes with you and then stays;
Just at the corner, you can't go wrong—
    Here the wood, there the water, no two ways—
But it's there I always get my song,
    Out of the wind-whiff, the strong sun-rays;
You'd hurry faster, I wait and feel strong,
    These are the moments that make my days.

Who could have left it? The Dryads are dead,
    This is no scrap of their pic-nic cheer;
On a bit, often, strange sounds it is said
    Echo, all hasten, and none rest here.
Or is it a fragment of thought that fled
    From a singer set musing and left in the rear,
When a shout broke it off, to the winds since wed,
    Hovering till he shall reappear.

Nay, for it's new, and chimes in with the hour,
　　Chimes with one, and the way one feels;
Surely when song-seed rhymes out a flower,
　　Some tiny bud through its sheathlet steals,
For me to take up at my level; a Power
　　Takes us both up and itself reveals.
What if two storeys in one tall tower
　　See the same sun—'tis the cornice conceals !

AFTER RAIN.

THE wind went out with dewy breath,
And swept the rain drops to their death
    Upon the ground,
The grass sprang up to meet the shower,
The rushes waved their withered flower,
    Life fell around.

The earth her hard hot lips expands
And stretches forth her arid hands,
    To grasp the rain,
And every brooklet bubbles brown,
And all the river rushes down
    Upon the plain.

The wind has pass'd, the rainbells lie,
Glittering fragments of the sky
    Among the grasses.
Whole clouds are rent, and in between
Brings the blue heaven her painted screen,
    Whence tempest passes.

Now lives the world a life renewed,
Nature revives her happy feud
     With care and ill.
The stream refreshing sent from bliss
Has planted a bewitching kiss
     On vale and hill.

And everywhere, by wood and glade
Some song-bird lends a willing aid
     To cheer the earth.
He sits upon a greener bough,
Sees fresher things around him now,
     And trills for mirth.

The dust is laid upon the path,
The air is sweeter in the strath
     And up the glen.
The moss is steeped in emerald dews,
That heighten half her velvet hues,
     And glows again.

Here plays the rabbit by his home,
Right glad is he the rain has come
     Upon the field.

Dragging the long grass 'tween his paws,
He eats, and licks his dewy claws,
    And then has mealed.

The wild dove plumes her tarnished breast
And, in her purple bodice drest,
    Takes speedy wing.
Over the mount her course is laid,
Deep in the hazel's fragrant shade
    Her praise to sing.

The flowers have bathed their modest form
And in the sunshine breathing warm,
    Unfold their fronds,
And to the breezes cast the smell
Piloted on through every dell
    By fairy wands.

Father, I thank thee for the rain,
And all its blessing to the plain,
    And to the mountain.
May my poor thanks with those arise
That happy nature upward cries
    To Thee the fountain.

"UNTO THE HILLS."

Schiehallion clearing from her snows—the sight!
  You fancy how she stretched one seamless sheet
  Daily the sun did into diamonds beat
And every evening to red rubies smite,
Till 'twixt the flakes at foot, grown faded quite,
  The heaven's and heather's answering eyes did meet,
  While the robe rose from her far-planted feet,
Crept to the shoulder and past, one crown of light.
  So have I witnessed some immortal theme
Rise on the mind and have the mastery,
  Perfect and in one piece without a seam,
Challenging all and always conqueringly,
  At length shot through by a superior gleam,
And it and all the heaven see eye to eye.

FLUX.

THEY change, all change, they perish evermore;
The new is fairer than the old before;
They change, all change, and shall not man the more?

They change, all change, they perish nevermore;
This ceaseless death is glory's noiseless door;
They change, all change, and shall not man the more?

They change, all change, He smileth as of yore;
With Him no now, no after, no before;
He changeth not, and shall not man the more?

They change, all change, unknowing o'er and o'er;
We know their changes—naught is as of yore;
They change, all change, and shall not man the more?

They change, all change; Him changeless we adore,
And smile His smile in the face of the dark before;
We change, all change, immortal all the more.

HOME FROM THE CONTINENT.

(AUTUMN OF 'SEVENTY-SEVEN.)

ENGLAND, 'tis something to come back to thee,
  On billows of despisal homeward borne,
  Full to the ears of bitter foreign scorn,
And find thee sleeping on a summer sea,
Free as of old to all abuse, and free
    To welcome thine abusers any morn
    Tyranny turns them suppliants forlorn
To the one soil whither all exiles flee.
    England ! and yet I join the charges now,
For these dumb signs are not thine ancient mood,
    There lies upon thee our great fathers' vow,
Never to slumber at the cry of blood,
    Bestir thee, nor to darker hands allow
The birthright and the bliss of doing good.

EVOLUTION.

FAR space 'tween us and Him as 'tween us and the ape,
But each to the other turns, lifts hand, holds lips agape,
The image fills the eye, though neither gain the shape.

We ever liker grow, but never strike the level.
Each glimpse of the beckoning glance is goodbye to the devil.
We know He is our crown, but faint through weight of evil.

The life is but the form that fringes on the soul;
For matter is not all, and mind aye lacks the whole;
The age begins to open and hurry on the goal.

Christ is arisen far-off, the days do draw us near;
He is the missing Man, He is the higher sphere;
We circle round Him darkly, yet He shall appear.

A HIGHLAND FUNERAL.

"LORD, THOU HAST BEEN OUR DWELLING PLACE IN ALL GENERATIONS."

ONCE more we meet in the old retreat,
  The home roof over us once again;
But the old walls wake to the bearers' feet,
  And the old rooms sob with the mourners' train—
  'Tis the old, old home again,
  But the old dwellers will not remain.

So we bear her out to the mountain side,
  For the hills are an older sort of home,
And better, they say, will the mountains bide
  And the heath thatch over the dark peat loam.
  Oh! this is an older home,
  Where the feet of her childhood used to roam.

The hills rise round us as we rise,
  As they rose to Him who gave them birth,

Creation's dawn-look in their eyes,
  And their witness-feet fixt fast in earth,
  Attesting as at birth,
  Till our thoughts are spurred to the heaven's far-spanning girth;

His heaven whose home is everywhere,
  And all within His ken is home,
Who sleeps with the dust we scatter here,
  Who sleeps not, over that crystal dome,
  Where she is awake and at home,
  Whither her spirit in living slowly clomb.

So we aye shall meet in an old retreat,
  A home-roof over us evermore,
One house to the lords whose rest is sweet,
  And the servants busy about the door,
  One dwelling-place evermore,
  In whose going and coming we rest and rejoice and adore.

BIRDS OF PASSAGE.

(FOR A FRIEND SEA-FARING.)

SWALLOWS built in my balcony,
Long and late awake lay I;
Morning came with a call and a cry;

Wakened me out of my dream about you—
Was it not tender? will it come true?
You and your friend's distress—these two.

In broke the cry of the birds uncouth,
Barely-fledged, unquiet of mouth,
Brought up here, but bound for the South.

And through the sameness of their notes
Some of your chequered story floats,
And makes a mouth-piece of their throats.

So what I send you does not seem
So much my own—you may call the theme:
What he dreamt and the swallows did with his dream.

I dreamt the swallows were bidden go
From the balcony they clung to so;
There came a wailing deep and low.

Why leave the nest, the cosy nook,
The grating above, where the still stars look,
The water-pipe doorway, our perching-hook?

Why seek the South? If friends are there,
We do not know of them, and where
Were friends like these so fond and fair?

So spake they, when the Summer smiled,
But God's great heart touched theirs and wiled
Them, as a father does his child.

His suns set daily further down,
He gave the Northern skies His frown,
His breath blew all the leaves to brown.

And beckonings in their bosoms grew
To meet the South that beckoned too;
A Hand came out from far and drew

My swallows to a warmer home.
I did not see them start to roam,
But something whispered: Winter's come.

F

Then in my dream I looked and saw
Their far-off course that hand did draw,
Who followed it and fulfilled the law

Within them. And, since they obeyed,
Behold a gradual change was made,
And these in glorious guise arrayed.

The Southern suns smote into fire
About their necks, and higher and higher,
Ring by ring, rose the grand attire.

In every lovely lake they crost
Some poverty was plunged and lost ;
They robed them at the country's cost.

With every tint of flower and tree
Royally revelling they made free.
Ah, what the wonder that will be,

I sighed, beyond those hills that rise,
The barrier of my eager eyes !
Then something whispered : Paradise.

'Twas then the morning woke, and I
Harked for the swallows' altered cry—
The old twitter seemed to laugh reply.

But still it could not steal the sweet
The dream did leave, though incomplete.
My waking must add something meet.

And, as I mused, there came a sense
Of Him whose love means permanence;
Who knows no whither and no whence;

Who liveth everywhere and moves;
Home is wherever He most loves;
Who draws us on by noiseless grooves;

Who leadeth the light-minded bird
By some blind motion inly stirred;
Who leads us by the voice we heard;

By no dim influence of a law,
But by a Figure that we saw,
And cords of brotherhood that draw,

And, drawing to a stranger shore,
Make Him less stranger than before,
Make us grow like Him more and more

Till law and love are scarce disjoined,
And both in likeness intertwined,
And even upon the path we find

Christ grow to our enlarging eyes,
And Valparaiso, with changed skies,
Be but a Vale of Paradise.

IN THE DARK.

DEATH doth make us draw together,
Like weary birds in the wild weather,
　　Till we scarcely know
The once dread difference of feather
　　We felt so much a little ago.

Death wins from us our weekday dress;
We can't do common things; life seems less;
　　There has past away
That blessed use of littleness
　　We live in, day by day.

What cause for quarrelling (he speaks true),
Or talking loudly, as if we knew?
　　All that man saith
Hath been said to him long since. Very few
　　Have been found to answer Death.

Sit still together. The sunbeams pour
In on us, past the swinging door;
    And, under our breath,
Say: Life's not less, the Immortal's more—
    Be kind to us, Death!

"LOST—A LITTLE CHILD."

I never feigned such tiny hands
    Upon these massive doors.
I never heard such little feet
    Tread up the burnished floors.
The child-friends in my Father's house
    Had grown away from me,
And for them, in this darkened world,
    I had these darlings three.
    .   .   .   .

The Hands that fashion out our lives
    Had not gone very far,
And what these Hands had made so fair,
    That Heart will never mar.
The very tissues will compact
    In some diviner way,
And faculties of thought and act
    Have fuller scope and play.

All will be finer, fittinger,
  But nothing changed will be,
Or nameless; but the same old stir
  Will lay strong hands on me.
When I shall see him, so preserved,
  And so improved, I'll cry:
O happy people who deserved
  A child at school on high.

ON THE MARCH.

Ps. cx.

WE are going home,
  We are almost there,
No more to roam,
  Not anywhere.
We are going home,
  The house in view;
That last hill's clomb,
  This will be too.
We are going home,
  Convoyed by love;
Out of the womb
  Of morn above,
Like dew, so thick,
  So fresh, like dew,
We are dropping quick,
  We are sparkling new,
Yeomen the youthfullest
  E'er drew sword,

Bowmen the truthfullest
  Ever warred,
All Thy young soldiers
  With one accord
Are coming, are coming
  To Thee, O Lord,
Garlanded feast-like,
  Helms concealed,
Filleted priest-like,
  Stole upon shield,
Fail not nor falter,
  Once offered to thee;
Thou art the altar,
  Sacrifice we,
Bound to the horns by
  Love's own cord,
Catching the kindling
  Look of the Lord,
Ready to leap up
  At His word.
Devoted, desirous,
  Lord, we yearn,
Fire us, inspire us,
  Till we burn!

Quick ! the home rises
  Clear in view ;
Shine we, sparkle we,
  Fire and dew.
Kindled in common,
  Together poured,
Coming and coming
  To Thee, O Lord.
Spotless and numberless,
  Lord, we come,
Countless and cumberless,
  And almost home.

THANKS.

Give thanks, give thanks, my soul, and sing,
   Give thanks, give thanks always.
Give thanks, for the least little thing
   Is great, if turned to praise.

The lute is larger, not for length,
   But for its range of tone;
And thou are greater, not for strength,
   But how that strength is shown.

The lute is larger in its scope,
   If pierced at one place more;
Then sing for love and faith and hope,
   And for them o'er and o'er.

DEO QUI DAT VICTORIAM.

LORD, I thank Thee who hast wounded, for the mercy that
  abounded,
  For the multitudinous mercy flowing forward like a sea,
For the deeps that, rolling o'er me, arched into an arm that bore me,
  For the thunder-step of time that woke thy peace, eternity.

And I thank Thee that the thunder never woke one word of
  wonder,
  Only hushed the murmurous thought and drove rebellion far
    away ;
That the wrath revealed outside me showed a rest where I might
  hide me,
  Till the inward clouds rejoined the outer darkness black as they.

Therefore Thee I praise for ever, merciful Taker, mighty Giver,
  Taking but to give, and giving none but Thou to take away ;
And if darker clouds encrust Thee, though Thou slay me, I will
  trust Thee.
  For Thy hurt is simple healing, and Thy darkness simple day.

A PREACHER.

I HEARD him speak, and at the subtle sound
Of music such as manhood only knows,
Winning the words a welcome, as a rose
Reaches you of her smell, I felt the ground
Yielding beneath me and 'neath all around,
Sceptic and scholared Christian. We were those
Who, drawn by the common need—the common woes
Of youth who let faith go and nothing found—
Leaned hard together toward the common one
Reality left remaining. Then gleamed out
The single certainty all are sure about,
Our childhood's Trust and God's dear eldest Son,
Who schooled ourselves His brothers—I could shout
To learn from bettered books that lesson new begun.

THE GLORIOUS FOURTH.

(Farewell Supper of the Fourth Year Students, New College:
Darling's Hotel, Edinburgh.)

ONCE again in the old places,
And again the old, old faces,
   About a common board !
And, friends, 'twere mere dissembling
Not to tell you with what trembling
   The last glass is outpoured ;

Not to let the lips deliver
Their last with their own quiver
   Thrilled through from thrice three years ;
To trust the heart's denying
That somehow it was crying,
   And somewhere there were tears.

O days and names and places,
O happy, tear-stained faces
   That throng on us this eve !

O dear, delightful seasons,
O loved for fifty reasons,
  The College days we leave!

Come back, my friends, together
To the gay, glad, glorious weather
  When we were yet but boys;
When the cheek had yet its rounding,
And the foot had yet its bounding,
  And life was loud with noise.

Come, sign with slow, stiff writing,
Like one his doom inditing,
  The College Book again;
And ask, or ere you close it,
Your neighbour if he knows it—
  How things have changed since then.

And ask of your old Being
If aught was to its seeing
  As things this evening seem;
Do College skies beam o'er you
Bright as they beamed before you
  Or was it but a dream?

A truce to such sad comment
On the gold-engirdled moment
　That links us here to-night.
If it was not all fair weather,
Yet we went through it together,
　And that makes it all seem right.

Oh, this those years have given,
And better gives not Heaven
　That gives us all the best:
The love of the leal-hearted,
A link not to be parted,
　Two heart-beats in one breast.

O friends, be still and listen,
Though it make an eyelid glisten,
　To the voices of your lives,
To the head with his hard wrestling,
And the heart with her soft nestling,
　And the hand that strikes and strives.

And better—blown across 'em
Like a bit of bee-sucked blossom
　The presence of a Friend;
G

A busy brain beside you,
An heart wherein to hide you,
  The help that brothers lend.

Oh, this was the best learning,
To find such fires were burning,
  As nothing ere shall drown !
Oh, this was the best schooling
To feel the rays uncooling
  Of the sun that goes not down !

What though the Year be broken,
Our bosoms bear the token
  That binds, that binds for aye.
South Afric suns may smite it,
Australian stars may light it,
  We'll wear it night and day.

Then here's to the old places,
And here's to the old faces,
  Be every glass outpoured !
Here's to no cloud between us
Till some kind Hand convene us
  About a higher board.

March 27, 1879.

THE NIGHT BEFORE THE BATTLE.

(University Prize Poem, Rhetoric Class.)

THEY are gone; the last word spoken, ere we meet in dense
array,
Yet I seem to sing—such music is in darkness more than day.

'Tis the song we sang as striplings, when we mimicked war's
alarms;
'Tis the song will thrill to-morrow through the thundrous clash of
arms.

Strange, that aye before the conflict quivering calm the spirit
whelms,
Like the whispers rolling, rushing, through the depths of evening
elms.

Ah! the palm supplants the elm, the aloes screen the beechen
lea;
But the heavens are one above us, big with stars for them and me.

O ye silences of earth, how dread and deep are ye to bear!
Easier in the sweltering noonlight prodigies to do and dare.

Nights that mock us with your stillness, days that deafen with
    your roar,
Stirring thoughts you will not answer—What behind us? what
    before?

Fancy, O thou second dawn, thou meteor blazed about the sky!
Swifter than the shafts of sunrise runs thy lightning, Memory!

Angel of my country, why dost vex the angel of my home?
She is pale with woes and weeping, thou art flushed with wrath
    and doom.

Out upon this frenzied flutter, has a song the soul unbent?
I will quit this world of visions clustered in the stifling tent;

I will step into the midnight, silent save the leafy hum;
I will see how fair the earth is, ere the battle-curse be come.

I will step into the midnight, consecrate to God and me;
Hear Him send His voice before Him, ringing through the times
    to be.

Burning thoughts into the future still my wildered fancy flings,
As into a well a pebble, listening for the sound it brings.

Low and lurid lower the watch-fires, gleaming through the forest
bars,
Flaring up their gross pulsations to the trouble of the stars.

Hush! a whiff of wind, a whisper, blowing from a distant sea,
Calm and cool, as a new star from breathless heaven had yearned
o'er me,

Blotting out the fire, as mother's kiss her fevered infant's dream;
And the tranquil mind returning, tears the veil from things that
seem.

What is life? A flash of steel, the dim delirium of a wound.
Am I here? or, Have I passed? And life is gone while I am
swooned.

What is war? A maniac's ponderous rattle at the gates of Truth;
Tapestry reversed; a monstrous infant uttering tones uncouth.

Something crude, confused, imperfect, marred by turmoil in our ears;
Wiled into a subtler song, when echoed down the rolling years.

War is not our own. A bird may bear the thunderbolt of Jove ;
Who but *He* can trace its pathway when the splintered oak is clove?

So the battles shake our cities, but they die away to heaven ;
Softest snatches, blent in beauty, to the upper spheres are given.

Hark ! what says that wind of whispers busy with the wanton buds?
Is it not some fringe of tempest threshing forests, whirling floods ?

Is there not some spot of fancy, be it space or be it time,
Where the battles make a music, deeper peace and more sublime ?

Verily the ages tell it—war is but the shell of peace,
Till the blossom, grown to fulness, bursts the leaves, and war
    shall cease.

War is but the severed cadence, voiceful, for its mates are dumb ;
So our note be full and true, what matter when the others come?

Is the old to go by dying? Is the new to come by birth?
Where the uproar and convulsion? Where new heavens and new
    earth ?

O thou world so big with dying, therefore art so big with life !
Stars may point the path, may comfort, but they will not quench
    the strife.

Angel of my country, how dost clasp the angel of my home!
Ye are one, the civil manhood, fraught with social herodom.

Certes, gory is the gauntlet, but it graspeth life about;
Certes, blows are on the harness, but they beat a music out.

Let the fires then flicker heavenward, let them sink to ghastly
    glare,
I will never call back darkness; let them burn—they cleanse
    the air.

Better is an English song than shrieks that trouble yonder camp;
Better is the rail and trenching than the vapours of the swamp.

Better the Martini rifle, that I burnish here alone,
Than the spear or blundering firelock that these rebel races own.

Better than discordant clamour, clanging fierce of lance and targe,
Rings the "Forward, Forty-second, *this* way, on your pins and
    charge!"

All is well. This life is little; little can our vision seize.
Time is larger than our out-look; there are other worlds than these.

Therefore I will trust the future, turn my face toward the sun,
Where in front the dawn, Perfection, lights and leads the ages on.

I will trust: for, not as painter, poet, or musician He,
Having well begun and prospered in His masterpiece to be,

Falters fearful at the crisis lest the promise fail the end,
When the plot's detail has thickened, craves a master-stroke to
    blend;

Throned in silent sense of triumph, clad in consciousness of
    might,
He can watch His purpose, pressing through our darkness to His
    light.

LATER POEMS.

CHANGED ARE THE THINGS I SEE.

CHANGED are the things I see
  To my window come back grown older,
Ay, field and tree, they are changed to me,
  And still more changed the beholder.

Say is the light as warm,
  Is the day as bright as ever,
Is it past the glimpse of perfect form,
  The flush of a full endeavour?

.   .   .

So sank the sun, and with him
  My heart sank down with sorrow,
But heaven grew bright as earth grew dim,
  And the sun came shining thorough.

Still 'tis the same, the same
  As when first the sight was given,
Still a crescent of silver flame
  Hung in the height of heaven.

Changed are the things I see
From life's low window corner,
And many a truth is changed to me,
And still more changed the learner.

But oh, God's heavens, ye shine,
Ye shine and do not alter;
Turn more that way then, eye of mine,
Foot less in the footpath falter.

Bonskeid, Dec. 28, 1889.

DETERMINATION.

"C'est bien puissant le 'je veux' de la Volonté."—*Eugénie de Guerin.*

A VACANT hour! a wintry day!
Green fields! a sky of ashen grey!
A horse there on the towing way
  Straining along;
Not worth so many words you say?
  'Tis worth a song.

Ho! brother, in the traces there,
With starting thews and steaming hair,
How bravely dost thou forward fare
  Up the canal.
Thy load says, "Further if you dare";
  Thou say'st, "I shall."

O heart upon life's towing road,
With cares that drag, and fears that goad,
Tug on, toil on, 'tis well bestowed,
  This strife and strain,
One more mile onward with thy load,
  Is surely gain.

Between Winchburgh and Linlithgow, Feb. 3, 90—2 p.m.

IN THE GARDEN AT FINCASTLE.

Not but under showers,
  Under sunshine sealed,
Do the fairest flowers
  Fullest fragrance yield.

Not but from the cloud,
  Light that makes him dark,
Pours his loudest loud
  Pastoral, the lark.

Not but from thy pain,
  Thorn that tortures still,
Struck and struck again,
  Poet, pipe thy fill!

Sept. 1, 1890.

THINKING OF A FRIEND IN TROUBLE.

' O WHY for me this starry light,
When others tread the starless night?
O why for me this perfumed rose,
When my own brother flowerless goes?'
Thus speaks to me a brother's pain;
Answer me, gracious God, again.

Is't that th'abyss had whelmed my bark,
Compelled to voyage in the dark?
Is't that my steps had strayed from Thee,
If no sweet flower had bloomed for me?
Say, speaks it *thus*, my brother's pain,
' Beware thou stray, or sink, again?'

Is it that, with no pain to see,
My heart had heartless grown in me?
My star, unmarked, had fruitless shone?
My rose, unshared, had bloomed and gone?
Say, speaks it *thus*, my brother's pain :
' Beware thy selfishness again'?

Is it that, had I known to trace
Some merit congruent with grace,
I had been lifted up with pride
And Love's pure sov'reignty denied?
Say, speaks it *thus*, my brother's pain:
'Adore Omnipotence again'?

O Sovran and Unsearchable,
Who doest all, and all things well,
Thou wiser than the wisest mind,
And than the kindest heart more kind;
My very doubts Thy wisdom prove,
Thyself dissolves them: Thou art *Love*.

Friday, Sept. 26; Sabbath, Sept. 28, 1890.

SURSUM CORDA—A SPRING SONG.

I.

LIGHT slowly lengthening, life slowly strengthening,
  Green coming back again, vivid and young;
Breath beating fast in us, death fleeting past in us,
  Powers meeting vast in us, proud to be sung.

II.

Hope, how we bound with thee! joy, how fly round with thee!
  Spring, how are crowned with thee spirits of men!
Earth, how thou ravishest! heaven, how thou lavishest
  Songs on the minstrel who greets thee again!

III.

Freedom fall'n low with us, right moving slow with us;
  Haste ye, and go with us, rouse ye and sing;
Strike, fife and drummer, in; speed the late-comer in;
  Welcome the summer in, welcome the spring.

Jan. 27, 1890.

H

IN AMOREM.

"Every sacrifice shall be salted with salt: every one shall be salted
with fire."—Mark ix. 49.

When thy cup is at the brim,
And thine eyes for gladness swim;
When thy darkest doubt is stilled,
And thy dearest hope fulfilled;
When joy is heaped and cannot higher—
Ask the baptism of fire.

When the lips that thou dost love
To their sweetest utterance move,
When the soul, with longing sore,
Knows it does not long for more,
When thou hast thy heart's desire—
Ask the baptism of fire.

ON THE OPENING OF FREE ST. JOHN'S CHURCH, DUNDEE.

O Thou that art engaged to be
The unfailing Guest of two or three,
We name Thy name and wait for Thee,
    Thou promised Saviour, come.

O Thou whose word we strive to keep,
And love Thee, and are led like sheep,
Bring us God's love, indwelling deep,
    Thou and Thy Father, come.

O Thou that at our door dost stand,
And knockest with the wounded hand,
Open Thyself, the feast command,
    Come in, Lord Jesus, come.

O Thou that wilt not see bereft
The little ones whom Thou hast left,
Give us, we cry, the children's gift,
    Thou, by Thy Spirit, come.

                  Feb. 7, 1884.

FRIENDS.

ALEXANDER DUFF.

Nat. 1806, *Ob.* 1878.

" BLESSED ARE THE DEAD WHICH DIE IN THE LORD."

THE histories of heaven and earth are still,
  And through the silence, through the shifting scene,
  A fragment from a chorus breaks between,
Pure melody, 'mid the mixed strains which fill
The Apocalypse. Heaven has a sudden thrill
  From earth. We know not wholly what they mean,
  Those lips of benediction that o'erlean,
Those drops that on some open grave distil.
Yet so could we cry peace to the world's noise,
  The rush of all things racing on their goal,
And hear, above, beyond, another Voice
  Bid it all cease, to list a passing soul,
And know how such a dying not destroys,
  But only marks the march by which His plans unroll.

II.

Saints' deaths do but give dating to the world,
  They are the human points of that one plan
  Which moves unhindered and unhelped of man,
On whose sure surface he and his are whirled,
Obedient ripples that a breath has curled
    And quieted again.   For when the span
    Fulfils, and goeth back where it began,
Into the interval God's own voice is hurled.
For He will have them forth to write in heaven
  How far His purposes have reached the full.
These deaths are dear, for that the dead are given
  Entirely up to Him, being home from school,
And henceforth needing to be drawn, not driven,
  The subjects of His reign, while others of His rule.

III.

"BEHOLD A WHITE CLOUD" (REV. XIV.)

Oh, well it seems that this same snowy cloud,
  Wherefrom the final blessing falls in dew
(Much like the mist that once before was loud
  With words of "My Beloved"), sudden grew
  Into a fair white throne whose wintry hue

Took nought of shadow from the golden-browed,
    Keen-sickled Reaper-King, who rose and drew
His weapon down earth's harvest heavy-bowed.
Oh well for us, who bend sore hearts to-day
    To hear that benediction for the dead.
We weep, for the best sickle is away;
    We shout, the King of Reapers comes instead;
"Had we but him to lead us!" do we say?
    Look you! the Lord Himself! We shall be led.

IV.

TWO RIVERS.

The restless Tummel runs about the feet
    Of these fair heaths, fresh-springing at his birth,
The restless Tummel goeth wild and fleet,
    Nor halteth him to help the needy earth
    To any show of fruit or flower's gay mirth,
Nor swerveth save a brother stream to meet,
    Hurry it on, and gather force and girth,
Never, till name and course are gone, complete.
The sluggard Hoogly creepeth sad and slow,
    Washing his rice fields, laving groves of cane;

He steals no strength from the far hills to sow
The easy flats, producing without pain—
Such and so different do the rivers flow ;
Who knows what currents mingle underneath the main?

V.

Spring, doors of peace, spring open, we are come!
We bring him to his resting-place and peers.
Were sorrow not so sown across the years,
What company his, the cream of Christendom!
And even now we catch a gathering hum
From the great dead who greet him. Ringing cheers
These plain inscriptions sound—Miller and Spiers,
Guthrie, Chalmers, and Cunningham, we are come.
Oh, master of the pen that sprinkled fire,
Oh, gentle knight whose words were lances thrust,
Oh, golden mouth inspired to inspire,
Oh, hammer head that did our foes to dust,
Oh, princely prophet than the highest higher,
Take this last hero-heart! His sickle shall not rust.

The Grange, Feb. 18, 1878.

VI.

GOD OF THE DEAD AND OF THE LIVING.

Cry "Blessed" to the dead, but bless us too,
  Who must go orphaned over vacant ground;
  Bless us, O God, in listening for the sound
Of these lost footsteps, that we follow true,
And do not quit us as lost children do;
  Whose tears and trouble turn their senses round,
  Until they cease to follow and be found,
And out of very weeping miss the clue.
Yet let us linger a little near the spot.
  'Tis pleasant, and we think the hand that took
  Our brother just from here will turn again,
Having housed him safe, and we would miss it not
  When it returns, for like a child we look
  Just *there* to get what went amissing then.

New College, Feb. 14, 1878.

IN MEMORIAM W. G. ELMSLIE.

DEAR friend—for 1 may call thee thus; the name
   Will sound not strangely where thou art—dear friend,
   Whom here I honoured with the cordial bend
The boy's heart gives the student grown to fame.
" Friend," that first night I saw these blue eyes flame,
   And heard these lips their rapid arrows send,
   Swift to attack but swifter to defend,
" Friend," said my heart: to-night it says the same.
Dear friend, who seest the truth now through no glass,
   Who readest now no Scripture but the Word,
   Who ridest now to triumph, not to fight,
Would that my soul one day to thine might pass,
   Would I might be for ever with the Lord,
   Changing this darkness for that light of light.

Nov. 16, 1889.

IN MEMORIAM J. F. EWING.

ONE more who made this earthly pilgrimage
An arduous mountain climb, a stubborn fight,
Fought till the nightfall! Yet it was not night
That fell, what time a voice cried: "Cease to fight
My warfare; enter on My heritage;"
Nay, but full daybreak, "day most calm, most bright,"
Boundless and endless, rich with all delight
That heart can hunger for or mind can gauge.
One more at Life's clear fountain drinks his fill,
And feasts his eyes out on the Face divine;
One more ascends into His holy hill,
Beholds His beauty, worships at His shrine.
Brother, let Christ call *me* too, when He will,
If only my freed spirit be with thine.

May 7, 1890.

PROVOST SWAN.

(and L. S.)

December 17-18, 1889.

Written at the Club Meeting, 3 Park Circus, Glasgow, 14th January, 1890.

OUR head has fallen; fall'n is the ample tree
Beneath whose generous shade this friendly band
First gathered. Brother clasped the outstretched hand
Of brother; but who joined all hands was he.
Fallen is our head, and in our sorrow we
Stand orphaned. Bare to all the winds we stand
Trembling, as if the next our face that fanned
Might be the chill breath of eternity.

Is *this* it? or what is it? this soft breath
That blows from out the South, and with it blown
Something?—a lily from an English lake?
This is the breath of life, and not of death!
Welcome already for our brother's sake,
Henceforth and always welcome for thine own.

G.A.S. TO L.S.

LILIES are of flowers most rare,
Lilies are for all things fair;
But I say, deny who can,
"Lilies are for Lilian."

Lilies lurk in hidden wood,
Lilies are like maidenhood;
And I say, the happy man,
"Lilies are like Lilian."

Lilies are the songs of spring,
Lilies bloom what poets sing;
But what song is sweeter than
"Lilies are for Lilian"?

Lilies flower for spirits meek,
Lilies fan the lowly cheek;
But, the best that flower or fan,
"Lilies be for Lilian."

Lilies are of flowers most rare,
Lilies are for all things fair,
And (I sing it; join who can)
"Lilies are for Lilian."

AN ELIZABETHAN,
''THE FRIEND OF THE BRIDEGROOM.'

MUSIC FROM THE MARRIAGE OF R. AND E.

Two streams I knew together—
One rose among the heather
　Where a south moorland lies;
And one rose near the city,
Full-breasted one, one pretty,
　Under the self-same skies.

You could see them both by climbing
A height not meant for rhyming,
　So call it what you will;
The spots from which they started
So slenderly were parted—
　It seemed a single rill.

And when you saw their severance,
How one was grave, like Reverence,
　And one was wild, like Mirth,

I

So likely lay their courses,
You said : The natural forces
  Have mated them from birth.

You said : A kindred motion
Will link them ere the ocean,
  Or marriage must be wrong ;
For all the stars intended
That these two should be blended,
  So also said my song.

Still they kept strangely sundered
Till everybody wondered
  Why nature disobeyed ;
But if they knew not, I did,
Why one a bachelor bided,
  And one remained a maid.

Oh, sealed to common senses,
The subtle influences
  That shape these lives of ours ;
Oh, plain to their quick spirit,
Who, when the grass grows, hear it,
  Who hark the springing flowers.

Then meet and flow together,
Make summer in the heather,
    You wedded streams at last.
I understood—the stars too—
And wished away the bars to
    This joy that's flowing fast.

Oh meet, the stars will quiver
More brightly on one river
    Than on two severed streams ;
And I shall sing the better,
When once there comes a letter
    Fulfilling all my dreams.

And from the height I'll often
Gaze till the distance soften
    Around your wedded ways;
Shall I name the place—I dare to—
"The eyes a Poet's heir to,"
    Which has watched you many days?

Then meet, and flow, and murmur,
It makes one's faith the firmer
    To see one's hope come true.
To see you twain together
Brings a blush above the heather,
    Though that is blushing through.

                    Aug. 1877.

WITH A BRACELET OF BOG OAK FROM IRELAND, CUT INTO ROSE, THISTLE, AND SHAMROCK.

HERE, Love, 's a little gift for thee,
Carved from an ancient Irish tree,
Which bloomed in happier times, A.D.
    700 odd,
When Erin's Isle was owned to be
    The Isle of God.

Perchance it heard him, garbed in brown,
The herd boy from Dumbarton town,
With furrowed face and shaven crown,
    Proclaim the Truth;
Perchance it saw the Druid's frown
    Melt into ruth.

Perchance its fellow bore him forth,
The Dove that nested in the North—
Crown, lyre, and pen of little worth

He counted then,
To herald over Scottish earth
The King of men.

Perchance upon its neighbour leant
Grave Columbane, as on he went,
Hood, cloak, and girdle travel-rent,
    O'er sea and land,
While Gaul and German meekly bent
    Beneath his hand.

  .   .   .   .

So, Love, at length it comes to thee,
This bit of an old Irish tree,
To bloom upon thine arm, and be
    A signet broad,
That Erin's Isle again we'll see—
    The Isle of God.

                              Sept. 27, 1889.

"IMAGO CHRISTI."

As one who enters on the shaded room
  Where sits some watcher of the heavens, and peers
  Through his wise instrument, and straight the spheres
Flash on him. Up from the illimitable they loom,
  Enlarge, and pass into their spacious tomb
In shining sequence, till the ravished seer's
Eyesight is dazzled, less by what appears
  Than what lies hidden in the boundless gloom.
So through this kindly glass that thou hast given
  I look, and look; and lo, the skies are rent,
    And whole stars shine where points were seen before.
Yet with each vision of an ampler heaven,
  Much as the record moves my wonderment,
    The unrecorded moves me even more.

CHILDREN.

THE DAY WHEN RUDOLF DIED.

Oh! well for the Little Children, that they are gone away,
They never gave their missives up nor promised us to stay;
Just fingered a while with the fringes hung over them out of
heaven,
And in between their gazings at God a glance at us was
given.

Oh! well for the Little Children, they left their angels there,
Keeping a rapid converse up the blue way of the air—
Keeping a wistful watch till the child was home again,
Glad that he came himself, nor cost them a journey's pain!

Oh! well for the Little Children, they patter along the row,
And seek out each his minister, and tell him he may go;
Tell him, "I'll stand for myself now—you needn't keep room for
me,"—
And send him on errand elsewhere, who knows? they send him
to *thee*.

But, oh! our Little Children, they could not stand upright,
Will the angel hold them in his arms till they are grown up quite?
Or will he take them by the hand and run with rapture wild
To the Angel of the Presence, who waited on Jesus-Child?

Ah! ill that the Angel of Presence is angel of absence for us,
That, his face being turned to the Father, we see but his back
    parts thus;
His back and a bit of his wings, all pink and transparent with joy,
And folded round something—you see it?—the form of a little boy.

Oh! well for the Little Children, some office hath fallen free,
Heaven would take in some wider note, some novel order see;
We gave him to a service—small part on earth appears:
Oh! well for the older people, who have children in two spheres.

December 13, 1877.

AN ORPHAN.

MOTHER is dead: she simply said
With a slight droop of the curly head,
Just like a flower at fall of rain
Bent to be lifted up again.

Mother is dead: I had no dread,
Saw no other to ask instead,
Spoke to the child as if naught had occurred,
Saw it all in a single word.

Mother is dead: two little feet led
Where the turf was newly, newly spread.
Then, with a sob that startled me:
Mother, O mother, to have died with thee.

GOD'S NURSERY.

I WAS in God's nursery to-night as the evening was getting dim,
And I sat with God's children, and they were talking of Him;
And another Child was with them, though Him I could not see,
They say that God has an Elder Son, I think it was He. ·
It was bedtime before I was there, and all was done for the
 day,
And the children were going to bed, but first they were going to
 pray;
And that strange Child who was with them the other children led,
But He did not say 'Let us pray,' but He went on talking
 instead.
"Father," He said, first of all: though I could not see for the
 gloom,
Yet the instant He said it I felt there was Someone else in the
 room;
And the room itself must have grown in a very little space,
For the Child called to Father in heaven, and heaven is a far
 away place.

But oh, what an echo was left by that one single sound,
It crept into every corner and wandered round and round,
The very air felt holy wherever the echo came,
Cried the children, "Oh! that it ever were so. Hallowed be that
name!"
With that they smoothed their dresses, the frocks their Father had
given,
Marked with His name and made to be kept clean for Father in
heaven;
They seemed to prepare for a feast, though everybody was
dumb;
When all was ready I heard, "Now may Thy kingdom come."
And then did they talk of a playground? or what were they speak-
ing about?
A place for spending days in, for running in and out:
But might it be under His eye like one somewhere else they had
seen,
Strong and sheltered and safe, but pleasant and wide and green.
Wherever He wished it to be, they would play in it under His
eye,
They would not have two playgrounds, one on earth and one for
the sky;
The same would do for both, and so the word was given,
"Let us do what our Father likes on earth as they do it in
heaven."

And was it hunger now these little hearts perplexed?
Though it was not long since last meal time nor far to the next,
For fathers lay by for the year, mothers lay in for the week,
But 'tis only of the little each day that the children speak.
A little makes them hungry, a little satisfies,
So "Give us to-day our daily bread," was one of the children's
  cries.
And then a rustling of ravens, that after the sower run—
No more noise than the lilies make when they drink in the
  sun;
So each with a piece in his fingers, the children were put to
  bed,
But first there came a meeting of lips and little voices said,
"We have kissed with one another, kiss us, our Father in heaven,
We have forgiven each other, we want to be forgiven."
And then I heard the sweetest sound any on earth can hear,
A face hung over each little head, coming quite close and near,
Leaving a rose on either cheek and either eyelid wet,
And the mouth of God and the mouth of the little children met.
But, when the face was lifted, there was something clasped them
  still—
"Surely it will not lead us wrong but rescue us from ill."
Then came low regular breathings like footsteps dropped in a
  dream,
Led past every perilous place, lifted at every stream;—

But the things they said in their sleep were the strangest things
of all,

Angels round them, heaven opened over them, words let fall.

The feast had come His hand had prepared, His brightness made
it shine,

And "The kingdom, the power, and the glory," said the children,
"all are Thine."

Begun Bournemouth, April 27,
finished on board the "American," Oct. 12, 1879.

ON RECEIPT OF A CABLEGRAM.

UNCLES, when new nephews come,
Some give gold, and silver some;
Uncles who have nought to give
Ought to play the fugitive.
I who neither pay nor flee,
Should I send some poesie?
.   .   .   .   .   .
Shall I an epistle frame?—
But I do not know his name!
Praise his voice, portray his mien
Whom I've neither heard nor seen?
Ah! but one suggestion slips
Through my pursed and puzzled lips—
Do you ask it? think of this:
Take and give the boy a kiss.

Wynberg, Cape of Good Hope,
June 1st, 1880.

WELCOME TO BABY.

(EDWARD PEASE.)

WHAT is the weather we welcome him in?
Chilly without and cosy within,
Into our new made, lovely nest
Baby came—the loveliest.

What is the cradle we twist for him?
Mistletoe mad and holly trim,
Wreathed with Christmas roses round,
And the first snowdrop from the ground.

What are the christening robes he'll wear?
See, they're weaving in the air :
Frosty flake and crystal star
Baby's earliest broideries are.

What is our hymn for Christmas morn?
"Unto us a Child is born";
Sing it on earth as they sing it in heaven,
"Unto us a Son is given."

Dec. 15, 1880.

K

SCHOOL-GIRLS.

GIRLS are going to school—
  Looks high-coloured and cool;
Spring's sweeping by with a light in her eye,
  Beaming and beautiful.

Girls are going to school,
  Conning the crookedest rule;
Puzzle's a grace in a girlish face,
  Learning leaves woman a fool.

Girls are gone into school,
  Faces rounded and full,
Spring has swept by with the light in her eye,
  Leaving me sorrowful.

IN THE NURSERY.

ON EARTH.

M. S. S. W.   C. M. B.

"How is she, Nurse, to-night?" I said.
"Safe asleep in her little bed."
Yet not the cradle soft and strong,
Nor the love that watches it all night long—
Not these can quiet the heart's alarms,
Till I lay her again in her Shepherd's arms.

IN THE SKY.

R. F. B.   G. B. W.

"How is he, Lord, to-night?" I said.
"Safe asleep in his little bed."
But not the sight of the narrow tomb,
Nor the bitter blight of an opening bloom—
Not these can trouble the heart's deep rest,
When I see him clasped to his Saviour's breast.

Aug. 23, 1885.

A SONG OF SEVEN DAISIES.

WHICH name is sweetest, none agree;
I know the sweetest name to me:
It is another name—and yet
I love the name of Margaret.

One wears it with the angels now,
At whose grave knee I learned to bow
My infant head. My eyes are wet!
I bless the name of Margaret.

And one—we love thee for her sake,
Her life thy love will stronger make,
She loves thee for thyself, and yet
She loves herself in Margaret.

One we already sister call;
We all were rich if one were all;
But thou dost make us richer yet,
We have two sisters, Margaret.

And last I name them, children three,
" Five," " seven," and " two "—clap hands for thee ;
Our Meg she is a clinging pet,
But she will love " Aunt Margaret."

July 16, 1889.

A FLOWER MAIDEN.

FREELAND brings me all delight,
　Wealth of budding powers;
Joys of soul, and mind, and sight—
　Meg brings me flowers.

Robin flings me—seraph bright—
　Buds from Eden's bowers;
Baby missives, angel white—
　Meg brings me flowers.

Maida brings me, laughing sprite,
　Sunshine dashed with showers;
Rainbow moments, dark and bright—
　Meg brings me flowers.

Gwendolen brings—the darling mite—
　Smile that never lowers;
Tenderest clasps for day and night—
　Meg brings me flowers.

Men may bring me wrong and right,
  Thorny days and hours;
But I'm armed for any fight—
  Meg brings me flowers.

THE LITTLE RED SQUIRREL.

An account of his Death and Burial, and of all those who had any share therein.

(Written at the Age of Twelve.)

Published by W. Young & Co., *one wet afternoon at Bouskeid, in the Year* 1864.

A LITTLE red squirrel sat on a green tree,
And merrily, merrily chirrup did he ;
He climbed up the boughs with his sharp little claws,
And cracked the hard nuts in his firm little jaws ;
And oft as you walked underneath the green tree,
The shells falling down by your side you would see.

But one day as we passed—
'Twas on Saturday last—
We saw no squirrel there,
Though we looked everywhere ;
No nut-shells were falling,
No chirrup was calling ;
For the poor little squirrel, while merry at play,
Had been captured, and murdered, and carried away.

Who killed the squirrel?
'Twas I, said the cat,
I'd a right to do that,
    I killed the squirrel.

Who saw him die?
I, said the hawk,
Sitting near on a rock,
    I saw him die.

Who caught his blood?
I, said the stoat,
Sitting near on the rock,
    I caught his blood.

Who'll make his shroud?
I, said the rabbit,
I'll fold it and lap it,
    I'll make his shroud.

Who'll make the coffin?
I, says the hare,
I'll gnaw it out square,
    I'll make the coffin.

Who'll make the grave?
　I, says the pig,
　With my snout I can dig,
　　I'll make his grave.

Who'll carry him to the grave?
　I, says the toad,
　I don't fear the load,
　　I'll carry him to the grave.

Who'll bear the pall?
　I, says the fly,
　If it be not too high,
　　I'll bear the pall.

Who'll be chief mourner?
　I, says the adder,
　I'll daily grow sadder,
　　I'll be the chief mourner.

Who'll lower him down?
　We, say the crows,
　We'll stand in two rows,
　　We'll lower him down.

Who'll read the service?
 I, says the jay,
 I can chatter away,
  I'll read the service.

Who'll say Amen?
 I, says the owl,
 I can dolefully howl,
  I'll say Amen.

Who'll fill in the grave?
 I, says the mole,
 I'll come away from my hole,
  I'll fill in the grave.

Who'll tell his poor friends?
 I, says the monkey,
 I'll ride post on a donkey,
  To tell all his friends.

Who'll toll the bell?
 I, says the quail,
 If you tie the rope to my tail,
  I'll toll the bell.

Who'll deck his grave?
    I, says the ant,
    Some flowers I will plant,
        And thus deck his grave.

Who'll put up a tombstone?
    I, says the sheep,
    I'll fill it in deep,
        I'll put up a tombstone.

Who'll carve the name?
    Who but I, says the weasel,
    With a mallet and a chisel,
        I'll carve the name.

Who'll write his life?
    I, says the rook,
    I'll make up a book,
    Written so well
    That it cannot but sell,
        I'll write his life.

LETTERS.

BONSKEID.

BONSKEID.

Bonskeid, Pitlochry,
October 9, Evening, 1875.

I WRITE to remind you of your promise to let me have
the name of Craik's little book—not because I think you
will forget it, but rather as an excuse to my conscience
for omitting a small dose of Livy before shutting up for the
night.

I had a delightful plunge through mist and mud to-night
to my meeting in the Glen, where we had a pleasant hour, as
always, when there are very few. We talked together about
the words, "Thou wilt light my candle," Psalm xviii. The
energy of the walk rid me of an attack of discontentment,
consequent on an unsuccessful attempt to settle down to work
again, after my two days' (would it had been twenty) dissipa-
tion with you; when, instead of plodding, we indulged in
'vain and foolish questionings.' The pleasure of your visit
has not yet lost its evil effect on me; though, I hope, our
'night thoughts' of Wednesday have been ere this atoned for

by you in the shape of lengthy slumberings. You have been,
I have no doubt, already up at Edradour, and out for a ride to
make up for a six hours' stretch at Hebrew. Julius had not
overdone the 5th conjugation in your absence, I hope. It is
pleasant to think of the number of pheasants you have slain
since your return.

I have just been hearing from the under gardener
about the joy and peace of —— and his wife, who
were brought to the Saviour when Miss Savill was here.
Formerly rather a quiet man, he is now overflowing with the
warmth of first love, and the two talk of nothing else in their
daily work. When the Master is working at one's very door,
one feels lost in shame at the trustlessness and restlessness of
one's life. You feel as if your struggling and weary spirit
got some dim realization of what it is to be in the secret
of the Lord, wherein some lives seem to find their guiding
spell. It throws a bar of light athwart the seething unintelli-
gibility of our own little world, and the great world beyond,
of which ours is an image. It kindles a tremulous hope of
possible restitution, which is enough for me.

Forgive the madness of this epistle, and forget the nonsense
of it; but, oh don't forget me in your prayers; for the coming
session, I fear, will soon drown me again in a miserable
alternation of self-satisfaction and self-despair.

Candlish's death makes one feel very heart-sick, I was almost going to say home-sick, but you won't hear of shuffling off this mortal coil yet. And, indeed, after the first faintness has passed over, the emptiness and cheerlessness of the struggle makes one draw the girdle tighter, and resolve to live, rather than die. For, if He has blessed Chalmers, Welsh, Cunningham, Guthrie, Miller, and Candlish, surely he will bless you, Frank, and me ; and finding work and faith for them, neither shall be lacking to us.

The last words of the grand old doctor from the pulpit, about the Christian life being a 'walk,' quite startled and then encouraged me ; so like they are to what we were talking about together while he was dying ; saying how difficult it was to believe in progress, when one was toiling along in the darkness, forbidden to linger behind, unable to run on before and see the end of it all. Whose faith follow, considering the end of his conversation ; Jesus Christ the same yesterday (when He was toiling along, and we were dreaming), and to-day (when He is transfigured, and His death calls us to labour), and for ever (when we hope to be united).

L

Attic Tower, June 5, 1879, 1.30 a.m.

So I have stolen away to "my Den" through the hushed house and up the creaking stair, and am alone to meet the dawn of a new day for Bonskeid and me.

All round me are plain green-papered walls, with narrow windows let into the walls, through which one bar of landscape at a time can slide, of heaven or earth, according as I sit or stand. There is a little square tapestry carpet rounded with the varnished floor; a low cane-and-pine couch to match a reading stand for one reclining; a little oblong table covered with an old crotcheted cover of roses and lilies, and behind me a bookcase with books. Oh, *there* are all my select friends, seen and smiling to me, though my back is to them. A row of pure German theology: on Christian Doctrine, Christ's Person, Old and New Testament Theology, a couple of great Commentaries on the Psalms and the Life of Christ. Then there are select books of reference: dictionaries, grammars, and so on. Then there are my great Christian heathen—Homer's "Odyssey" and Virgil all; then my heathen-Christian Heine; my great Christians—Dante and Pascal; then the mighty singers of our century—Goethe, Tennyson, and Browning. Some lighter verse, Barbour's epic ballad of "The Bruce," "The Nibelungen Lied," a rare volume of

the best shorter Scotch ballads, and the master ballad
singer from Tübingen—Uhland. There are lighter things
than these : some volumes of German story, the "Promessi
Sposi," and a trifle of Corneille, Racine, and Molière. Then
come some things more sacred—"The Imitation," the
"Gesangbuch," and a volume of Beck's "Reden." Last
there are the words of eternal life themselves : my Cannes
Latin Testament with Beza's Psalms ; my Italian "Santa
Biblia" of '72 ; Martin Luther's, with me since Tübingen
in '76 ; and a Griesbach's New Testament with the Scotch
Psalms and tunes. These are almost all, and they have
not come there by careful forethought or intentional selection ; they have been floated in here by the everyday
tide of human affairs—one when a room was shifted ;
one when a sudden fit of sorrow took me ; one in a flush
of joy ; one when some thought struck me, or some wish,
or some recollection.

I have just come from two hours over my old college desk,
my shelves, my papers and letters, and I came up here to
get calm, and I *have* got it. For I could not turn over ten
years of my past life and touch, now college letters, voices
of men in trial, misunderstandings, makings-of-it-up ; now
essays, now records of societies, now the quartettes we made
to play away the tiresomeness of a *diligence* in the Pyrenees ;

now a passport to Italy, and a wax taper for the Catacombs; now exam. papers—bushels of them, and exercises—cartloads in Latin and in Greek; now relics of the French winter; now sacred records of the Revival time; now certificates—no end of them; I couldn't do it without being fairly unmanned.

Bonskeid, July 15, 1879.

. . . And then the drive home. You can have no conception of the summer that is here. The green is wonderful. The woods are crowded to an impenetrable mass; every wall is overleant, every water overhung, by the rank riches of summer; every mountain climbs to heaven, heavy with luxuriance; every valley is an unknown depth of verdure; here the birches flutter full of leaves through every trembling tendril, there the pines drop languid with large fans fringed with fresh gold; here the chestnuts are broad with glistening foliage, there the firs taper to a new, never before seen, top of spring. Every plane tree flaunts a thousand leaves of glossy lightness, every oak bristles dark with a myriad patterns of deep green.

" Wilt thou know of my doing to-day? Here are some of the σκόπιαι καὶ πρώονες ἄκροι which stand out in the sunlight. 11.15 walked to the school with Uhland, reading snatches of Swabian song and calling Carlo, our Dandie Dinmont terrier, to heel. Spent some time in school, hearing Bible lessons, infants' spelling, older boys' arithmetic, big girls' reading, examining books and " copies," and all school gear. Then a "blow" home, roaring "Graf Eberhard im Barte" to the glorious mountain air. Then a hasty getting "tidied," and then into the arms of — who? who but your old friend of the Rialto,—guess again,—Professor Blackie, with his hearty Πῶς ἔχεις ; καλῶς ; and my unhesitating Παγκαλλίστα. Then follow minutes of Elysium, were life only the academy, and the world made for students and professors. I hear him talk of foreign travel, of the pictures it gives to hang for ever in one's after-study ; and as the brave old snowy head falls back against the claret of the sofa, he brings me out, one by one, the pictures—Rome, Florence, Milan, Göttingen —latest hung therein. Then we go to early dinner, Mrs. Blackie and Miss Fraser being our other 'company.' After dinner the Professor and I have an hour and a half's stroll to the school, while I drink·in the delightful desultoriness of his talk, and try to stop just when he does—which is not always easy; for you cannot tell why this cistus should so seize his fancy, or that potentilla interrupt his thought. But it only breaks, to flower forth again more beautiful, as he talks first of Italy, its grace we lack so in Scotland, its lack of sternness we could so well supply; its few great hearts alive and active, its multitudes asleep and slow; then of its new literature; of Massimo d'Azeglio's Memoirs and Villari's Savonarola; then the parties—Cairoli's and Minghetti's, hurry (as he thinks) and moderation; then what poets should do now, not be so sundered from their time as Browning (who walked these roads), nor so bound to the mere accident of rhyme; let poets write short, sympathetic lives of men; let them write history, not stories. And so we come to the school, where the Professor has half an hour of cross-questioning the best scholar, to the advantage of the whole school; and such happy definitions, such funny "pokes" with the mind and the walking stick, and such instructive sallies and amusing information. They are rather annoyed when I tell them how great a man my master is. Then they sing to him in good Scotch, to his heart's desire, the alte Greis and junge Herr joining in, and then the little ones have "action-songs" which please him well. So at last he rises, and, asking them some things in a Gaelic too good, or bad, or both (or rather book-born), to be understanded of them, he breaks into a beautiful Gaelic lament, while the whole little audience stands open-mouthed-eyed-and-eared and hardly recovers to whisper "Goodbye, sir," ere he and I are out into the air again,— I apologising for having given him such little work for so long, and he humming out something in Scotch, which he breaks half sternly, to say: "There are four things a man must love: children, flowers, woman and — must I say it?—wine." He went on to tell me how hateful and horrible a nature Napoleon's always had seemed to him, who said: "I love nothing, I love not woman, I love not dice, I love not wine"; "Il n'aime que la politique." Then the hill came, and with the hill our thoughts could not help climbing. 'Was I licensed?' No, not ordained yet, of course. Would I preach the splendid possibilities in a man, to sink to the beasts which perish or to rise to heaven itself? No; he did not deny that the heart was deceitful and desperately wicked, but should we not call on men to realise for what they were made? Jugend ist immer bigot, says Goethe ; yes, but age will make the heart open, and you will always grow gentler. No man understands men who does not always leave himself more behind and go and sit by others, wherever they may be. He could not say what Greek one should read who had few books and less time; no, read only where the heart runs; read nothing except that about which you are 'passionate.' (Oh how my whole soul leaped out to meet these words; I did not once even gently deflect the current of the conversation, for to get the testimony of a true heart is a priceless treasure, κτῆμα ἐς ἀεί). So I got no lists of authors or works, and was it not well for either of us? I told him of my three loves—Greek, German, and Italian. Yes; Italian was living; there was a great language being spoken there at present—what would the issue be? "L'Italia è fatta, l'Italiani sono da fare." Then German, "Alles Gross ist Deutsch geschrieben." Read, where you are thinking; don't read where you are not feeling. This and much more on churches, war, and architecture; youth and new opinions in theology, and materialism (he had read some, he couldn't for the life of him remember it) and philosophy. He talked and I treasured up. But most the thing on the three tongues and what was work for poets. Then came afternoon tea, and raillery between him and my mother, who since many years has 'cared for his soul,' upon religion and growing ripeness in it. Then they packed into the pony phaeton—my professor a perfect picture, his broad Leghorn bright with a flower, scarlet of sedum, fringed by golden yew; and the ladies a good background.

Bonskeid, August 26, 1879.

. . . After dinner at 1.30 yesterday, I wrote letters for an hour till 3. Then Hugh and I walked up the Glen to finish our visits. We called on the gardener's wife, and old Mrs. Seaton, Balnald, in whose house I have kept a meeting these many years. I told her of aunt (she is 82 herself), and it comforted her to hear of another who at her own age was leaning on Christ and getting rest. She is my truest friend in the Glen. Then we called on the smith's widow, a comfortable little character who keeps chickens and has a queer accent; the tailor, an old soldier, brought to the Lord some years since, now near his end; the old land steward of a neighbouring estate; and Mrs. M'Lauchlan, Drumdagowan, a young wife with four little girls. Then Hugh and I hurried home to have tea with the children in the Temple, and had the greatest fun carrying down the tea things in the rain to the house. Then for an hour Anna and I watched the sunset wandering up and down the strath, and working every moment a fresh wonder with river and rock and tree. It struck out every little cranny in the hills into bright relief; sparkling with the rain, it came behind the birches, and traced every tendril of their matchless foliage out upon a fair background of brilliance; it caught up a mist from the river, and kept painting the hills and trees between it, and finally fixed it all with rose. It threw a rainbow light over all else, one foot of it upon the Giant's Steps and one on Ben-y-Vrackie.

Bonskeid, September 2, 1879.

Coming home from the little meeting instead of taking the Pass, I crossed the heights above Killiekrankie, and, as I came out upon the open, all the stars came out, and the heavens brake open to their highest, and through a sea of snow and azure rode the moon triumphing. In the midst of it all I stood by a sick woman's bedside and heard her say she was leaning all her weight on the Lord Jesus, and then wrestled with her husband at the door.

Bonskeid, Sabbath, 4 p.m., September 6, 1879.

At the Bridge of Garry on our road home from church we dropped off and climbed to the lofty plateau to ask after the poor woman. At 11 the Lord had come and taken her to Himself. We knelt by the bed, where the face was so thin and pinched, but peaceful, (I never saw any but an infant after death till to-day) and gave thanks and prayed, and then I spoke and prayed with the family in the kitchen. Surely the Lord was with us there. . . .

8 p.m.—What a marvellous joy possessed me in the pulpit to-night as I closed; to think, said my heart, that the joy of the Lord is the best joy, and that thou art to have this hereafter for ever. And so I kneeled forward in the pulpit until all the people had passed out, praying in the darkness. . . . It was dark to-night in the chapel after I began to speak, and I spoke with the more freedom and boldness, and they heard with the less confusion and fear. I forbade the lights at the close, and at the last we stood in the gloom together in confession and raised our voices together in song. It was "Rock of Ages" I repeated, and we all knew the words. Meantime the rain fell heavily outside, and I intimated in deep silence how to-morrow our whole Presbyterian Church in Scotland (Established, Free, and United) would join in prayer for fine weather, if it be God's will, and we should join too.

The poor woman at Tenandry said to Grace Stewart, who nursed her, on Friday morning: "But will I get away with Jesus, Grace?" Grace said her end was near, and, if she trusted Jesus, she would get away with Him. "Then I'm lippening to Him" (trusting to Him), she said, and so was quiet and spoke little more that was for earthly ears. I breathed into her ear yesterday, "Jesus is with you," "The Lord is your Shepherd," "In the valley of the shadow of death, Thou art with me." She nodded assent. When on the day before she was tossing and throwing herself about she cried, "Row (roll) me over to Mr. Barbour's side ; that's the strongest side." Then she began to wander.

Bonskeid, 1881.

These two days I have been going throughout the coasts of Bonskeid, from Ballinluig even unto where thou goest unto the Bothy, and from the hill that goeth up to Drumdagown even unto the oak that is by the well. Are they not all written in the book of our rambles together? I have pursued after the reapers and overtaken them, and smitten them with an exhortation great and sore. Yea, I have shewn unto them a new teacher, above all the teachers that have been in the glen.

Bonskeid, 11.30 p.m., 18th June, 1883.

I am writing in the saloon, strangely silent, and yet surrounded with so many voices of memory more eloquent than any speech. One feels here how little *past* he has had in his own home ; the *present* is all there, rich and full ; but here there rushes on you at once a whole world of association and allusion ; you enter a crowded room ; you are awed by all you have been, and others before you have been ; it is a long history you are conscious of, not an individual life. I never felt it so much before ; though the feeling is old enough to make me fancy it must be true.

Outside, things are to match. How poor Aberdeenshire is to Perthshire. Here the hills are wooded to the tops ; you have a delightful sense that all is clothed ; there are such hidden depths to explore, such recesses in which to hide and live a hundred fairy lives, far from men and hard, onesided, domineering reality. The rhododendrons are all in bloom, scented with journeys twenty years old at least, when we drove up from Dunkeld. Azaleas are at their best, redolent of Springland and childhood and πόθος ἀνεκλαλητός. The broom blazed like a golden lane along the railway line ; while the rowans and lilacs and chestnuts glimmer visible, though ghostly, even at this midnight hour. Just now I saw out of the dining-room window the moon riding, Diana-fashion, on great masses of white fleece cloud against a deep background of blue, right over the west wood. It was a great sight here now for anyone ; but it was also a splendid picture out of an old gallery for me.

Mr. Fergusson and Mr. Pittendrigh have just disappeared after one and a half hour's talk in the gloaming (after worship) over old Highland stories, wherein Mr. Fergusson told us, among many things, how he grew up a jack-of-all-trades in his father's house, and shod the minister's pony in the home smithy, and made two ploughs, one of which still cuts old mother earth at Moulin, and a set of harness, also shoes for himself and family, and did odd joiner jobs about the place ; and how the minister 'improved the occasion' by calling him out before everybody at a catechizing and saying, 'Ye have got great talents and ingenuity; just so much will be asked of ye.' Who knows what he owes to these faithful words ?

We had a delightful drive, abundant tea, and stroll thereafter to the view beyond the saw-mill. Everything is as it was.

Birnam, January 11, 1884.

I have just enjoyed a delightful drive down with Norman Mackay in the car. Bonskeid was looking its best, bright April sunshine breaking through the mists and falling on purple birches, brown oaks and larches, and green Scots fir. A slight peppering of snow covered the ground, hardened into frost on the higher grounds. Walking up to ——, I found Mrs. —— away at the doctor's. The old man (well over 80) looks sadly stricken, but is still a fine gentlemanly old fellow. Coming from rugged Aberdeenshire it was like being received in the grand Springland manner. The old woman, also a goodly bit of clay—with Gaelic shining through every second word, and the second-sight tinging her stern Calvinism. What these Highlanders might have been, might yet be, and bring forth—but for the poison with which Saxons have drenched them. She drinks—has always drunk, I am told—this grandmother stepping into the cold stream—has suckled and bred both son and daughter to drink (so they say) . . . . I sometimes wonder whether it is I who am mad on this subject—and all the world—who are taking all this murder quite pleasantly—are sane.

. . . The Vale of Athole was as beautiful as ever to-day, as we passed along. Only its beauty somehow seems less inspiring and more subduing than it used to. One begins to understand why people, as they feel life ebb within them, desire to see again the old sights and familiar spots of their first days. They soothe one somehow, like the faces of those you love. I still feel life strong within me; but I am thankful, too, for the sense which restrains, as well as the sense which urges. I need much holding back.

I was up at Robin's grave this evening, and did give thanks for God's goodness. The words on the stone seemed to tell of his life above. " The Lord took him up in His arms, put His hands on him, and blessed him." He did that two years ago, and He is doing so still.

My chapter this morning, too, told me something of him (Luke xx. 35-8). We shall not get new children there, but we shall have our own made angels. There is no more dying there for them or us, but a blessed life as God's children. What it will be, we know not; though Mrs. ——'s last words often come back with sweetness

—" Everlasting—spiritual—union." It seemed given me
as a watchword for to-day's life that part of the text,
" worthy to obtain that world." It is an extraordinary
thought that we may be, and by grace are being, fitted
here and now for such a world.

At 11.30 Mr. Ritchie came, and we climbed the hill
together to the Mains. . . . The Glen was looking
lovely, the young larches just breaking into green, and
the hills quite royal in their purple. . . . We walked
back by the new drive. The riverside was sunny and
warm as June. . . . At 3.30 we drove down by the
Falls to look at the new plantation there. . . . At the
bridge Robert Mackintosh and I came down from the
dog-cart and walked home by the footpaths along Garry
and Tummel. It was a lovely afternoon. The mottled
bed of the Garry showed brightly through its flowing
stream ; while dark Tummel in his full strength went
hurrying down and "leapt his falls with thunder rather
than glee." It was almost terrible to sit at the Queen's
Seat and watch the frothing water sweep sounding by.
The background was unusually striking. The Giant's
Steps stood out behind in black profile against the sinking sun, while clouds of spray curled up in front like
incense steaming from an altar.

M

All the way home was one wonder of beautiful bare birches ; their delicate foliage full of sunlight, shaking like fairy veils in the faint-blowing wind, and their straight stems flashing like spears of silver out on the hillside. I never knew Bonskeid more beautiful.

Bonskeid, Pitlochry, May 17, 1887.

We are having days of great happiness here. Every hour is filled, with errands to the Village, the Milton, the Cottage, the School, Balnald, the Farms, and so on, and so on, which bring back at every turn old scenes, in few of which you do not figure. From measuring fields to catching fish, from fetching home a minister to finding out what is wrong with the water-supply, from recovering a runaway tune in the chapel to restoring a strayed sheep to its park—what Bonskeid experience have you not shared? And now over all there is shed a strange halo from the green sward on the top of the West Wood, where he sleeps who gave its character to everything, and for whom it seems as if everything might still be done. God grant that it may be done in some measure as he would have desired.

The magic of spring was surely never more wonderful than it is at Bonskeid this May. Even while I am writing, and it is growing dusk by long delightful inches, the woods are still bursting open, as if for pure excess of life they would die. The green is almost too bright for earth, and far too rapid and varied in its change for earthly senses. You could shut your eyes and cry for want of human beings fit to match it, were it not for two little figures that flit about as familiar with it as angels with Paradise, two little souls that laugh and prattle, eat and sleep, and only know that it is their father's and mother's home.

Bonskeid,
Pitlochry, N.B., August 26, 1887.

I promised to tell thee of my ride yesterday afternoon.

I heard in the morning that the re-cast bell for Tummel Bridge Free Church was lying at Pitlochry, and that there was no sign of any one coming for it. So I thought I might go up there myself and see why it was not being sent for, and get some one to go for it. The man from the casting-works was waiting in the village, wasting his time, until it should be sent for.

At a quarter to four I trotted off with Polly by the front avenue, in order to post some late letters and have a look at the new entrance to the gate, which Forgan has finished on one side. I trotted quietly up to the glen (4 o'clock), walking down all the hills, and letting Norma have a good look at everything. She showed a disposition to turn in at the west lodge (as she had done at each of the Faskally lodges the evening she arrived), and seemed to think the well was 'meant for her to drink at.'

It was a strange, still afternoon—everything covered with a grey-blue mist. At the Queen's View (4.15-20) I got off, and led Norma near to the edge of the rock, and had a quiet glance at the weird landscape. Land and water lay under the same heavy veil of vapour, reed-beds and glassy levels and jutting promontories (ἀκταὶ προβλῆτες), standing distinct, yet dim, in their gauzy dress. The very heavens were thickly draped and curtained, so that Ben-y-Vrackie, behind me, loomed faint and spectral against the sky. Only above Schiehallion the mist was caught aside, and a slight suffusion of red showed the grand mountain in its simple strength and massiveness.

Gently descending the hill, I felt the rich fragrance of the birchwood on Borenich, doubly rich with all the drought and heat of this tropical summer, and ready to exhale with the

slightest moisture. I passed the farm at 4.40, and beyond
Croft Douglas had a minute or two's chat with a lad,
carrying fowls to market, to whom I gave a threepenny-bit
to carry the fowls head-upmost for the rest of the way.
That was at a quarter to five—an hour from starting—and
at five minutes past five I made Loch Tummel Inn. A
little girl at a cottage beyond gave me some water in a tub
for Norma, who said she could go no further till this want
was supplied; indeed, she nearly carried me into the cottage
in order to emphasize her feelings on the subject. So we
went through the close wood of Portneilan, and, emerging
from it, caught the full blow of moorland air off broad
Rannoch and lofty Schiehallion. How I drank it in!

The last three miles we did in twenty minutes, for I was
getting anxious about my time. As we flew along, I was
only aware how the scents kept changing. Rich aromatic
birch, with bog myrtle among it, rose from either side as we
slanted down from the heights above the loch to the river-
level again. Then came the open moor, with honey-laden
heather in full bloom, among grey rocks and stones on the
one hand, and on the other the wide-running Tummel beginning to race and grumble again with the narrowing glen.

I arrived at my destination, a little way beyond the
peaked bridge on the Rannoch road, at 5.25.

Bonskeid, April 9, 1890.

Everything is bursting and breaking and sounding with young life ; starlings and 'merles' were crying in the oaks above me; doves, pairing, fled like surprised lovers from a spruce close by my side ; rabbits set off before me with the peculiar hop, step, and jump they only put on in spring. Every tree and branch and twig wore a favour different to its fellow, that looked as if it had never been worn before. It is God's world, and He still says in the hearts of those who keep His commandments, It is very good.

CULTS.

CULTS.

The Free Manse,
Cults, Aberdeen, October 17, 1881.
[After his Ordination.]

MANY thanks for your timely reminder of Wednesday last. It struck a dormant chord and met a real need in me. I had no time to sit, or stand still and think beforehand. Things were pressing in on every side, till the Martha in me was fain to exchange places with her meditative sister. But Mary had her hour at last, I think.

The minister, an earnest young man, took for his text, "This is the record, that God hath given to us eternal life," and he was helped to bring home to me in a new way what the outlook and the issues of the work that was being given me were.

And when he and the others, my brother among them, laid their hands upon me, my heart did indeed melt down, and I sought to offer up myself, all sinful and ashamed as I felt to be, to Christ and His service.

Yesterday Mr. Wilson was all his old self. The opening
prayer, going about like an invisible friendship among the
people and finding out what everyone wanted to ask for ;
the chapter (Acts xx. *ad fin.*) opened up like a pastoral
directory ; the sermon (Tit. iii. 8), 'the doctrines of grace
the only guide to a holy life,' full of large familiar ex-
pressions and masculine force ; the introduction making
such solemn engagements and undertakings for me as, I
trust, will be remembered and striven after with strong
wrestling and tears.

The Free Manse,
Cults, Aberdeen, July 29, 1882.

I must write and tell you how it went with us yesterday
[on the occasion of Mr. Moody's visit].

I had 100 great bills printed the day before, and a lad
and myself went over the whole place the afternoon of
Wednesday posting them and personally inviting the people.
I had been in Aberdeen each night through the week,
and saw some souls pass into the light at the Music Hall
meetings. Many of our best people went in too. We
had a special 'bus out at night each evening through the
week. Some of them were deeply impressed.

Yesterday forenoon I again spent in bill-posting and publishing. At three I heard Moody give his Bible Reading on "God's love," one long and moving appeal to Christian people to open their hearts to this revelation of love. We had a prayer meeting at the close.

At 4.30, he, Stebbins, Gray Fraser, and the "Christian" reporter, drove out with a carriage and pair to the manse. Charlotte had tea in the drawing-room for them and for some of our people. Moody had his arms open at once for Freeland, and said as he took him, "This is the fourth generation." I marvel at his absolute disengagement from everything except the matter in hand.

Twelve of the Aberdeen choir had come out by the train, and had tea in the dining-room. Then we drove up. I had great hopes of a good meeting, but a few fears they were all disappointed.

Our office-bearers were marshalling the people in their places, and Mr. Moody at once took the meeting in hand, making the people sing, getting them massed up about him, ordering all things.

Almost all Cults was there. I think every house had masters or servants, old or young, representing it. Perhaps this mixing of classes was the finest outward feature of the meeting. Town and country, rich and poor, saints and sinners, were all mingled together. By six o'clock the place was packed, without being crammed. Moody gathered himself together for a great effort. He would get hold of the youngest there and make him understand the way of salvation. If we were all to be in eternity to-night, this would be what he would do. We should never meet again until the judgment seat. He would so speak that no one could then say, I never knew the way of salvation.

Four words he took to tell it, ' receive,' ' believe,' ' take,' ' trust.' Under each particular he was extraordinarily full and explicit. Every word seemed given him ; like John Knox he ' spared no arrows,' and they seemed sticking ; you could hear them strike. In all my life I never heard the Gospel so fully and powerfully preached. My own heart seemed an index, registering the effect on others. I just drank it all in, and prayed heart and soul all the time that my people might drink it in too.

His wealth of Biblical reference was amazing, only more wonderful than his anticipation of every possible objection or question of the human hearts before him. It was the true prophet reading off the history of every one before him, and then reading the Scriptures into the face he had read. The effect of each successive experience, caught and carried back to you with a text at its heels, was very impressive.

Towards the end he began to plead with the people individually. I saw nothing, but I know now heads were going down all over the church; and then, to my intense delight, he began to call upon those who wanted prayer to rise. The Spirit of God seemed moving on the face of the waters, and raising, literally *raising* one after another. It was unspeakable to hear how he pleaded and pleaded for another and another before he should pray. *Twenty-three* rose and sat down again.

He did not spare himself. He spoke on for more than an hour. You would never have imagined that he had an audience of between two and three thousand waiting him half-an-hour away. *We* seemed to be the only people he had ever preached to, or would ever preach to. He might have been living among us by the way he took hold of the entire wants and state of the congregation. Young men, women, children, parents, all got their own message. His closing prayer was most pathetic. His petitions for my people and for me, and for the mother of our old minister, and for you next week, were just brimful of affection and understanding.

He told us he had come here in order to keep a promise to you; you were going to be among us next week (the words he used of you were very high but most discerning), and he had just come to make a beginning. The humble-ness, as well as the gigantic strength of the man, shone out radiantly all through his address. What touched a High Church lady who is staying with us, and who only knew him from hearsay, was his exquisite tenderness.

After he left I asked those who wished to be spoken to to come into the hall. Several did so, and I believe one or two found peace. I am just going out on a search-expedition.

I intend to have a noon prayer meeting each day of our meetings. In great thankfulness, in trust and prayer,—Yours ever.

The Free Manse,
Cults, Aberdeen, Aug. 8, 1882.

I think evangelism has got a standing among us, which, with God's help, it may never lose.

It was a little awkward ending with a new voice, and one pitched in a slightly different key to that of the evenings before. But even this could not interfere with the impression, or hinder God's hand from working, as it did; we had a good meeting, and I gave them Rev. iii. 20, as a close, and got one new one to speak to. What I learned most at the meetings was the absolute

indispensability of previous preparation and of prayer, and
the great advantage of keeping feeling under restraint. I
managed better, I think, on Sabbath night about that.

We had a good little noon meeting upon Friday—not
quite so large however. I took the account of the revival
under Samuel, 1 Samuel vii., with its completing touch, the
setting-up of Eben-Ezer. On Saturday night we gathered,
some fifty, to give thanks. I took the treasure, the trustee,
the entrusting of it, the security, the termination of the trust.

On Sabbath morning Milne was admirable, giving us
first a rapid Bible reading over John i.-xi., to bring out
how much might be accomplished *at one interview with
Jesus ;* then preaching on John i. 29 and 33 *ad fin.*—the
connexion between the outpouring of the blood and of
the Spirit, the connexion for the Christian preacher, for
Christ Himself, and for the believer; under the last
article he was most practical, showing how Christ was the
fountain of the Spirit both for pardon, purity, and power,
and meeting the difficulties about predestination, evidences
of grace, and assurance of salvation. The people listened
and liked him.

At night I was helped, taking your theme, "A Good
Man's Visit to a Revival." 1. The revivalists; 2. The
visitor; 3. His view of the revival; 4. His advice.

1. The central object of the Christian life—"the Lord";
2. The vital attitude of the Christian life—"cleaving to the
Lord"; 3. The essential organ of the Christian life—"with
purpose of heart . . . to the Lord."

Your words about the burden of life and work were, and
are, very helpful to us. It brings one strangely near to
another, to know of his conflict, ay, even to hear his heart's
sighs. I think there is a secret and irresistible sympathy
which knits us at such times. It reminds me of the scene
in *Iliad*, β, where Agamemnon summons the chief of the
Greeks to his side in dire need, while he makes prayer
and sacrifice. But his brother comes *uncalled*, his own
heart telling him what trouble Agamemnon is in. αὐτό-
ματος δέ οἱ ἦλθε βοὴν ἀγαθὸς Μενέλαος. ᾔδεε γὰρ κατὰ
θυμὸν ἀδελφεὸν ὡς ἐπονεῖτο. And if human hearts
thus answer each to the other's need, what of that divine,
sustained, untiring sympathy of the Brother of us all. *Non
enim habemus . . . qui non possit affici sensu infirmi-
tatum nostrarum, sed tentatum in omnibus similiter.*

Cults, March 15, 1883.

I have had a blessed afternoon, trying to do the Father's
business. After sending off the money I went to visit

poor Mrs. ——. She had wonderfully recovered from her terrible illness, when one day at church she caught cold, and three weeks' nursing her parents made it worse. The left lung is badly affected, and her cough was harrowing to hear. Yet she said she was 'contented.' I had no words of my own for such distress, but I took her back some grapes.

Then I carried Dr. ——'s message to old Dr. ——, who is standing, very calmly and happily, not far from where the river must be. I felt like a child at the foot of a rich old fruit tree, with beautiful, sweet fruit, falling off of itself whenever he opened his lips. He spoke much of the mystery of Providence; much of faith in Jesus Christ; but most of the great tenderness of God's love and of our need for great tenderness in telling it to men.

In the train to Perth, June 18, 1883.

It is a perfect day to travel in, so warm, yet fresh, so genial, yet stimulating—a day like one of ——'s ideal characters, who do you good without either ruffling or re-laxing you! On starting from Aberdeen the sea-effect was more brilliant and original than I ever remember to have

N

seen it. It was this. The light, penetrating the thick clouds with itself, cast, through their medium, a rich purple over the nearer part of the sea, which lay perfectly still, as though pleased to receive it, and content to rest a little after the rough play it had had yesterday. But beyond the clouds the light poured, straight and strong, upon the further surface of the waters, which were ruffled slightly so as to resemble frosted silver. On this silver the little brown sails of the herring-boats were set, like flies in amber. Only what made the silver so wonderful was that the purple ground appeared quite distinctly in it. It was, for all the world, like my 'Babylonish Garment' of last night, fine soft stuff embroidered with precious metal. . . . Reading to-day in the 'Journal' of the opening of the Episcopal Church at Mannafield, with its 'procession,' its 'priests,' its Presbyterian ministers put down among 'the laymen,' its inaugural sermon saying there were 'no means of grace' between Aberdeen and Banchory-Ternan, rather dis-heartened me. One must try to put the doctrines of 'free grace,' of the utter ruin and the unmerited redemption, of the 'One Mediator' and the universal priesthood, so plainly that such things may be seen to be manifest lies. Above all, one must testify more with the life, that these are truths to live for, and turn out better lives than delusions do. There is trial and discipline enough for a follower of Christ in these days, if he have but grace to take it up. Only the cross in the heart can conquer and keep down the cross on the sleeve—but it can and will.

The Free Manse,
Cults, Aberdeen, Aug. 10, 1883.

About more devotion to the work, I can join in your prayer for that with all my heart. I feel the need of it more every day. Old habits, easy circumstances, even earthly love, and a hundred other things fight against it. You know me enough, and yet not enough, to tell what my battle is.

I had to induct Barry last night, and took the opportunity to pour forth my own experience into the text, "Feed my sheep." The pastoral virtues I said were these : sense of responsibility, sustained effort, patience, self-denial. I know them from sore need of them, scarcely more.

You ask about my summer plans. I suppose you mean for work, as I have had my play. I am lecturing over Joseph again in the morning—miserable flogging of a dead horse, for the most part. I began it without sufficiently thinking, but chiefly in order to get sermons on the

Commandments written out for the evening. I have gone
through three or four of them. My greatest trouble is to
be clear and elementary enough.

But I am at sea about the whole subject of preaching.
I have been labouring these two or three years at your
plan of subjects and divisions, not without benefit, mainly,
however, in the way of checking indolence and slovenli-
ness. But I am not sure it is the right path for me.
Sometimes I feel as if Maclaren's plan of a succession of
explosions were the one for me. Yet there there is the
danger of carelessness, not to say extravagance.

I am in another trouble about the question of reciting.
It is a heavy burden sometimes. I read last night for the
first time for many years.

Another and a much wider question lies before me,
whether orator's work is mine, or poet's? There is not
much difference in the two, it seems to me. My nature is
not to reason, but to feel. *Reason* wrong I often do, but
feel wrong very seldom. I sometimes think I could help
in the work of the time better by singing in a corner
than by shouting on a stage.

But half of this is cowardice. I do not forget the
higher interests, sometimes the ἀνάγκη, thank God, really
ἐπίκειται, sometimes I can rise to the Οὐαί μοι. Nor do

I forget that a minister may sing, there being birds about the altar as elsewhere, ay better, happier birds, as David found, than elsewhere. Perhaps this, too, some day may be given me.

Freeland is getting 'strong on his feet'; he has a merry way with him, which comes from some ancestor who lived when there was a good, healthy humour and a jovial laugh among mankind.

Cults, December 24, 1883.

I had a pleasant journey north on Wednesday by the 'Ferries.' A number of Lord Randolph's hearers, fetched over from Fife, were returning to their homes. Having testified to the Conservative unity in Queen Street Hall, they were already indulging in local jealousies as they recrossed the Forth. "Na, na," said a farmer (Kirkcaldy man, I think), "Na, na, thae *Cupar fowk* need na' suppose they'll get the like o' *him*" (referring to an invitation the poor, proud little local capital had sent to his lordship.) After crossing the Tay (where Broughty Castle always reminds one of Knox's galley lying off it, in the estuary, and his prophecy, as he looked over to St.

Andrews, that God would yet make his voice to be heard there), I had two interesting talks with fellow-passengers upon temperance. The first was a young lady, who had grown up in a Christian family, where wine was moderately used, but who, with all her brothers and sisters, had become an abstainer, partly through her parents' care and counsel, and partly through a friend's example. She, however, would not hear of going one step further and encouraging those within her influence to do likewise. She prided herself on being above that sort of proselytizing (I think the want of a ministerial and congregational opinion on the subject had prejudiced her). I asked her if it was fair to have enjoyed the advantages and securities of her position (which she admitted), and escaped the many perils of a less decided attitude (which she admitted also), and not even to lift one little finger to bring others of her own age and standing and intimacy to a like situation of decision and safety?

Her seat was taken, at Montrose Station, by a man (about 35, I should say), who stood on a curiously antipodal ground. He was the father of a young family, and I opened the question from that quarter. He at once met me with a blank negative, enlarging on the mischief he had so often seen arise from an over-strict upbringing of children, giving me a score of ministers' children who had turned out ill,—those worst, who had never seen wine in their father's house ; stating that children were not to be governed by moral considerations ; they never dreamed of such things, and that they would start in life far more likely to succeed, if they had seen a moderate use of stimulants at home. Much of this was, of course, impossible to meet.

To the 'manse-child' argument, I could only reply with a list of manse children who had not done badly, from the University of Edinbro' in my time—such as Guthrie, Ritchie, Macleish, Sorley, Greig, Lundie, etc.; that no child, in manse or out of it, was born good (which he admitted); that a minister's child had as many censors as there were names on the church roll ; and that, from their position, they were more exposed in some ways, *e.g.*, to flattery and over-attention, and general spoiling, than others. The government by non-moral considerations I, of course, flatly denied ; and went, I think, within some little distance of his affections by the argument, that all a mother's influence was derived from self-sacrifice—an influence which a father could possess in a much smaller degree—and that, if he was not prepared to curtail his comfort, or go contrary to the custom of society, for his

children's sake, to this small extent, he was putting from
him one of the most potent weapons he, as a father, could
wield. But the 'manse-child' and 'Christian-child' theory
blinded him to the better part of this appeal. We parted
good friends ; he, I hope, to reconsider his position; I to
tell myself and my people at the prayer-meeting what is
the great obstacle to worldly men taking Christian ground
—the atrocious inconsistency of Christians. A minister
had led this man, an abstainer and disliking stimulants
up to the age of 21, to begin beer-drinking.

It is one great charm of travelling that you can learn,
as you cannot where you are known, what men's opinions
and positions are.

I was at Queen's Cross, relieving Smith, yesterday and
preached from 1 John i. 7 ; subject: "The Cleansing
Efficacy of Christ's Blood." Heads : (1) the *Place* of Cleansing—in the presence of an awakened conscience; (2) the
Time, 'cleans*eth*,' now ; (3) the *Cause*, 'the blood of Jesus
God's Son.' I gave my people the same at night. In the
Bible Class I am going through the Catechism, and am
profiting now by Dr. Whyte's peerless work on the subject.
It possesses the principal virtue of a book, readableness,
and the second next virtue, originality. You hear the tone
of the man's voice nearly in every line.

I asked Freeland if he had a kiss for 'Anda,' his name for you, and he held up his great loving mouth. I hope to be at Bonskeid about the beginning of the year.

I was helped in preaching on "A Desperate Case and a Divine Cure" (Rom. viii. 3); only I got harsh at times. Oh for some of the love of Christ in the heart to take the place of this wretched self! It makes me so miserable at times. If I could but look to Jesus, I should be so happy. I do get glimpses—just beginnings of glimpses —of Him, but they fade away; and I find myself speaking of what I do not know.

. . . At —— it came on to rain, pleasantly softening the frosty night air. I ran up —— Street to get an umbrella, and saw one in a clothier's, newly opened. As I went in, the man at the counter said to a poor outcast-looking creature who was leaving the shop, "Good bye, and mind you look after yourself." It was, as I thought, a poor victim, he had been trying to help and counsel.

The incident led to one of the best and most helpful ten minutes' talks I have had for many a long day. The clothier (a young man about thirty) and his wife, members of —— Church, have been married for four years and led a very happy life together, but they have both at the same time been very unsatisfied. During the last year a strange, new experience has come to them—through no express message or agency or special providence, but only as a growing conviction taking possession of them both — the feeling, viz., that they had not yet let everything go and wholly given themselves up to Christ and His service. He could not say that the satisfaction was complete, but a new desire and power for service (in the mission district) had already come and was making him very glad. The only thing he could associate with this experience was— the breaking down of a reserve which had always been between his wife and himself upon religious subjects.

Cults, Saturday Night, Oct. 10, 1835, 10 p.m.

Dear old Mr. Reid has gone up to his room. It felt very solemn, seeing his white hair and bent form in the pulpit to-night, and hearing his frail but clear voice pro-claiming the Gospel of God's plighted faithfulness from a text redolent of the "revival" memories of 1859 (Hos. ii. 20). He was very fine upon how we must trust God, even when He was doing what we did not wish.

I had a good forenoon at my sermon, and a merry afternoon with sober J—— over the bills. I felt as if the joy of the Lord was moving me to make puns, but, as J—— had nothing wherewith to respond to them, it was not a very satisfactory frame to be in.

3.45.—We have had a blessed day. After going over my sermon last night, I felt it would never do—it was too philosophical and special a discourse for the occasion, and also too high and advanced a theme for me.

So at 11, on going to bed, I turned to Rev. i. 5-6—the Ascription of the Redeemed to Christ—and much enjoyed meditating upon it. I soon fell asleep. Margaret wakened me at 7 to a most perfect morning. Autumn excelled itself indeed, and the first yellow sunshine on brown leaves and golden sheaves was like a benediction to begin the day with. Mr. Reid at worship was again very reverential and helpful. I left him to finish his breakfast, and had three quarters of an hour to myself. Then came the hour with the young men over Luke xxii. (the Last Supper). On the way I took dear Freelie's painted beasts to give to poor Johnnie, who has the sore foot. I thought

Freeland would like the sick little boy to have his beasts. Dadda will get him some more.

Old Mr. Reid and I walked up together, the whole family of F——'s going before us; it was a goodly sight. I was much helped in prayer and meditation—though it was all unpremeditated almost—on "Christ's love, Christ's cleansing, and Christ's dress." Some seemed a good deal impressed.

I also enjoyed the Table fully more than I have yet done. I spoke on Mark x. 45—Lady Macneill's text—on how we must just let Christ serve us and not try to serve Him. Mr. Reid was ripe and fragrant and impressive on "It is good for me to draw near unto God." The singing throughout and parting prayer were unusually enjoyable. A large number communicated, though the church, as usual, was not full.

Study-Room, 9.50 p.m.

At tea Mr. Reid and I had a long talk on the history and work of the Free Church. The evening service was largely attended; the devotions were, if anything, a little long, but the sermon on 'Abide with me' suitable, and, at the close, searching. 'Ye gates, lift up your heads' went with great vigour.

'Another meal!' as the old gentleman greeted it, came at eight. Margaret has been excelling herself. And since then we have had a pleasant fireside chat, chiefly on his own experience, which covers the entire period of the evangelical revival in Scotland from '32 onwards. His visit has much encouraged and, I think, instructed me. I think one should always have one old minister a year at a communion. 'No man, having tasted old wine, straightway desireth new; for he saith, The old is better.' There is a rich mellowness and chastened calm about old saints which far surpasses the fresh wit and 'scampering' activity of the younger ones. I should like Freeland to know some of the 'Fathers' before they are quite extinct.

[The following letters refer to a deputation of students which had come to Aberdeenshire to hold a special Mission.]

Cults, Tuesday Evening, 1885.

I have been trying to remember the meeting to-night, and it has been strongly borne in on me that I should try and do something to bring you (the deputation) and our young men—and also the audience—nearer together. At least, the prayer given to me has been that you and they may, if it is God's will, be led very close to each other to-night. The fire generally kindles when the sticks rub hard.

I thought at first that it would be best for me to stay down here all the time. Only I am not quite sure how that might look to those outside. So I am coming up to the meeting at 8.30, and shall spend the half-hour before in prayer for, if not with, you.

1. I am anxious—very anxious—about my own young men One great prospect about this week has been the hope that they might get to know one another as Christian men, so as to stand together afterwards and (perhaps) form a nucleus round which others might rally. The beginning of such a fellowship is sometimes laid in united (audible) prayer. It would be a true heart's-joy to me to know that they could so join with one another. That, I am well aware, may be not at all the best way for them : it may not be God's will. But, on the other hand, it may. How to compass this end I hardly know. If they could have joined you alone in the vestry for ten minutes before 8.30, while the other deputies waited and did their work at the door, one of them (or two) might be persuaded to join in, and so the ice be broken. Perhaps you might manage it by saying the deputies would like to get to know the

fellows' faces (I mean the strangers), as they come in, as some of them gave them promises on their outings to-day, and that would be a reason for asking——(whoever of them, that is to say, happened to be up in time—it wouldn't do to delay the hour, to get them all into the vestry beforehand) to come into the vestry.

This is a long rigmarole. You will consider whether there is anything available in it.

2. About the thing that is next your own hearts—I mean reaching those outside. I could leave the meeting before it ends (for the vestry), and so practically let you be alone with the rest. Perhaps you could then press the men more earnestly, just as your fellow young men, if they have any desire to begin the New Life, to stay and have a few words with you about it. The Christian young men, and other Christians there, will, of course, be a difficulty ; perhaps it might be lessened, however, by entreating them to cry to God for their fellows as they go home.

This also may be impracticable. I only mention it because it is on my mind. Such burdens are a happy load, being very real proof that One above is moved by a lively concern for ourselves and our fellows—a small portion of which He is communicating to you and me.

[*On return to Cults after four months in Cornwall and Egypt.*]

Saturday, 13.3.86.

. . . I had a welcome from Mr. and Mrs. Donald this evening ; the doctor was out.   But my chief recognition has been a nod from a little girl as I drove along the road.

Sunday after church, 1.30.

I have got through my first sermon with God's help, not to my own comfort certainly, but I trust to His glory. The place was sweet and, at moments, sacred to be in ; and I gave what I had sought and got, though with much conscious weakness and want.   Oh to have love in the heart to Christ and His people.   So many faces were there that wore the grave, sweet look of true worshippers.   I could not name them all.

Cults, March 19, 1886.

I have had a busy, happy day.   The thaw continues, making everything dismal and bleak without, but all is warmth and peace within. . . . I had 33 boys and girls at the class.   They behaved better and sang better than before.   I told them about our journey as far as

Cairo. . . . Looking round on the children to-night, I felt as if I might be getting more of the pastor's heart than I knew. I seemed so to *love* these lambs—perhaps it was because of our own little ones, perhaps because of the Good Shepherd.

7.30 p.m.

R. M. preached with much calm convincing power on our sin: its disease, bondage, debt, and guilt; and how the only deliverer is Jesus; and how we are either welcoming Him and only sinning against our will, or refusing or neglecting His help, and sinning wilfully (Rom. vii. 24).

9.50 p.m.—I have just come up from worship, after a long chat by the fire on a point in R. M.'s book. We both parted where we began—on our own ground. His spirit is good to be near, especially for me. So clear and truthful, and thorough, and withal so earnest and humble. It is a great opportunity and privilege for me to be with him.

Cults, April 5, 1886.

I have had a blessed time to-night with the young communicants. All four who came said they were prepared to come to the Table; and, as far as I could see, they are true and sincere. —— said he thought he heard

o

singing 'like the church,' as he was at the harrows to-day; and he had been happier these weeks past than ever before. He said he never had understood so that Christ had suffered for him. *That* he must have been taught from above, for I have not dwelt much on Christ's sufferings. Would I could enter into them more.

——, who is very reserved, said he believed he had entered Christ's service; and, when I asked him why, answered 'because he felt it easier now to do right.' ——, when asked to pray for me, put up a beautifully simple request for 'him who is trying to make me Thine, and for everyone that is connected with him.' Amen. With —— I had a long talk; her heart seems like Lydia's, all 'opened.' She picks up what is said with the eager sense of a living soul. 'It has been put into my heart by the Lord,' she said first thing, 'to come to His Table.' 'Why?' I said. 'Because I love Him.'

Cults, April 9, 1886.

. . . It is incredible how blind we people called 'Christians' are to everything most real in life. Mr. Stalker has a touching passage about the *painfulness* of all the truest work for Christ, in the little memoir of Mr. Brown Douglas.

And next to our blindness about things as they are, surely most marvellous is our deafness to the simplest teaching of the Saviour. To *leave the ninety and nine* respectable persons and wander, and KEEP wandering, after *one lost* person—who follows Jesus in that eccentricity? (Luke xiv. 21, 23, 26, 27; xv. 2, 4-7, etc.) It seems as if I heard him saying (Luke xiv. 34) mournfully: You 'salt' of the earth, yes, you are very 'good'; but suppose, there's not an atom of saltness in you? What then? where shall I put you? What can I make of you? And isn't this the secret of all—our *infidelity* about what Jesus offers and promises? Nobody dreams of a woman overtaken with intemperance being recovered; every Christian you meet says so; and you catch the 'infidel's' spirit yourself,— secretly you cherish it. Christ does not pardon sinners, nor does pardon *change* them. We don't believe it for others, because we don't believe it for ourselves. 'Lord, I believe; help thou mine unbelief.'

I only ran over the outline of Gladstone's speech, and knew my prayers were heard. He may not carry it, but God will. I felt as if all our heroes in the Scottish Kirk were cheering that grand statement that Christian justice would never see another Establishment of religion set up anywhere within our realm.

Cults, April 19, 1886.

. . . Mrs. B. was worn away to a girl's face, just able to smile and speak. But what words! and what a smile! "I'm so weary, weary," she murmured, after a fit of coughing, "I wish I was at rest." "You'll get rest," I said. Her look was so lovely as she answered, "Yes, rest—delightful rest."

I was peeling some grapes for her, when her sister said, half shyly, "If it wasn't too much to ask, might she get a little of the soup Mrs. Barbour sent last summer; it did her so much good; Mrs. B. has taken a fancy that she would like some of it last night." I said nothing, but saw by my watch there was just time to catch the Cults train at 3. So I left Mrs. M. the grapes to peel, and took a cab to the station. Margaret had no soup ready, but was so pleased to make it in an hour. So at 4.16 I took it in and drove to the house again. I shall never forget the look the dying eyes gave me and the firm, loving clasp of the dying hand: "Thank you for your great kindness," she said. I had the delight of putting three tiny spoonfuls between the wasted lips. I took her hand in mine—"I'm leaving you with Jesus, Mrs. B." She smiled again. May I die the death of the righteous, and may my last end be like hers.

At 4.30 four children came. We read picture books together, and then had tea, at which one of the deputies, Mr. Maclagan (first year Divinity, U.P., nephew of Bp. Maclagan) turned up and entered into our society very nicely. We had the wild beasts' class and letter games as usual, and closed by singing a hymn together. We are to have Gospel addresses at the evening service to-morrow.

I have had a strange time the last hour. Coming home from our meeting—which was good—I fell in with Mr. ——'s prodigal son, and helped him home to his father's house and to his bed. May God have pity upon his soul, and show me more what I have been that I may have pity upon poor wanderers. . . . There are many poor wanderers for us to minister to here, if it be His will to give us strength to do it. The poor woman —— opened her door and heart to me so gladly, almost reprovingly, to-day. I had passed it for years. May God forgive my unbelief, and help my faith. Work for Him seems only beginning.

[*On the occasion of a second Students' Mission.*]

April 27.

Two young men's figures have just disappeared through the gate, Simpson's and Maclagan's. "He began to send them forth by two and two" (Mark vi. 7). They are going to prepare for to-night. We have had a delightful time together—reading, praying, and communing. . . . On coming in at 5.10 to dinner, we found a third man— Hamilton, from Canada—arrived out of town to help us, and during dinner Mackay, of Thurso, second year medical, turned up, more dead than alive, after travelling all night and day to be in time for the meeting.

We had delightful intercourse and a blessed meeting— the hall nearly full, and many farm lads there. The addresses were simple and telling, Mr. Mackay's especially touching a number. Three girls came back to talk with me. Oh! may the showers continue.

Wednesday, April 28.

In the morning the Aberdeen meeting 'men' came out —such a noble set of fellows—one New College, second year; one big, broad-shouldered medical; and one honours man in philosophy from Belfast. We had a talk and

prayer together; then they took coffee and set off for a
stroll round by Countesswells and into Aberdeen.   I went
to see the persons who stayed behind last night.   ——
turns out to be a splendid character every way.   She is
sure she found Jesus last night.

Thursday, April 29.

We had a good time to-night, though no one waited
afterwards.   Mr. Maclean (med., from South Wales), a
fine, manly fellow, told his story with singular simplicity
and beauty, and Gray's address (New Coll., Edinburgh),
also went home.   I am sure God is blessing us.

Cults, April 29, 1886.

I had a prosperous afternoon in town seeing Mrs. W.,
Mrs. B., F.S., and some other people in trouble.   You feel
nearer Christ Himself on such errands.   The 'overtaken,'
the diseased, the wretched and miserable, the conscience-
stricken, are specially His.

Friday, April 30, 1886.

At 7 I went to call for the lads at the Mains.   At
7.15 we gathered for prayer in the vestry.   The meeting
was hardly so large as last night, perhaps, but the impres-

sion seemed much deeper. Mackay was much helped to be simple, faithful, and pleading; Maclagan told of some mistakes he had made about coming to Christ with great clearness and quiet force; while Simpson was very direct and earnest. Many remained afterwards to pray for themselves and one another. I spoke to several; most seemed Christ's already, but one or two were seeking peace. It felt so blessed to be amongst seekers.

I went up afterwards to have a talk with the lads in the bothy at the Mains. They promised to pray by their own bedsides to-night.

Saturday, May 1, 1886.

Simpson and Mackay went up to the thanksgiving meeting at eight, and were helped there. Mr. Maclean came out from town and spoke also. Not so many were there owing to its being Saturday night and the other meeting; but it was beautiful to see the one or two radiant faces of those who have been 'helped.' " The Lord hath been mindful of us, and he will bless us."

Sabbath Night.

I took the Bible class myself to-night, as I wished to speak alone with them about the Great Choice. I spoke of

faith as receiving and resting on Christ—of the simplicity
of the act and the joy of the rest. It was a good time to
some, I trust.

Church was unusually full at night to hear the young
men's last addresses. We four went into the pulpit. I read
Isaiah liii., and then Caldwell spoke, gravely and weightily,
of what he had found the new life to be—how it had given
definiteness and decision and earnestness to his life. Christ
gave you something to live for; that thing must be the one
thing; there was nothing indifferent in the Christian life;
everything questionable had to be settled one way or other;
all must be submitted to Christ's will. Simpson followed;
and then came the pearl of the evening, such a moving
little last word from Mackay, thanking the Christians for
having prayed for them, and telling them they would find
unexpected jewels in their crown in the great day. It had
been the happiest week in his life and a foretaste of heaven.

At eight a little company of eighteen or twenty men
gathered to bid the young men farewell. Caldwell was
greatly helped to ask all to begin the new life there and
then, who had not yet done so. . . .

Since then we have had a great supper, and are in high
spirits. . . . They spoke so touchingly of the bright
spot this week would be in their after-lives.

I write in case I don't see you at S'haven.

I can't tell you what a help the deputation has been to me personally and in my work. Ps. cxv. 12 expresses my feelings and hopes for us and you.

About the future — I think something should be attempted. I have tried once or twice to project a Y.M.C.A., or something of that order, but the time was not yet.

I don't know what you will be *guided* to do; do *that* whatever it is, even if it = 0.

I would suggest the following. Sound your men after the meeting to-night, and tryst them to meet you in the school-room (where you spoke on Wednesday) on Sabbath morning at 10.15, to meet *for an hour* (that leaves time to attend F.C. at 11.30 and E.C. over the river at 12) before church, and talk over *then* the idea of their having such a meeting regularly there themselves. Say the room, you believe, will be got, to meet there at any rate, on Sabbath first, if it is not available, you'll adjourn *here*. I've asked the teacher to consult his managers to-night. He believes it will be all right. You'll have to look him up to-morrow evening (or any time before Sabbath) and see how it has been arranged.

Then, having got them to meet you, *ask them whom you should tryst besides,* any of our young church members, members of choir, and whoever else they say ; *drop a note to these to-morrow forenoon,* and post it *before* 5 *p.m.* (to-morrow Saturday), asking them to meet you, or leave the notes yourselves with J——. Besides those, write (on your own hook) to the following, unless they mention them themselves. . . . You might arrange at the Sabbath meeting one meeting forward, and let Committee meet during week to arrange more if think good.

Excuse me—I know you will—giving so much trouble. It looks as if you were being left here to try and throw the thing into some lasting mould. Don't fear for Sabbath, nor be too elaborate (I should say), God will help you mightily. D—— and I and many more will be praying for you all the time, so you won't be alone.

Cults, May 1, 1886.

I almost tremble when I think of the many 'schöne Seelen' I have been allowed to see in this world of woe unspeakable, but I never think of them without devout thanksgiving also :

> " Mir ist's als ob Ich die Hände
> Auf's Haupt ihnen legen sollt' ;
> Betend dass Gott sie erhalte
> So schön und rein und hold."

Yet even as lovely and even more wonderful is it to see the virgin white coming upon darkened souls again, as they welcome the Light of the world. . . .

I am almost afraid sometimes when I think of the life ——— is leading, that it may be near harvest time with him. Yet why should it ? Surely God needs him and such as he *here* as much as He could need them anywhere. I think both he and I shall "live and not die" for some time, "and declare the works of the Lord"; though I have lost much time, and he not much.

[*Resignation of the pastorate at Cults.*]

Polmont Junction, November 18, 1886.

We have had a pleasant journey with bright sunshine all the way. . . . The country has been looking very lovely as we came along. The first white veil dropped on the hills from Kincardineshire inwards,—the blue waters and yellow reeds and black water fowl of the loch of Forfar; the mossy green of the banks and the bright emerald of the turnip fields; all are beautiful. Winter takes away much, but what it leaves seems to become more. Now the easterly air is coming up the Firth and shutting out the landscape. That is the way dear old Edinbro' shows you her affection.

52 Queen Street, 4.30 p.m.

At 4 o'clock Dr. Stewart came and Dr. Arthur and Alick and he had a talk together; then I was called in and examined and they had another consultation. They called me back about 5, and Dr. Stewart said they were all fairly agreed that I must give up Cults and take entire rest for a year. I was not prepared for this and it has come upon me as a heavy blow. . . But, ' He knoweth the way that we take.' Oh that He would bless to us this trial, and make me now a better man, and, some day, if it be His will, a better minister.

November 19, 1886.

After the doctors had spoken, I felt stunned. I do not yet realise it, though every fresh sense of reality brings pain. The chief feeling is the solemn one that my work at Cults is at an end. May God deepen that feeling and sanctify it.

. . . . After a talk with Alick I was sitting by my fire, drinking a cup of cocoa and reading the end of Romans viii., which I had come to in the morning: 'The Spirit helpeth our infirmities—all things work together for good—who shall separate us from the love of Christ'— when Hugh brought in Mr. Stalker. His visit was very comforting. He said, 'I am convinced that it is the right thing. You have not sought it, God has sent it. It may be the preparation for something far greater than anything you have yet done.'

He did not stay long, but said, 'Let us pray together.' So we knelt down, and he offered up such a tender, fervent prayer :—"O God, we have come to a point where Thou hast gathered everything into Thine own hand ; we have snatched at other things and they have gone flying past us. This is Thy doing, the work is Thine ; we never were so certain of it as we are to-night. The race is not of our running. The battle is not ours. It is the Lord's. . . . Bless the people ; we thank Thee for the bright past up there ; it will dwell in their minds for ever."

It was so sweet and solemn, like a benediction coming down on our heads.

11 George Square, November 20, 1836.

. . . The more I think of it the harder it seems. When others speak, they seem to be looking at something quite different to that which I see : they do not seem to see the great black shadow, to feel the wrench and the gaping wound. But that is the way with all sorrow : the heart knoweth its own bitterness. Oh to feel His sympathy who sticketh closer than a brother. . . . Dear Hugh sent me this to-day.* I believe it all, tho' I am no eagle, but only a sparrow that cannot fall to the ground without our Father. It is just being put to sleep that I need, a sleep under a juniper tree with a cruse of water at my bolster and no wish to wake till the angel says, "Arise and eat." My passage to-night ended with :—
" How unsearchable are His judgments and His ways past finding out ; and of Him, and through Him, and to Him are all things, to whom be glory for ever and ever. Amen."

* " Be sure that God
Ne'er dooms to waste the strength he deigns impart ;
Ask the gier-eagle why she stoops at once
Into the vast and unexplored abyss,
What full-grown power informs her from the first
Why she not marvels, strenuously beating
The silent, boundless regions of the sky !
Be sure they sleep not whom God needs.'

July 10, 1890.
[His last visit to Cults.]

Had a most satisfying and uplifting day among my old people at Cults on Sabbath last. Not *one* is wanting to the good cause whom we left attached to it, and several have been added. *Laus laudesque Deo!*

TRAVEL.

P

TRAVEL.

Bei Herrn Pfarrer Pressel,
Lustnau, Tübingen, Wurtemberg (1876).

MY last note told of arrival here.

When we climbed up to the dining-room, the Pfarrer left the piano, and greeted Sorley and Smith successively as "Herr Barbour"; the proper party being at length produced, he was warmly welcomed, and constituted at once part of the family. The other members are—the *Mutter*, a fine middle-aged lady, housewifely and hearty; the eldest son, Gustav, in business here; the second, a student of medicine under Quenstedt and Hoffmeister; the youngest, Wilhelm, a lad of fourteen at the Gymnasium; a boy from Glasgow, Willie Mure, who has been learning German here all winter and returns to Scotland next week; an Established Church student, who, like myself, is preparing to attack the language and divinity together. The dog Hector, like M. Roch's "Mouton," brings up the rear.

We were at home in a moment, the visitors getting the place of honour on the sofa; the Frau Pfarrer insisted, good soul, on tea; and, as it was Scotch tea, that was not to be rejected. (I have smuggled through my two pounds, but it looks as if I should carry them back again.) When my friends left me, I felt a little strange, being for the first time cut off, as it were, and among strangers; but I promise myself better times than even in a friend's or acquaintance's house; for there are no antecedents here to tie one down, save the general report of Scotchmen, which is on the whole high (one hundred and fifty have dwelt with or visited the Pfarrer), so that there is room for a fresh start in everything.

I kept to English for the first night, and we went over all the famous names that were common property to us all— Somerville, John Ewing, Heinrich Drummond, David Ross, etc., etc. The Pfarrer walked up and down the room, cigar in hand, while I talked by turns in either language with the *Mutter*, who was shelling some unknown vegetable at the table. The room is scrupulously clean, uncarpeted; a flower-stand holds the corner; a semi-grand piano lies between the windows; opposite it is the sofa with the table drawn in to it; along a bit, at one side, is the polished stove (not in use), at the other a press and chiffonnier. Bookstands are scattered about, and engravings are on the walls. In the next room is the family meal-table, opening in here by a folding-door. An old Swiss clock that cuckoos at all hours is in the corner of it, and more books and papers lie about. The view from that is the same as from my bedroom, which lies above. From the first room one sees a stretch of undulating meadow, fringed with hills, and these with woods in the delightfully distracted colour of spring. There are patches of vine on the hill sides, but as yet these are scarcely more than a mist of green. Clean muslin curtains hang about the windows, ready to exclude light while allowing of air. The roof is low and long, the paper a light lilac, the chairs strong cane-bottomed affairs, meant to be sat upon.

We had been lighted up the street by the bright windows of Wirthhauses, and directed by the sounds that came from them. Now, when I had climbed another stair to a loft like that you see in an ancient farm-house, but very neat and clean, and after bidding *Gute Nacht* to the servant also who lighted me upstairs, and taking off my hat to her (as it happened to be on), I went to the window of my room and looked out into the moonlight. They were the same lighted houses which lay below me roofed with red tiles, peaked and gabled, with the black beams and rooftrees standing out against the white-washed walls. The big church rose from among them, and the bells rang a quarter

past ten. A mile away over the valley lay Tübingen,
also ringing itself to rest for the night. I found my lamp
and arranged it, then inspected affairs, and finally sat
down to meditate on the new little world of which this
will be the centre all summer. The roof is low, but the
room is long and airy. There are two presses for my
things in the wall. A neat little wooden bed, five and a
half feet in length, is covered by a feather quilt, bounded
on the north and south by two sheets to keep it from
going off in a heap, on the east by a pillow half the length
of the bed, and on the west by a stout brown board,
against which one feels bound to beat a tattoo every
night. The eternal sofa faces the everlasting table, a
smaller copy of which supports some ink in the corner.
Along a bit is the little washing-stand, with glass above
it; beyond that is the polished stove on a smaller scale;
another lamp depends from the white ceiling just over
the place where one brushes the hair, so that the operation
is one of considerable strategy, as I am in imminent danger
of getting hair-oil. After looking about, I went off to
bed about eleven, and examined the spire and other
objects visible in the moonlight before falling asleep.
Things had been painted and renewed evidently in my room,
so I felt clean and comfortable. There was no waking till

the morning. I heard some quarter hours from the clock, the servants climbing up higher to sleep among the pigeons, whose cooing and pecking I can hear above, somebody breathing heavily below, and then dropped off.

Sharp at six I sprang out of bed, with a sleepy reply to the maiden who waked me. A cup of coffee was waiting down stairs, and, after taking it with a roll, I found my way in the drizzle into town. The *Aula* (University) is on the great street, just on this side of the town. I found Sorley and Schmidt there, and with them adjourned to the first floor, where Professor Sigwart was to lecture on Metaphysic. There might be a hundred there, silent and business-like, with little black leather cases holding their notes (they wrote in the centre of a large page, leaving a margin), with yellow wooden ink bottles. Several had on the students' caps and sashes which mark them out as members of some club (generally containing members of one district), blue, white, and red; these were mostly the better-living sort of men, and some had their faces fearfully gashed with sabre cuts in duel. After waiting a bit, looking out at the green trees and white houses one sees from all the classrooms, the door opened, in rushed a little, wiry-looking man in mixed tweeds, swaying somewhat in his walk. As we all rose at his entrance, he barely stopped to close the door and nod his head by way of recognition. He mounted the rostrum and began ; no reading, though he turned over notes ; the students wrote almost continuously, though the hurry was most when he dictated paragraphs of special importance. He flung down his grey wide-awake beside him, and writhed with his little body, and worked with his little hands, and put his finger alongside his nose in moments of deep argument. He looked like a slim Scotch mason; there was something of Hugh Miller in his face, and he gradually twisted himself up to a given point, at which he made a circle with his fingers and seemed to have grasped the truth. He was of course difficult to follow from his jerky style, but interesting to watch. We have an introduction to him, but will wait for its delivery till we know more of the ways of the place. The way his eyes twinkled, the familiar illustrations he threw in, half in playful style, the good-natured size of his person and set of his face, seem to show that philosophy is not the thing of toil and anguish it once was to men.

At eight o'clock we adjourned to Teuffel's class (the Principal's), whose Latin history was a text book of mine, and for a dreary hour heard him lay down the pros and cons of Homeric unity with all the regularity, but little

of the interest, of the array of combatants in the Trojan
War. He made a very inferior Fate indeed, and seemed
afraid to say anything himself, while unsparing to the
combatants on either side.

After him, we trotted off at nine to the *Stift* (Educational
Institution) to hear the great Sanskritist, Roth, lecture on
the universal history of religions. He knows Muir well,
from whom Smith has an introduction to him. The subject was the first beginnings of religion among the early
Aryans; he spoke distinctly, hand in pocket, and looked
like an improved edition of John Stewart, who built
Bonskeid. The class is very large; we notice the desks
cut with the favourite feminine names of the German
students; but except for that, and some outlandish outlines
in ink, there was nothing to distinguish it from home.
The students hang their caps at the door; the professor
wrote out hard names on a black board; there was no
fussing, but the utmost order prevailed.

Being in the exploring mood, we went back to the *Aula*
at ten in time for Milner's English class. There were
half a dozen men in it, and they were translating Goethe
into English with a precision and sweep that astonished
one. At eleven we went upstairs to the hero of the place
(Beck), an old fellow of 72, who holds on like a youth.

The class might hold 300 (there are 1000 students in all—
many non-theologues take it) and, although he speaks broad
Swabian, his very appearance is interesting. He prelected
sitting, with a burst now and then, in which he left his
slowly read MS. and warmed up to some great argument. We couldn't understand much : he was on the
difference between ordinary and Christian morals—the one
being a culture of the *old* personality, the other being the
taking on of a *new* one. He ran briefly over the notices of
the distinctions which occur in the Church before the
Reformation, tripping down the centuries with an easy
tread—the fathers, scholastics, mystics, etc., being briefly
characterized and passed. We noticed several young fellows
in military dress : they have been drawn for the army, and
are allowed to go on attending college, Government having
established a station near Tübingen to admit of this. The
professors wear no gowns here.

Feeling funny after five lectures, we adjourned to the
Lamm for dinner. After soup and meat, for which we were
mulcted in the sum of one shilling, we called on the Pedell
(University secretary) and enrolled as theologues. Thence
we marched to Smith's lodgings ; the dyer had great widths
of indigoed cloth the height of the house hung up to dry.
The river Ammer—size of the Glen burn—flows at the front

door down the street, and acts as bathing establishment, gutter, drain, and air-cooler (not to say odorifier) all the way. We saw some Scotch papers there, and then went up the hill behind with him—Tübingen lies between two —and looked over the little town and Stift Church to the other one, with castle and wood thereon, and beyond to the Swabian Alp; in the other direction to Stuttgart, round a little to Hohenzollern, etc. Descending to the post-office, we blew up the functionary, having passed the poet Uhland's dwelling on the bridge over the Neckar, and had a turn down the long avenue of trees. Thence we went to Lindenmaier, a delightful bookseller (whose shop will be the ruin of us, I fear): he knew all the old Scotchmen, and walked with Smith and Sorley teaching them to speak German. They go out to some neighbouring village and get milk and wine in a *Wirthschaft*, over which their tongues seem to be loosened. At another shop we possessed ourselves of note-books and pencils. The shops all shut here from twelve till two for siesta, and again for altogether at 7 p.m. Things are middlingly cheap; but have risen much since the soldiers came. We next attacked the Museum, saw the library, and in the reading-room got the last news, in German, from London. It was now time (4 o'clock) to hear Diestel, so we went. He lectures on Hebrew Exegesis; takes up Genesis just now; going word by word over all, giving new translations and discussing every line in the light of contemporary or analogous records and of modern science. He burst out into a great fit of cachinnation now and again, is satiric and speaks no good of his opponents, and is the most lively of the lot. After this we read some of Heine's songs together in Sorley's room, and I trotted off home. I was in time for tea at 7.30, a great feast, of *real* tea, if one takes it, meat and rolls. The Pfarrer and Frau sit as in Germany together at the farther side and not separate at each end of the table, as in England. The grace is a pretty German couplet of which I am not yet sure. The politeness here is great. After separation for the day a "Grüss Gott" (God bless you) is expected, and a shake of the hand. So on returning to a room after bidding good-bye, you are expected to repeat it. In shops and such like, you bid good-day to the shopkeeper on entering and lift your hat on retiring, etc., etc. After prayers, in which we read all round and merely bent forward towards the table during devotion (the servants sitting in the darkened ante-room), I read some of Uhland with Frau Pfarrer, while Herr and Halliday laughed over chess in the neighbouring room. The former is re-writing his articles for Herzog's *Encyclopedie*. He is quite a don in Hebrew, Egyptian and Palestinian literature generally. After that I went off upstairs rather tired, but slept well.

Next morning on rising at 6, it was plain from the feeling that there had been frost. However, the sun was bright, so I walked off to Tübingen, heard Schwabe lecture on Greek Art, was back at 9, and after writing for an hour, read from 10 to 12 with the Frau, translating and retranslating. We finished the day in a café, where the comic papers are kept, though we did not make much of these. The others walked home with me at 9; I had a long talk with the Pfarrer about his books, half in English, half in German, and, after writing, turned in for the night. Yesterday (Friday) morning it was Scotch mist in earnest and very cold. I heard Sigwart at 7, Reiff on Modern Philosophy at 8, Roth at 9, and Beck at 11. We dined at table d'hote in the *Lamm*. Thereafter I went home; the others waited to give in the lists of classes. We intend to take Reiff and Sigwart in Philosophy; not however in the sense in which one takes an English professor; for all our getting will be knowledge of German at first, and it will be long ere we know enough to enable us to work for the classes. After a game at nine pins (knocked down by a swinging ball), afternoon coffee and conversation, I returned to Diestel and also attended a stray lecture of Weiszzäcker on New Testament Introduction. After being in Smith's room from 6 to 7, I came back to tea, receiving a letter from Greig who is now in Switzerland. Shakespeare was being read in the Museum at night, but it was very wet. After tea here I had a long talk with the Pfarrer, when he played and sang some of his brother's songs and part of an opera (oratorio). I unpacked afterwards and found my way into bed.

Not being up to the mark this morning, I have not been in Tübingen, but have been busy reading and writing. Otherwise I am very well. I go to see a confirmation service in Bebenhausen to-morrow.

At Andernach we saw the head Moravian settlement, women in colours according to age, a quaker-like, calm set of people. Wood floats and rafts then met us, and, as the river narrowed, the cliffs closed in, to lift up upon their very brow the splendid boundary fortress of Coblentz. (Did I tell you we heard Christlieb on Sabbath, a noble sermon on "The joy of the Lord our strength"? I understood a good deal; there were soldiers and English schools in church, the latter behaving pretty well; the singing was like ours in Scotland, only with a peculiar

German fall at the close; the organ was grand, and almost all joined.)

Of the home life much might be said; of the greetings on going out and coming in; of the patriarchal relations between servants and superiors; of the housewifeliness of the *Frau Mutter;* of the way things are cut and served at table (the eldest son doing the first slicing at a side table, and every one being invited to a second portion as the plate *en masse* goes round); of the afternoon coffee for visitors; of the family game after dinner; the universal gathering at *Abendessen,* when everybody seems to see everybody else for the first time; of the prayers, when that is over, at which we all read round, the Pfarrer coming in with his beautiful, all-embracing collect at the close; of the Pfarrerin's *Gute Nacht* at nine o'clock; of my talks thereafter with Herr Pfarrer, while he sits in the dark at the piano, and plays alternately chorales, Scotch songs, and snatches from his brother's operas; of the later evening alone, or in one another's rooms, given to newspapers and the German Bible; of the final *Schlafen Sie wohl* to the old *Magds* as they stump up to a higher loft still, which might be among the heavenlies, and *is* among the cocks and hens—all this and more might be made the subject of a series of idylls, but being in no mood for verse-making, the mention of them shall be strictly dramatic, *i.e.*, only as they touch upon the progress of my life-play in the little world here.

Outside of the house are Idylls more. Indeed, though, save to Tübingen, I have never walked beyond the *Hof*, that itself (and I get it all from my windows) is a study. So it was to-night; the second attempt at a sunset (it has been dark and bitter since my last) just threw the different points into their proper places, so that I can go over them one by one. First, in the furthest corner, the great square church tower, springing above the houses into a spire (as if it waited like the other houses till it got above them, and then set about more original aspirations), its presence is with me even in the darkness, in the form of the constant quarter-hour bell, which never lets one get lazy; under its shadow the other houses are grouped, with delightful difference of roof in the way of tiles, old and new, red and brown, with just a sprinkling of slates to prevent the church seeming at too great a distance; their gables are white, with black beams appearing, giving you a sense of strength, which, however, does not stand out too strongly; the windows are muslin-curtained at the top, with flowers in some, and now (nine p.m.) all bright with the 'best flower in the garden,' rosy fires; at their foot they grow distracted, separating into sheds, out-houses, waggon-stands, etc., leaving only so much bare wall as convinces one that the upper storey does not rest on nothing. One half of the court is green with bushes, carried up into the woods behind the houses (the far view is Tübingen itself) by glimpses of green poplars and fruit trees scattered among the buildings everywhere. We may pass over the manure heaps before the houses (easier to do with the pen than with clean feet on a dark night), going no nearer them than the goose pond, where half-a-dozen of these fairy-book creatures are waiting to be turned into *Mädchens* à la Grimm ; a mädchen, however, *does* appear, fresh and ruddy, and turns *them* into a little wooden house, not without a remonstrance which is something worse than the drawing of a blunt pencil over a greasy slate; they are out again in an instant, following the old *Magd*, who, with pitcher on head, marches into the court from a stable, followed by a score of great, relieved-looking kine, who again are pursued by a youth, clothed as to his feet (so are all the children here), but bare on the head, and driven out to pasture for the night. There is a large waggon underneath the windows (like a wash-basket on wheels) from which the *Bauer*, in dress somewhat like a dirty night-gown, is loosing the grateful

Q

oxen, which bend their necks into the box of mixed rye grass hung from the cross bar which keeps the heads together. Another boy is working the pump (going like a rusty saw) and then staggering along, tub on head, half tripped up by the geese, into the low-linteled enclosure whither the oxen have just disappeared. Said geese are finally sent flying by a herd of cows with calves, which come scampering down the steep causeway, past the end of the square, sending their bells before them and leaving them behind them with a surprising sense of what is most attractive about their persons. This *émeute* rouses the feelings of the Goose-mädchen who appears, dashes down the outside stairs to the tune of an admonishing mother and admiring baby brother, seizes a broom, and making said animals show the white feather, finally succeeds in locking them up to cackle and hiss to their hearts' content. Bauer has by this time finished operations, and is now going up the same stair to the crowing of the afore-mentioned child, and hastening of the Hausfrau, the last of whom I see when she crosses the room, with lattice left open, carrying a bowl of something that steams and needs stirring. Looking higher, there is a black thing like Milton's Satan in the Sun ; on coming nearer it turns out to be the gentleman stork, who is welcomed by his wife on the handsome edifice erected for them, I believe, by the corporation. The sunset is going now; the sparrows are getting quiet; Wilhelm comes to my room to let down the pigeons' trap door (through a hole in the ceiling); they are calling for tea, and it is two hours before I get upstairs again to begin this letter.

The old lady is really a good soul, tells me about her dead daughter, hears about home, reads me her husband's hymns (she, too, has written a book), feeds me *ad lib.;* offers another bed in the same room for Sorley or Schmidt, in the event of my having the *Heimweh;* manages her house and her children (the second son is a genius, fiery tempered and difficult to keep in, but she lets him blow over and come round, and he is proud of her and loves her like a queen; she explains the ways of the Herr Vater to him, hears his woes—he is medical—and gives him money when it fails elsewhere). She plays a little, but works a great deal; is very gentle in teaching me; we help each other out with French which they all know so far. The eldest son was a transit officer in the war, and saw thousands of prisoners over the frontier in 1870-71; they lost none of their own then, though every family they speak of misses someone; it seems to have been a deep spiritual experience with many of them, and they speak of it as a

solemn thing and yet a triumph. Just now, in the event
of a Russian war, there is a great watchfulness and preparation everywhere, and, though much apprehension, no
fear. Bismarck is believed in, after God, and is an
Evangelical of the Evangelicals. Salmond's pamphlet has
been issued in German, and everyone has heard of him
here. The youngest son talks most with me, shows me
his Greek and Latin versions for the Gymnasium, wakens
me in the morning, etc. He brought me in some of the
first of the *Maiblumen* (lily of the valley) to-day, and has
just been in to tell me how he liked the circus which he
begged his mother to let him see to-day, she sent him on
to his father, who heard, I suppose, of a previous permis-
sion, and gave him *Pfennige* enough to go. To-morrow
(Sunday) a marriage will be in the church, and a children's
service in the afternoon ; Sorley and Schmidt walk out
after dining at the *Lamm* and spend the remainder of
the day with me.

Sunday.—The only change in the weather has been a
little hail, with south wind freezing from the Swabian
Alp. There are funerals almost every day, mostly, however, old women and children, from the delayed summer,
and the number of sick people which the Frau Pfarrer
goes to see is striking. She has just shown me a beautiful

book of hymns with tunes which one of the old wives
had been feasting upon, and telling me about the *Stunde*
of the Pietists in the village, to which I must go some
day, and of some others up in Wankheim who are like
Plymouth Brethren, and quarrelled with the Pfarrer when
he was settled there. With remembrance to such as
remember me.

Tübingen, Friday, May 26.

. . . . Halliday was at a duel this morning;
and saw eight young men of high rank engaged in carving
at what little of the divine likeness remained in their
faces. It took place in a lovely wood, which had to
be cleared of singing birds for this piece of work; and
resulted in:—1st round, scalp removed; 2nd, cheek cut
clean through; 3rd, eight head wounds; 4th, cheek and
chin slashed; the wounds were sewn by fellow-medicals
on the spot, and then the spectators and those of the
combatants who could bear the pain, drank beer together;
it was no affair of love or war; only one belonging to one
society had spoken with a forbidden member of another
and 'Hinc illæ lacrimæ'—this is what came of it.

I missed a delightful canter to Reutlingen with a party of them to-day in order to be at a garden concert, where the *élite* and beauty of Tübingen were to be beheld. They were merry enough in little domestic or erotic circles under the trees, talking and drinking, the young ladies filling the pauses of tatting or *tête-à-tête* with potations of red or white Rhenish. In spite of very neat and expressive clothing—a custom they continue beyond childhood here—they are not wonderfully good-looking; the loveliness they had when children—and they are almost *all* lovely then—seeming to be thinly spread over their faces as they grow old, and never being renewed. It reminds one of butter as respectively laid on a child's 'piece,' and sparsely distributed over that of an old one.

Yet in some things there is a deeper sense of harmony in them than among ourselves. With us, ministers on meeting generally make it the sign for a discussion on divinity. Here it is otherwise. For instance, Mrs. Pressel's brother (a pastor) arrived to-night. He is musical, as most of them are. And if there is less reason than usual in this last sheet, you must lay it, not at my door, but at that of the dining-room below, where the two brothers in Christ have been signalizing their reunion by a series of splendid bursts on the piano, sacred and profane; all the while, I have no doubt, darkening the room with two rich cigars, and laying them down now and again to suggest a new method of meeting the world, flesh, and devil. Somehow their Christianity comes as naturally here out of their fingers' ends as anywhere else, the mouth in private being generally otherwise filled. And if their religion, nay their whole life, has one strength or one weakness (and it has many), the secret of either lies assuredly in the place to which the body is admitted in both. However, on the whole, if a German is saved, it is a complete thing, for the soul without the body is an idea they never thought much of.

Lustnau,
Tübingen, June 4, 1876.

I'm afraid, if I don't now, I shall never get a letter begun. I have just got free from a troublesome cold and am going about, walking and working as usual. Of the latter there is precious little; some German reading and, alas! less speaking, filling up the pauses of my much-outing every day. However, I think I am getting impressions now; and it is a state the most pleasant, fruitful, and hopeful that man can enjoy. It has taken longer than I thought to get rid of English, not so much on the tongue as in head and heart; to isolate one's self so far from home ways and ideas and lie open to the *Einfluss* of other and new ones. I have great advantages here, too, in being utterly free from ordinary surroundings, so that the isolated watch-tower of observation, which jars on "our ain folk," is neither so much ascended, or, if it is, doesn't do any harm to anybody's feelings. It is a great grace, too, to be allowed to begin anew in a few things, though the difficulty and the circumscribed extent of change are not without their pain. It is good, too, to see one's old self slightly at a distance; one's church I must add, for I have been looking back and forward at her with you and others, while your much-prized pictures of her present position have kept me within call of the realities.

Of the life here, it must be said that in many ways I must regard it as a thing to put within brackets—*e.g.* the Sabbath-life, though I couldn't protest against it, will give me arguments for sincere devotion to Scotch ways when I return; and in other things, where I might have been tempted to press against home bounds and barriers, experience here will help me to be more respectful and content with them than heretofore. But, on the other hand, in many ways there are rebukes for one in the ordinary life here; the relations between parents and children, the mani-

festations of open feeling, the rules of courtesy, the strong
and deep patriotism, more than a century in sweep, and
the general religiousness, in matters like the late war,
deaths, high tides, and so on, give one much cause to im-
prove. Of course you will say observance is not morality;
the family tie is strong among the lower animals, emotion
is in the majority there also ; politeness is a poor substitute
for personal respect ; the empire and love for it is a piece
of hard uncalculating cruelty, etc., etc.; but while much
of this is true, and it were easy to construe still more in
the same unworthy direction, yet there is a possibility and
a reward in engrafting observances upon deeper feelings,
purer motives, more real and living commands.

Anyway, I trust I am beginning to learn. I had intended
to write pictures of the places I have seen and studies of
some points of character for the *Review*, but my illness
has put that out of my head. And I daresay the thoughts
which do us most good are those which, rushing up out of
our hearts spontaneously in moments of new and pure
experience, are possibly turned back again in upon the under
being which they sprang from, and for whose nourishment
they most are needed.

With which generality I pass to details. I am keeping
the Schwartz Wald for some later time, when the weather is

more settled. Smith and Sorley go off on Tuesday. I follow the professors now pretty well, all except Beck. But I am going carefully over the 'Seelenlehre' to get his standpoint. I have read Faust, Götz, Don Carlos, Monologen (partly), and looked at my subjects for next winter. Aren't they splendid? Isaiah vi. (Davidson) and "That Rock was Christ" (Macgregor).

Thursday Evening,
Lustnau, Tübingen, June 8, 1876.

On Monday and Tuesday it was from 80 to 90 in the shade, so I dosed over a German novel under an awning in the court with the Frau, who read to me dreamily about knights and monks, etc., etc., I keeping her awake by timely interrogation about some queer-looking word. She is ill to-day; Halliday's and my studies have half killed her.

Then came yesterday's thunder-storm, with rain in sheets: everybody disappeared, but the geese made a public washing out of it. Gustav says it only went six inches into the soil; he is gardener among other things (was up at four this morning catching a creature known as the 'early worm'); but any way it went deeper in the 'drooked' dresses of some ladies I saw; but then they are more impressible.

I caught my worm too; for being in the woods this morning, I caught a young mole, washed out of 'house and hole'
by the floods, and walking in the sun to dry its moleskin.   I
haven't, however, got *the* animal yet; he rattles a crust in the
cupboard every night, and plays a war dance 'on the top' of
the trap, thinking that is far enough.   The cats, too, in number legion, build houses (at least it sounds something like it)
with the piles of firewood just outside my door at midnight,
till there is a rush, a crash, and 'fuffings' fearful to hear, and
I know that Hector has forsaken his sleep on the mat outside
Heinrich's (the medical's) door in order to straighten up
affairs among the felines.   I can testify to the success of his
attempts; for when I meet said animals after Hector has
been talking to them, they look *very* straight, especially the
hair, alongside of which one might lay a rule without hesita-
tion.

> Tuesday Night,
> Lustnau, June 13, 1876.

The time of night and position of my pen, in the
dark dining-room underneath, must be my excuse for
this pencil note.   Three days' rain and no outing must
similarly account for my want of news.

There is only the inundation to speak of, and since that event has been frequently repeated since Noah originated the idea, a few words about it are enough. Suffice to say, Cause: rain since Wednesday last. Buckets, drench, steady downpour, drizzle have all been 'on,' and seem only to have given in for sheer want of water. One day it drove like pellets of hail; but, though not a leaf is left on the trees at Heilbronn, we have been mercifully spared that here. The streets are rivers; we went to bed last night with the Neckar 12 to 13 feet above high water mark. This morning the whole valley was seamed with canals, which, as the day advanced, clubbed together to form a sea. I went down after lunch and saw a boat being carefully steered about by fences and ditches, to keep it clear of currents, carrying dinner to people whose dwellings are, like champagne bottles in summer, up to their waists in water. The clouds seem quite rotten, can't hold in any more, and so are moving about in shreds about the hills and close to the ground; while the sun, thinks Wilhelm, has drawn up too much water, like Jeanne's fish, and is quite drunk. I had a great talk on Sunday night with the Pfarrer over Baur, Schwegler, Strauss, and Zeller, all of whom he knew. If the river is passable, I shall resume the 'Aula' (college) to-morrow.

There is an eighth Scotchman come, an F.C. from Glasgow. We half propose getting up a Scotch club to rival those of the German students. I had a good game at foreign billiards with Halliday last week and beat him. I am gathering a list of good books for Jeanne and Margaret, a number of evangelical stories, cures for neuralgia, and sudden deaths for Mamma, agricultural facts for Papa (they are all, I am sorry to say, under water at present, along with half the Swiss railways and the cricket pitch), and observations of the medical students for yourself.

Lustnau, Tübingen,
Saturday Night, June 27, 1876.

On Wednesday it cleared and the flood abated, so after my lesson I strolled out to the *Aula*, picking my way among remnants of burns (still in rebellion and keeping hold of the high road), and heard Beck on the morality of free grace. He is an earnest old gentleman, and talks the truth out to his men in a way that makes one wish oneself at times under the table ; he was scolding them about duelling, etc. In spite of this, however, there is a large increase of students on the evangelic side this year (there is a Romish faculty as well), helping to swell the number of students to 1060, being

200 more than it has ever been. Beck has a bigger class than Baur ever had, the northern students coming most to hear him and Weiszzäcker, a New Testament expounder, successor and student of the great Baur, who made the school here.

At dinner, however, that day the storm renewed, and we had a rattling thunder (*Gewitter*) again (8th day). The effects of the flood began to fill the newspapers here and in Switzerland. The peasants are about broken-hearted, having lost everything, and some of them weep like babies about it, and no wonder, for their bit of land is more to them than wife or child, and the attention paid thereto would be the salvation of any human being if turned in that direction. They have it direct from the State—there are no landlords— paying a small ground tax for vine- or hopyard. The Barons are not like our landed proprietors; they have, indeed, patronage of country churches, people having no vote or voice in the matter, but otherwise 'well apart' from the people, though they do not on this account resemble 'stars' (see Wordsworth's Sonnet on Milton), except in the fact that they are 'fading away.' Speaking of peasants, I must tell you of one respect in which they exhibit regard for their children's well-being. No child is allowed barefoot, or with torn frock or coat in school ; the children are kept very clean, in order to distinguish them from the streets where otherwise they might be run over. Now this is how they do it. They wash the children on Sabbath morning, but at the same time they wash the clothes too, of which *every* child possesses one set, and *none* more. Now it happens that walking down the street at an early hour, one sees little cherubs in a state of native innocence set out upon the threshold or in the centre of the street to dry in the sun, while the outer 'hull' or tabernacle, from which they have been temporarily unclothed, hangs above them drying in the same sun. The doctor says it is the senna-quinine (I think the English of it is *sine quâ non*) of health to do so. A philosopher whom I consulted on the subject, says the incident comes under the rule of 'divide et impera,' which, being interpreted, reads 'split your washing into two, and the thing's done.'

Returning from the 'naked lie' (as Halliday remarked to me, on observing one such asleep at full length by the kerb-stone) to the naked truth, let me tell you of a wash I had, without separating beforehand unhappily.

On Thursday after dinner it was so cool that I thought no more storms could come, and so sauntered in the cool afternoon wind into Tübingen. When about half-way ($\frac{3}{4}$ mile) however, it became suddenly calm, and soon a few first drops, flung like teacupfuls of water on the ground by a

woman before she begins to brush, told that something was
'up' and would shortly be 'down.' I quickened my pace, but
before finishing the *Wilhelm's Strasse* (the long, lime-edged
avenue which unites that and this), the rain was lashing
down and leaping up from the ground as if driven by wind,
though not a breath was there, and it came down straight as
stones. It took a minute to fill the cracks of the rent ground,
but, ere I had got under an overhanging verandah, the street
cleared like lightning, and I was left alone with one or two
labourers sheltered in similar fashion, and the town water-
man, who kept rushing about clearing gutters, lifting gratings,
and opening drains. It got dark and a great band of thunder
undid itself gradually to and fro along the heavens, which
seemed bowed quite down with the weight of what was
rolling above, whatever that might be ; while, in the rough
seams of the cloud, three-forked lightnings worked up and
down, lacing the ragged edges of the two conflicting clouds
with a hem that was needle, thread, and seamstress all in one.

Bei Pfarrer Pressel,
Tübingen, June 28, 1876.

I am owing letters all round, but yours are mostly
received and read out-of-doors, where answering is out

of the question, and I seldom am elsewhere except when opening my mouth to feed or snore.

We are much in the open air; I went through the delicious process of getting my 'pow' cropped to the quick the other day, and have begun an epic on the subject. The boys at school here have a trick. It is this: on a promising evening, when it looks like being a very hot to-morrow, they go and get themselves shaved 'ad unguem.' The reason is, that the master, losing his temper in the hot weather, makes a frantic grab at the heads of all and sundry, and is fearfully and wonderfully surprised to find himself—like Æneas with his mother's ghost —grasping nothing. One boy who crept to the window last night saw the master watering his nails to make them grow.

Did I tell you of our fun a week ago? The last of the Scotch was come; so we fixed to have a Scotch evening. It took place at Henderson's. The coffee took two hours to make, so we drank it as dessert to the other things— cookies, rolls, cake, etc. Smith had brought his machine along to club with Henderson's (carrying it in a dressing-case) and we were about stifled with methylated spirit before the thing began. There were nine of us in all: the hosts, Cullen and Henderson, Smith, Sorley, Halliday, Hunter (Glasgow, E.C., ready for licence), Sutherland (Glas-

R

gow, entering F.C.) and I. There was not much talk during tea, our attention being chiefly attracted by the ongoings of the *Wahnsinniger* (*i.e.*, idiot), as we have dubbed a mad student who lives *au quinzième* of an hotel opposite, and takes a ghastly interest in our two friends, his attention being divided between them and peppering big papers on the road. After a while he lit his lamp in order to get us to do the same, so that he might command a view of our conduct, but we voted no light, to his infinite chagrin. By this time Sutherland was getting loud; he imitates animals like one of themselves, only much better. Forthwith he set up all the dogs within call by summoning them to a fight with a supposed dog; which, however, they couldn't find when they came, but were thrown into fury by the 'meows' of an imaginary cat which seemed everywhere present in the midst of them. At last they fell on one another, and then '*disparurent.*' The *Wahnsinniger* drew his chair and lamp to the window and pretended to study. Sutherland, however, did for him. For we saw him spring up at the sound of a supposed bugle and look out to see the street full of soldiers, having stealthily filled his pockets with pellets wherewith to pelt them. But, when he slipt from behind the curtain and craned his neck over the sill, the military—oh, where were they—he was greeted by howls of laughter from the other side of the way ; a crowd of children collected ; we left him to 'orate' to the assembled crowd and visit them with his vengeance. We drew in to the table. The first toast was the new Tübingen school and its revival by the Scotch, which Sorley and Cullen managed between them ; this was capped by the " Braes of Banavie" from Halliday.

Then came "three universities and churches" (Edinburgh, Glasgow, and Aberdeen ; F.C., E.C., U.P.) which Henderson and Hunter looked after. Thence we broke into the chorus of a hunting-song from the last mentioned. We noticed that more than the *Wahnsinniger* had by this time drawn close to the opposite windows; for a Scotch chorus is, after all, not a German one. Then came a temperance recitation from Schmidt in reply to his health; and this was felt to be a peculiarly fitting opportunity for introducing some more beer. Then came Sutherland (who had been splitting our sides all evening, by acting the part of an imaginary general audience, which sometimes seemed to be in the gallery, at others in the reserved seats) with Blackie's song of Good Greeks; we had already begun to warm to a chorus, and the thing went really well. It was getting dark, and of course we were rapidly becoming grave, when Sorley gave " The Professors, and success to

their efforts in the direction of Foreigners." I forgot that
we began with an enthusiastic one, "The Girls we've
left behind us," which was drunk with honours and 'Good
fellowing' to the full ; the others had *prosit*, clinking
of glasses, and other customs of the country, for, though
our hearts were at home, the willows must needs be
Babylonish, and the harps discoursed the language of
Babel. A long breath, a fill-up, and then we gave one
for the Queen, and a deep-throated "God save our gracious
etc.," sung in splendid style (we had six parts going)
shook the roof, and made the other side of the street
look up. By this time the *Wahnsinniger* was frantic, he
couldn't see us, couldn't shy anything at us, and, by the
light of his lamp added to that of natural reason, we saw
him pacing up and down the room, with his arms rolling
vehemently, and his shirt sleeves rolled up stringently,
while his eyes were a match. Sutherland was sent to the
window, and communicated to him in a series of sounds
the desire to have a duel ; that made him, if possible,
wilder still. When S. came back, we were clearing our
throats by instinct, and when one of us gave (in a *mēlan-
chōlisch Tön*, it must be admitted) "Bonnie Scotland," we
felt bound to clear the room by three hearty cheers for
what was to follow. Then we stood up in close circle

round the table and sang, as never before, " Should auld acquaintance be forgot." The last verse and chorus were repeated, till our arms rattled in their sockets (Henderson had on purpose opened a side window which overlooks another house, where the Frau comes from Schottland; and, as we rose from " Auld Lang Syne," I fancied a figure slid from the window *vis à vis*); after 'good-night' all round, we broke up. It was only to meet again at the city gates, however, where, under the quiet moon, we marched out (singing in streets sends you to prison) along the *Wilhelm's Strasse*, with " Old Folks at Home," " South Carolina," " John Brown," " Tramp, Tramp," " Rule Britannia," etc., etc.

On Sunday afternoons the same party meets for discussion, critical and exegetic, of the " Romans," which we are enjoying greatly.

The story of my matriculation, address of rector, and diploma (everybody gets a thing like a newspaper here) must be untold. Also of my Sunday's walk to Bebenhausen, of the Reformations Predigt there, the singing of *Ein feste Burg*, and the catechizing of the children about the story of three hundred and forty years since.

I must tell some other time of Monday's garden-party, of games with a score of Tübingen beauties (such as they

are), ending—sting in the tail as usual—with a Polonaise,
which you are not to fancy I took any part in ; for the
thing is a fact.

Tübingen,
Würtemberg, July 26, 1876, 11 p.m.

My good angel turned up in a half invalid Balliol man
(between Mods. and Greats) who wanted a companion in
the Black Forest. So, as my only hearty friend in the
house, the Frank, was down with heart disease (a result,
I believe, of desperate attempts to instil the irregularities
of the language into said Englishman's thick head, you
will add, that of somebody else as well), I accepted ; and
leaving Beck up to the waist in Baptism (he was just
emerging, and that gloriously, when I picked him up again
to-day), Diestel deep in the 4th "I-v-st" of Genesis, and
class wrestling with Schleiermacher's notion of Immortality, I got into the open air. I can never hope to
tell you what a time we had. For the first moment
since coming here, I got really free from my cold ; the
weather was wonderful ; and the walking ground even
more than we had imagined. Just think of one hundred
and fifty miles in five days ; of getting lost, and having
adventures with peasants, wood-rangers, and charcoal-

burners; of taking short cuts which led nowhere, and leaning on guide posts which pointed everywhere; of climbing twice each day a range of 2500-3000 feet; of waterfalls and precipices; of strange inns and characters enough to fill a photograph book; of sleeping on straw in a barn with workmen, and bathing in brooks of every size and shade; of feasts on blaeberries, wild strawberries, and rasps; of talking German, French, English, Latin (to a priest) and broad Scotch (in the trains) to mystify the people; of meeting in with at one boarding-school one madman, two drunkards, and the daughter of a Russian millionaire; of seeing the sick world in Wildbad, the naughty world in Baden, the religious world in Freiburg, and the ordinary world everywhere; of dining on beer and hardboiled eggs, and smuggling the uneatable things into one's pockets; of blisters treated with brandy and cotton thread; of 'puggeries,' bad jokes, and classical quotations; of 'winding' rival student walkers till their faces grew as long as their breath was short; of being 'done' by hotel keepers, and eventually arriving with a few *Pfennigs* among the party. One of my feet went the third day, with descending three hours of broken stones; so I removed the top of my shoe and walked, a wonder to many, for the remainder of the way. On Tuesday when we started we were respectable travellers, on Wednesday we were directed to an asylum (*Gutlenthaus*), the next two days 'vagabond' was written on our brow; we finished up at Strassburg as 'spies.'

To ascend to the solemnities. Hebrew is buried; Schleiermacher and Beck are being waded through, with skippings over Schiller and Lessing (the former of whom turns very poor after some reading); the lectures are easily followed now. Roth is extremely interesting upon the remains of Celtic religions, while Weiszzäcker is retreating with the Gospel of John to about the year '90. After all, the world is improving and men with it. I intend to take a month's grind at pure philosophy when I get back (D.V.) and then another at mixed theology.

After all, I shall be sorry at heart to leave this old place, spite of its much imperfection, and more failure on my side. I am beginning to believe that the heights where your last and higher effort leaves you, are the very spots (the only ones perhaps) where you get lifted up; that there is no point of worked-out aspiration that does not hold out wings to something higher; and that all such experience is *spiritual.*

With which sermon 1 am done. The storks are clapping their beaks from the nest on the church tower, the servants are snoring sonorously through the wall; and I must have off my slippers, not to wake the Frau Pfarrer who sleeps in the room under, as I get to rest for the night. With remembrances to all who remember me.

The Katberg,
S. Africa, March 2, 1880.

They will have told you that we came up here to rest during the last month of summer, intending to descend to the plain again this month and spend the next month or two of cool at Lovedale. It is the first of a series of ribs which run up the centre of S. Africa, parallel to the sea. We are upon the side of one of the spurs which run into the range of mountains, here called the Katberg. Some three thousand feet of elevation leave us with an immense sweep of land lying below; accordingly, you sweep the horizon, and find your eye rests on range after range of hills. To the right are spurs from this mountain; beyond them the faint blue of the Beaufort district ; to the left are great flat tables of stone, the edges of them sheer precipice. Over these again peep further heights, cones, and ridges—in front the rough peaks of the Chumi which looks down on Lovedale as we look down on it. But best of all is the view behind. For full two thousand feet the Katberg climbs above us, first in slopes of green velvet, divided off by deep glens, filled with forest trees, finally,

in great upright, almost overhanging, basaltic cliffs, like
"Samson's Ribs," only ten times higher and continued for
miles, like the turrets on the brows of Cybelé. At last, on
the far right, the mountain goes up 700 feet higher yet, in a
needle-like point, from which it descends in a ragged shoulder
to the lower ground. In one light alone, and seen for a brief
instant in passing, this mountain must fix itself for ever in
your mind. It did so or ever we alighted from the coach.
But how much it grows with the inexhaustible play of feature,
the resources of expression, poured into every part of it,
drawn forth from every corner, at every change of the weather,
at all hours of the day. It is a ceaseless panorama ; or rather
it is a stage, upon which daily dramas are done by sun, moon,
and stars, cloud, wind, and sky.

We have been reading Homer's descriptions of scenery in
the *Iliad*, and are greatly struck by the resemblances between
the country he describes and this. A dweller here would
understand almost every line, would appreciate each allusion.
Some of these seem perfect *voces signatae* for the place and
the people. The simple agricultural and pastoral life, the
virtues and qualities of the natives, the outs and ins of the
country,—you find apt words for each and all in those old
lines. The sixth book and the ninth recall readings with you
at every verse ; part of the first, too, you taught me to scan at

Cannes, from the little copy we read out of—a cheap *Trübner* bought at Paris, and bearing the lines and handwriting of this month ten years ago. My present seems to "copy fair my past" in a way not easy to describe.

We are just finishing the closing lines of Homer, and I can understand Shelley's outburst about the closing books—their "perpetually increasing magnificence." But I have hunted him through from the first line, in search of bits of S. African scenery, of which he seems completely full. I think to write a paper on Homer from the point of view of these hills.

You will maybe think I am not attending to theology. I trust it is not so. Here you cannot help getting "Introduction," of a kind, to all the books, from every walk in the open air. If Homer might have set his heroic life down in this district, the Scripture seems just here—as it does, I suppose, more or less, everywhere—to have been on the field before everyone else, and said all about it.

From the thunderstorm of Psalm xxix. to the gorgeous lilies of the gospel field, which the thunder brings to bloom in a single night, everything under the African sky speaks that same *Muttersprache* of us all which is transcribed in the Bible. The forests on the mountains, the locusts on the green pastures, the oxen ploughing, the watercourses, like Jordan himself, every one of them, for steepness and thick growth, the springs, the drought, the head-dresses, the heat and the shadow—all of them make the old well-known words as if heard, or rather seen, now for the first time. I know not how the colours in which Revelation is steeped, were chosen ; or in what single rich conjunction they were first found ; unless it have been by that "wisdom of many hues" ($\pi o\iota\kappa\iota\lambda\dot{\eta}$ $\sigma o\phi\iota\alpha$) which has made two things—the daedal earth and the divine word.

Perhaps this is very elementary divinity—and only so much as saying that nature is a theologian, as long ago some one said she was mathematical ($\dot{\alpha}\pi o\mu\epsilon\tau\rho\epsilon\hat{\iota}$ $\dot{\eta}$ $\phi\upsilon\sigma\iota s$). Beyond this, however, we have been reading Farrar's "Paul" pretty carefully, and are now half-way through vol. II. One cannot ever sufficiently wonder at the erudition of the man, the wealth of reference, the flood of side light he throws upon everything. I feel the classical parallels in themselves to be a reminiscence to me of everything I have read, besides the thousand instances where I can barely follow. It is, without doubt, a noble work ; as far above the *Life of Christ* as possible,—unless it be that the latter subject is "as far as possible," $\dot{\upsilon}\pi\epsilon\rho\epsilon\kappa\pi\epsilon\rho\iota\sigma\sigma\hat{\omega}s$, above any writer.

The point in which he is strongest is his "preparatio scholastica" for such a work ; it puts him on a perfect level

with the whole region, sphere, and outward relations of
Paul's life. Farrar's patient years as a teacher have been a
great help to him in this. The point in which he seems to
me to be least sure-footed and steady is his treatment of
passages where the circumstances and issues lie most nearly
within the *spiritual* domain, *e.g.* the descent of the Holy
Ghost at Pentecost, where a word of Neander's is worth a
world of criticism, elucidation, and explanation; the conversion itself—where the psychological analysis is interesting,
but the transition point—the real *Brennpunkt* of the whole
—is vague and therefore inadequate ; the dispute at Jerusalem
and the point of Titus' circumcision. His eschatological
views, though nowhere very prominent, colour his treatment
at times, as in I Thess., "taking vengeance on them that know
not God." His giving of the gist of the epistles, so far as I
have read, is beyond all praise. His translations rest upon
the accuracy of a scholar, but they have all the forcible
freedom of one who understands in his heart the language
spoken by Paul. Such a work as Farrar's is a great apology
for the Christian faith, a vivid exhibition of how completely
the doctrine of Jesus can saturate, and captivate, and occupy
a human intellect and soul. I should like to write a review of
the book, perhaps for the B. and F. ; I wish you would; you
know Conybeare well.

Besides this, I have had a little of the highest privilege of theology—to preach. At East London thrice, and here each of the last three Sabbaths at a little afternoon meeting in the inn, I have spoken, sometimes on old subjects, as often on new. "My yoke and My burden"; "Seen the promises, been persuaded, embraced, and confessed"; "The word of God—its scrutiny of us, the Son of God—His sympathy" (Heb. iv. 12-15)—these have been the new topics.

I have had the still higher privilege, while staying here, of coming very close to one or two young men; one led to another, and I trust God has given us to help each other. It is very striking to find how almost all ὧν Κύριος διήνοιξεν τὴν καρδίαν, προσέχειν τοῖς λαλουμένοις, have had a godly and goodly upbringing; sad and encouraging it is at once: for one sees how bread cast upon the waters comes back again; and yet—that it should only be after such tossing and wandering, and going astray.

Last Friday night a young German—come out here for his health—asked me to accompany him as far as the top of the mountain; he was going to cross it to meet a friend. It is a grand ride. You must go back to that never to be forgotten route from Pau to Eaux Bonnes, to find its equal, and even that, I fancy, must be enhanced by memory in

order to match this. You climb along the sheer side of
the mountain, mounting up all the time, rounding shoulder
after shoulder and fold after fold. Below the road, banked
up by a retaining-wall and partly cut out of the solid rock,
with no barrier, but now and again a big stone, the hillside
pitches down for hundreds of feet, thick with every kind
of undergrowth, overgrowth, creepers and streamers of lichen,
and filled, after these rains, with an innumerable noise of
waterfalls, subdued by the distance, the echoes, and the
intervening foliage, to one soft murmurous sound like a
blind wind finding its way over and through a thick forest.
On the other side of the ravine a similar bushy wood
ascends ; and above it again are reaches of light emerald
velvet, to the very feet of these magnificent basalt bastions
that crown the hill. As far as you can see there is this
waving land of shoulder and hollow, slope and glen,
presided over by the keen grey glitter of the cliffs, and,
over that, the eternal blue. Above the road, over the wet
stone walls, living with moss and many flowers, rises the
same entangled bush, too brilliant for shadow to damp it,
too deep for sunlight altogether to enlighten it. Monsters
of trees, fallen or hewn down, peep out of beds of green, into
which they have been pulled by the constant embrace of
parasites and weeds. The bright lamp-like blooms of the

Letters.

sugar bush ("protea"—from its many forms) look out of their branches, snowy-hearted, pink-tipped, and crimson-sheathed.

As you rise to the heights the land levels out underneath you, ridge on ridge of distant purple discovering to you on how much you are looking down. My friend and I walked our horses all the way up for an hour and a half, talking of Homer, Greek life, and the poets. Then we had some earnest words, and reining in our horses, prayed before parting. A storm had been gathering for some time, and as I opened my eyes they were filled with lightning. Bidding good-bye I cantered off, and watched the thunder-cloud making for our inn. Every moment the growls became louder ; we had a race for it. In half an hour I came down the four or five miles we had climbed, and galloped into the yard just as the big drops came down, followed by a deluge like those we had in the Pyrenees.

Katberg,
South Africa, March 23, 1880.

Our greatest event since we last wrote has been the visit of Dr. and Mrs. Stewart and Ida Leigh (baby) to carry off Mina. They spent a whole day with us, roaming through the woods and gathering trees and roots to plant at Love-dale. This session is a very successful one there, in spite of the drought—there are more boys and girls than last. The feeling is again running high about the natives; the Basutos are to be disarmed, though they have fought for us and done nothing to deserve it, and many fear a new war. Dr. Stewart has a great deal to do and to bear in his fearless defence of their rights. He does not flatter the natives, but he does wish to see fair play, and to give them a chance of standing on their own feet in all this hurry and press of Europeans, eager to get more land, and threatening to over-ride the coloured people altogether. Pitiably enough, the subject is made here, just as at home, a matter of party. I see in England Sir B. Frere is being made the scapegoat of all that has happened, and I fear a new Government may send out some one to go against everything he has done simply because he has done it. Now, this will only irritate the colonists, and justify them in saying England changes about and interferes with us whenever a new minister comes in. Whereas, it is forgotten, there is a strong feeling among colonists themselves, especially among farmers, against the natives, and the late wars with the Kaffirs were not Sir B.'s doing alone, but the Colonial Ministry's, for the Cape has as free and respon-

s

sible a government as England has at home. I see by last night's paper that to-morrow writs will be issued for another home Parliament. I have no doubt how it will be constituted; but I do trust that righteousness will reign in it, and not revenge. Some colonists think the Liberals neglect everything out of England, and that Lord B. sees beyond. I wish any Government were in that would help to train up and send out of England a nobler sort of men, who would make our name more unmistakably the name of freedom and intelligence and earnestness all over the world.

Our time in the open air daily varies from eight to nine hours. We start with the herd of goats that saunter about the grass near here, and come home with them. In wet weather they run into the verandah and play pretty tricks, boxing with each other, tipping over one's umbrella and scampering off in fun, chasing the hens, and in turn chased by the dogs. These last have the best of all the farmyard games that are daily and hourly played here; they stir up the sleeping kittens, send the cats helter-skelter up the willow trees, pursue the piglings (one of whom we call Orion, because he has a broad white belt on a black ground, and one Pleiades, because he has seven dark spots on a light body), steal their meat from the ducks, hunt the calves, and even trot the horses up at dusk. There are so many dogs that no one has yet finished counting them; we began when we came. The kittens are dying off day by day—the mortality comes from their being made presents of. The latest additions to the establishment are a silver peahen and a blue peacock; the latter gave it to a cat who came too close the other day in a way that would have amused you. We have found out the feud arose from peacock's thinking the cat's ' miaow' was an attempt to take off his ' piaow'; it was really very natural when one came to think of it.

Lovedale, April 27, 1880.

Mr. Watson's farm lies quite on the top of a rise. It is a great white, square building, like a Scotch shooting-box. For many miles from it stretch the ostrich camps, immense enclosures of bush and veldt railed in by three wires supported on sneex wood. Inside these roam the younger birds in flocks, while the older ones are paired in paddocks nearer home. Their nest is a deep pit of gravel, level with the ground, and there they lay perhaps twenty eggs like immense ivory balls. When they are all laid, the hen and the cock keep them warm turn about, by night and by day. When the little ostriches come out, they are such oddities, just like hedgehogs set up on hen's legs, with brown serpents coming out of one end. These serpents are their necks, and they are the most deliciously soft, downy things, all speckled over with black mottles upon a brown ground. Then Mr. Watson takes them away from their father and mother, and they run about the farm-yard, with two little black boys to feed them. They get chopped-up cabbage many times a day, and peck it up as if they were hammering tacks every time into the ground. The ones we saw like this four months ago, like babies, are now grown big girls and boys. They are now like an armful of feathers fastened on umbrella sticks, with one big claw, like the claw of a mahogany table, at the bottom. The serpents are grown longer, and go arching about like india-rubber canes, while all the little mottles have died away. It was near sundown when we saw them last Wednesday, and it was the first time they had been out for a long walk. They appeared far off among the bushes like the tops of guns on soldiers' backs when they are marching. One little boy was behind them and one before. Mrs. Watson called another little boy to go to make them come faster. He went away like the wind, and instead of chasing them as little boys do at home, he ran backwards in front of them quite fast, and called to them and cheered them on, and on they came, careering and flopping and flouncing, stepping on their toes, and moving as if on springs, till they came to the farm-yard. They had great handfuls of maize thrown them, and they darted out their necks and picked it up like lightning. It was a funny sight to see all these feather-cushions crowded together, while the long necks went dab-dab-dabbing in between their legs. You could pull their feathers gently, they were so tame, and the cocks and hens crept out and in between their big limbs, to try and get a corn of wheat, but the crush was so great they had to get out of the way. Each of them was worth about £20, for very soon their feathers will be clipped and sent home to go in ladies' hats, and trim dresses, and make soldiers' "shakos"; and that will bring the farmer a good price.

On the "Melrose," lying off Port Elizabeth,
May 27, 1880, 9.30 a.m.

We are on our way home, being about 444 miles nearer you than we were last Sabbath at Impolweni.

Our last letter, which is lying somewhere in the mail bags on board, was posted after two days in Maritzburg (Thursday-Saturday), when we left to go on fifteen miles further to Impolweni. On the Friday morning, at 10.45,

we started off in a spider with two fresh horses from the
Egyptian House, of which you have heard. It is a most
exhilarating atmosphere that of Natal; the sun warm, the
breeze cool, and everything as clear as crystal. We drove
out of the trees that surround the town and out on the open
hillsides to the east of Maritzburg, with the summit of
Table Mountain standing up on the horizon beyond. We
passed a native kraal or two, ran down into a donga, and
up again to the crown of a small hill, on the end of which
lies Bishopstowe. We saw the Bishop's house among the
trees to the right, and turned towards it through a field of
maize skirted by native huts. Many of them were of the
ordinary Kaffir kind, differing from the Fingo in being
thatched down to the ground. But further up the hillside
we saw several neat square cottages, such as mark an im-
provement in their owner's mode of life. If all we have
heard of the German missions in Natal be true, Mr. Glockner
should not have cast the first stone at Bishopstowe.

We passed a beautiful little rustic chapel, and then
rounded a low-built spreading gabled house, overgrown
with roses and creepers, and embowered in trees. We left
the carriage and went up the gravel walk, but, before we
reached the steps, a stately figure came out upon the
verandah and welcomed us without any introduction.

Bishop Colenso is a splendid looking man, about Uncle Robert's size, with the same beautiful white hair and large mild eyes, over which he now and then draws down a pair of eyeglasses. He led us through the dining room with its bare polished floor and simple furniture, where one or two boys were cleaning. They saluted us as we went past —one of them was the son of the chief Langalibalele. In the corridor Mrs. Colenso met us; we were introduced as " a minister from Edinburgh and his wife."

Soon we were sitting in the parlour and were very courteously questioned as to how we found the country and other things. We had known some lads sent by the Bishop to Lovedale, so that was something common between us. In a little the Bishop invited me out through the window door, as we used to go out and in to the drawing room of Bonskeid, and took me round to his school. There was a small attendance there. The lady teacher accounted for it, as our own in the Highlands does, by so many of the children being taken away to "scare crows," "herd beasts," or kept back by sickness. She said, too, that from the poverty of fuel, the children were kept late in the day collecting grass and rubbish enough to make a fire for breakfast. Of course there is no compulsory clause here, and the Government of Natal has no system of recognition or inspection of native education as there is in the old colony.

While Charlotte was talking to the mistress—Mrs. Larkins —the Bishop took me to his printing office, where I saw an interesting man, Magema, his head printer, who was sent into Zululand last autumn to recover some things of the Prince Imperial's. He learned a good deal there that throws light on the late war. I inquired of him how he found the people : were they settling down? He said the one thing they were longing for was to see their king. He said the common people loved him and many of the chiefs now in possession. He could be brought back without disturbing the new settlement, only John Dunn would object. He said they never expected war when it happened, unless it were from the English side, who seemed to want all the lands for themselves, and would not let any one else have them. The stories of the king's cruelty were quite new to him. He had often heard of his trying to save those who, by the laws of the nation, ought to have been put to death.

After having learned this for myself, for the Bishop left me to talk with him, Dr. Colenso himself returned and began to speak of the Zulu war. It seemed to touch his inmost soul; he did not speak wildly; he was very calm, but that only made his words more impressive. He took me into his library and showed me from the blue books how everything had been done to bring on the war, telegrams being sent home to prejudice men's minds about the king, officers having been arranged to co-operate or actually to enter the country—all this before one of the charges alleged as *casus belli* in the ultimatum had occurred; how the country was entered before the days expired, although the king had done everything in his power to collect the indemnity asked for; how his messengers were ignored, and in one place put in irons; and how dynamite had been used to blow up men, women and children after the war was said to be ended. He put into my hands the authority in detail for each of these statements, and they make one's ears tingle, and one's heart sick and sore. Everything you have read at home of the treachery and horrors of the Afghan campaign has had its counterpart here. No one can believe that the authors of these things intended to bring about such awful effects; it is one more instance of the inviolable law, that what begins in injustice ends in cruelty; that where righteousness has first been outraged, no other virtue under heaven is secure. Two hours passed very quickly as we talked on these things, Miss Colenso making a fifth, and not the least outspoken, in the conversation. We felt how grievous it is that the Bishop's isolated position in other things should have separated him from good men at such a time as this, when every voice that can murmur should be raised to thunder, and every hand that has the least life left in it should be lifted up. We felt how much judgment and observation of all sides was needed in a matter such as this, but I believe they are not half so much wanted as common honesty and unflinching courage. There is a time to hear all sides, and there is a time to take *one*.

If you wish to get a short statement of these things, send for a book called "Cetshwayo's Dutchman," by Mr. Vijn, edited by Bishop Colenso (Longmans), and read it carefully, especially the notes.

The last thing we saw at Bishopstowe, a thing I shall never forget, was a handsome morocco case, with the royal arms of England engraven upon it. A book in rich scarlet binding, resting upon a purple ground, lay inside. It was a copy of a report of the installation of the King at the hands of the representative of Her Majesty in 1873. On the outside, lettered in gold, ran the following: *Queen Victoria*, etc. etc., to *King Cetewayo*. I remember how it startled me, in closing the best and most impartial history of South Africa, written just before the beginning of these troubles with the Kaffir and Zulu tribes, to find the last sentence state that Zululand was then in peace and quiet, and that a new ruler, Cetewayo, had been crowned by Sir T. Shepstone in the name of our Queen. Little did I dream one day to see such a seal of friendship between ourselves and the Zulu nation wet with the dews that fell on it as it dropped from the hands of the same king in his flight before an English force, which had invaded his land, ignored his overtures, and by help of traitors, worthy to be descendants of Judas, hunted him down. Until this last accident, the book had evidently been carefully kept with an equal chivalry to that which forbore to cross into our borders when Natal lay at his feet, which spared the mission houses in his country till they were turned into forts against them, which protected white people within his borders while the war still raged.

Dr. and Mrs. Colenso asked us to come and stay with them on our return from Impolweni if we should have time. I told him Mr. Fowler was my father-in-law, and he recognized the name with pleasure, remembering his work in the Aborigines Society. The courtesy and kindness we received at Bishopstowe touched us much.

The drive up the hill to the north was delightful in the fresh morning. We were on the Greytown road, which winds along up and down over a rolling plateau, covered with grass that reminded me of the south of Scotland. Only here and there little patches of trees with neat houses and plots of tilled land make a welcome diversion in the view. The dwellings are much neater than in many parts of the old colony. There is much less roughness and neglect in Natal; some say it is because the Dutch element is less prominent there. After about twelve miles we descended into the valley of the Umgeni, the large and beautiful stream, the mouth of which we saw on our way to Verulam. It has a broad, deep mass of water, of a pale green colour, as though it came off snow, and, just above where we crossed, it comes over a low fall in the whole length of it with about a dozen distinct tresses of water descending between green bushes. On the rise above it we turned off the smooth road to the right to seek for Impolweni, which lies some three miles further on. Our road was a self-made one, leading through long grass and fields of maize, with water sprouts and mud holes to vary it. It was the wrong way, of course, we found afterwards, but the right one is not nearly so amusing. However, nothing could exhaust the horses who went through thick and thin. We came out upon the face of a stream running parallel to the high road, and just below us joining the

Umgeni is a "meeting of the waters," that reminded me
of another place. This was the Impolweni, and in front
of us it made one of those sharp serpentinings you so
often see in South African rivers; the opposite banks
being rocky krantzes, with a small kloof coming down
from the other side, where the river bends furthest in.
On the flat meadow left by the stream is a little cluster
of trees at the nearer end, sheltering the old mission house
where Mr. Allison lived. He brought a settlement of
Swazis here from another place where he worked, near
Maritzburg. They were part of a tribe that he brought
over into the colony to escape destruction among their
own people. He leased this piece of land, which was one
of the 6-7000 acre farms given out to the Dutch in the
first settlement of Natal by English in '50, from a Boer
named Maritz, whose brother's name the neighbouring town
bears. The Dutchman's house became a manse, his barn
the church and school. When Dr. Duff passed there, Mr.
Allison joined the Free Church Mission, and the land is
now ours for mission purposes. We saw more square
cottages round about than at almost any mission station
we have seen. A German workman at a large building
on the hillside above the river, which turned out to be
the new church, stopped us on our way down.

We are speeding along due east with a favourable wind, which is ruffling up the dark blue waves with white caps under a crescent moon somewhere to the south of Malaga. This has been a day of great excitement and delight to us, for it brought us our first sight of Gibraltar.

Yesterday towards afternoon the coast began to grow nearer and clearer, running out northwards in a series of rocky promontories. At the corner of these came a great headland crowned with a heavily-built lighthouse like a fortress, which every one recognized as Cape St. Vincent. The shore continued to run on in a low line of sheer cliff, surmounted by bare downs for a considerable distance, till it ended in another cape ('St. Mary'), after which it gradually trended again to the east. As the sun went down we were entering Cadiz Bay, reminding us vividly of Browning's description of the same scene in his "Home Thoughts from the Sea." Those few lines reproduce the place, and the feeling of it perfectly.

At half-past seven Charlotte and I went forward to the other cabin to have a short service with the soldiers, which they had agreed to the evening before. About a dozen came, and we had some nice hymn-singing, their strong deep voices sounding beautifully. We had "Hold the Fort," "Only an Armour-Bearer," and so forth. Then the English clergyman offered up prayer, and I gave a short address from the words, "My son, give Me thine heart." We were very thankful for the quiet and attentive way in which every one listened. They assented pretty warmly to a proposal to have a meeting again on Sabbath next. This morning at six the steward told us we were already in the straits. By the faint red light we could see through the port-hole that we were passing a fine bold, mountainous coast to the right. I thought of old Ulysses, or the first Phœnician seamen, creeping through this wonderful gate which joins two worlds. But we were both still more eager to see what lay on the other side. So by a quarter past six we had climbed on to the highest deck, and there, in the north-east, in pure purple outline against an orange sky, " dawned Gibraltar grand and grey," as Browning sings. It was quite something to take your breath away—the heroic place you had heard of since a child ; a great bit of Mother England hundreds of miles off from the rest of her—all suddenly, unmistakably visible, palpable, and far grander than the best you had looked for.

Thursday morning.—Tuesday was a quiet and uneventful day. We sped along within sight of the rugged outline of the

African coast, feeling rather inclined to be sober, like children after a holiday. Toward evening it freshened, and as we passed a light (C. Bono, somebody said it was), C. thought something was coming on. Whatever it was, I could not sleep, and as I lay awake became conscious that we were beginning to get into an uneasy roll. About three I rose and shut the window in front of the 'port,' which we had been told the night before might remain up all the way now. The motion steadily increased, and at four we heard the men overhead letting down our ports from the deck. As no one came in to screw ours fast, and as the waves were dashing up, I got up, and by dint of 'fighting with it,' as papa would say, got it pretty tight. A little broken sleep and one woke at last to all the sad consciousness that we were lying across a heavy sea, which 'sea-sawed' with a regular motion like a swing, first to one side then to another. I went on deck at once, and for a time enjoyed the adventures of the occasion, holding on, as Ulysses did in Charybdis, like a bat— νύκτερις ὥσπερ—to a tree and watching the vain antics of those who tried to walk from point to point, and only succeeded in showing a wonderful similarity to their physical ancestors. Then the cold (for it blew a *gregali* or misty air from the north-east) and the uncertainty of one's tenure made me move into the upper saloon, where I lay curled up

on one of the sofas, and moralized on the situation.   In truth
it was a marvellous sight.   This seething chaos, far as the eye
could reach, no inch of it for a moment stable, no point in it
fixed, and through and over it all our vessel pursuing her
trackless path, shaken but not turned aside, opposed but not
overthrown.   It reminded one of Gerhardt's fine paraphrase of
the 37th Psalm :

> " Die Wolken, Wellen, Winden
> Sind lauter Strass und Bahn,
> *Der* wird auch Wege finden
> Wo Dein Fuss gehen kann."

One moment we were slanting like the roof of a house down
to the water's edge, the next lifted as high in the air.   And
with this that sinking at the heart came on which seems
inseparable from any sudden motion of the kind, and makes
a child cry if you swing it beyond a certain point.   " They
mount up to the heavens, they go down again to the depths ;
their soul is melted because of trouble."   That is all that can
be said about it, as about every experience that the Bible
touches ; it always hits the centre of the mark.   At another
moment it was an unseen spirit one fancied descending from
the snowy heights of the north, and urging this chill army
towards the warm shores of Africa ; while every now and
then some great broad-backed leader among them came

T

striding up out of the ranks, caught us on his huge shoulders an instant, shook us all over, and passed on in the track of the others, triumphing as he went.

By this time the wind had gone round to the north-west, and the seas were coming up after us on the port quarter with increasing strength   It was a picturesque sight watching the troop of nimble native sailors reefing the awning over the quarter-deck ; while a great burly tar climbed atop of it to keep it from flapping out of reach.

Monday Morning, January 18, 1886.
11 o'clock (about 9 with you).

Off the low coast near Alexandria ; wind south-west, with a falling sea, light blue sky and veil of haze on the horizon.

After dinner at 7 p.m. on Thursday evening last, we heard the engines stop, and going on deck, found ourselves lying just outside the harbour (or rather harbours) of Valetta. To the left was the opening to the grand harbour, through which in the distance we could just see the climbing lights of the hillside city glimmering like fireflies through a mist. To the right was our haven (the quarantine harbour), while on either hand gleamed the lights of the two guardian fortresses (St. Angelo and St. Elmo), reminding one of the

'Twin Stars' under whose auspices St. Paul sailed away from this very spot 1800 years ago. We had passed his bay about 9 miles westwards along the coast,—dimly discernible in the moonlight. The planet Venus, large and luminous, was dropping down into the eastern waves, like an imperial pearl into Cleopatra's cup.

It felt like being in fairyland, as we were urged on over the glassy surface by two stalwart figures standing barefoot, looking forward and working their long white sweeps with leisurely strength, away from them. Prose, however, shortly set in again, on our arrival at the landing place; and we set our faces to the long ascent of steep stairs leading up to the principal streets of the town. At this point there emerged, and pursued us without intermission for the next fifteen hours till we departed again, what may be described as perhaps the characteristic phenomenon of modern Malta.

Maltese lace still exists and flourishes in its original forms of wonder and beauty. But the other special product of the place—the maltese terrier—has undergone a striking transformation. To cut the matter short—he has assumed a *human* form. No longer does he sportively attend your steps, careering joyously before you, and turning round every now and then, salute your friendly countenance with a yelp of delight. He 'dogs' your footprints still, it is true, with an assiduity that is invincible, and a tolerance of rebuffs that excites your admiration (to say nothing of *stronger* feelings); but the only sounds to which he 'gives tongue' are muttered inquiries such as these—'Gentleman, want to see Malta, sir?' 'Gentleman, find best hotel, sir?' 'Gentleman, need a guide, sir?' 'Only a sixpence, sir'; 'That's nothing to gentleman, sir'; 'Number 199, sir'; 'No, no, not a guide, sir'; 'Gentleman find me to-morrow morning, sir'; 'Not forget number, sir': and so on *ad infinitum.*

Indeed this 'animal de combat' more often reminds 'you of a lower order of life than the noble canine.' He is generally *brown*, and crawls silently, almost invisibly, but his entomological antitype shall be nameless.

Climbing up the flights of steps from the sea, we passed under a narrow, high-arched portal, which reminded us that we were on the borderland of Moor-dom. Emerging on a narrow street, the high built houses, with their lofty, rounded doorways (a pattern which always carries one's thoughts to the desert palm), deepened this impression. At last we emerged on the parallel lines of main street (Strada Forni and Strada Reale successively) which skirt the face of the hill on which the city is built. There the full oriental vision burst on us. We were in Moorland at once. Far as the eye could see ran the narrowing vista of high house fronts, their clear white limestone mosaiced into the clear blue sky. Half-way down, on both sides, were tiers of projecting windows—" casements in balcony " is the only name I can think of for them—supported on brackets of stone. On the street level opened countless shops—doorless and windowless—less shops than show-rooms, open to the street. The blaze of light from these was the more striking to eyes coming out of oceanic darkness. At the doors or in the street stood the merchants, glibly rattling off their string of English syllables like a shower of small beads on the head of the passers by. Lace, filigree work, tobacco, coloured cloths, all passed before ear and eye in a panorama that was perfectly bewildering. And all the time there was the consciousness of this other obsequious something which stuck to one like an alien shadow hurrying behind, ready on the faintest occasion, or on *none*, to resume its midge-like " sūm-sūm-sūm "-ing in one's irritated ear.

At last, after much hasty, silent inference (inference with a margin of error, of course) and some little bold stationary interrogation (most successful of which was from a raw lad mounting guard at some barrack entry, whose broad Forfar-shire burr sounded sweet as northern porridge to the skim

milk of "Maltese Dog"), we reached our hotel—nominally
"The Grand," actually the old-fashioned, many-staired, half-
staged, Albergo-like institution familiar to the traveller in
North Italy. Only, anything in the shape of a real hotel
with foundations was welcome. What a luxury it was even
to see a four-poster, though the posts were only hollow tin
tubes immersed in clouds of gauze drapery supposed to keep
mosquitos out, which, of course, they didn't, but only served
to keep one fine, musical, muscular specimen *in*. One
could almost fall upon these hollow tubes and cover them
with tears. It seemed superfluous, if not wrong, to undress
and go to bed—how ungrateful not to go on all night
feasting one's eyes on the delightful object. As it happened,
one paid the penalty of not being content with joys in prospect. For when morning came in through the window on
the square court open to the sky, behold the white drapery,
yea, the four solid walls themselves were rolling and pitching
about in all directions, or, at least, the sleeper thought so.

We were early astir, for only a precious hour or two had
to elapse ere we must be on board again. Happily for us,
the chief sights of Valetta lie close together. We went
over the governor's palace, formerly the residence of the
Masters of the Knights of St. John. These brave repre-
sentatives of the Crusades, at first not only a martial, but a

nursing order (of which the modern Red Cross still keeps up the tradition), made a gallant stand for four centuries (the 12th to the 16th), first at Jerusalem, next at Rhodes, then at Cyprus, and finally here at Malta, where Charles V. had the wisdom to plant them in 1530 as a last bulwark against the then overwhelming tide of Moslem invasion. A splendid bulwark they proved, contending on this little spot for over a century stubbornly and all but singlehanded, unless when like-minded Venice came to the rescue in behalf of the Cross. As one looked down the noble hall, where stand ranged in order the arms of each noted champion (from Spain, Italy, Germany, England, as the case might be), preserved here with the wearer's name on the dissolution of the order a hundred years ago, one realized more vividly than ever that episode most strange and momentous in the history of Christendom ; dark on the whole, yet broken with bright gleams of faith and heroism —the 700 years' conflict between Mahomet and Christ. The presence in the armoury of some of our red-coated fellow-travellers bound for Egypt lent an additional interest to the scene. One felt how truly they and we were engaged more or less worthily in another act of the same gigantic drama. Ay, and beyond us, beyond all this stormy and obscure present, one could not restrain the flight of a trembling hope, the hope that by and through it all there was slowly, surely coming the kingdom of God's Son, the greater Peace, the larger Christendom.

Yet, here too, as everywhere, starvation and misery go hand in hand with drink shops innumerable. There may be barely a farthing for bread, there are always pence in abundance for wine, spirits, and beer. Never has one felt more the need of the little badge of blue in his coat, or at least of its equivalent in his heart, than at every stage on this voyage hitherto. Wherever our countrymen go, they carry with them this terrible complaint, and every race they mingle with is infested afresh with it. There is drinking on board the steamer on every occasion—on leaving, arriving, and leaving again ; in fine weather, to pass the time; in rough weather, to keep the spirits up. And these two most heroic possessions of England, which we have seen, the very mention of whose name quickens the blood of any true Briton, what are they when you look into them ? Every tenth house in them a place of temptation! O you young countrymen of mine at home (such is the cry forever rising from the depths of my soul), would God I could persuade every one of you to abstain, were it only for the honour of this noble history, this goodly inheritance He has given to you and me.

Shepheard's Hotel, Cairo,
Thursday, 21st January, 1886 ; 3 p.m.
(10 minutes to 1 with you).

We are writing in a large, airy room on the east side of the open court-garden of the hotel. Looking out, one sees the upper boughs of thick acacias, whose stout stems and broad foliage make you think they must have thriven on the mud and water of the Nile. A few birds, with wings of a pale brown—a kind of crow, apparently—flit among the branches ; while overhead a keen-eyed hawk occasionally hovers or sails. The sun would be an August one in Scotland, but the air is June ; in the morning and at night it is delightfully crisp and cooling, while the edges of the light-stone buildings seem to fit, rather than fade, into the azure sky like the finest mosaic. Last night, as the after-glow came on above the roofs opposite, in colours one has not seen the like of since those wonderful autumn sunsets two years ago, and the feathery tops of two solitary palms stood out against it in pure and perfect outline, with Venus every instant looming larger, like an advancing seraph, through mingled pink and purple and blue, and the sound of water plashing up from underneath just noise enough to set off the silence, the spirit of the place seemed to come over one like a bodily sensation, and shutting one's eyes one seemed to sink away into one of those Arabian nights which were lived here half an æon ago in old Mohammedan Cairo.

Thursday evening.—We have spent the afternoon visiting two of the mosques—one of the earlier and the latest, dating from 1356 and 1856 respectively. The sight of them also has greatly impressed us.

Cairo abounds in mosques; they are reckoned by the hundred. Many, perhaps most, seem going to ruin, unrepaired; but some are well kept up, though we have been told it is chiefly by strangers.

The mosque of Sultan Hassan, to which we went first, is a large building, of a rough oblong shape, standing at the foot of the Citadel, or Castle Hill. Its high and almost unbroken walls, together with the chain-like barring of its one or two windows, give it, from without, something of the air of a prison. Whether the original idea was to keep the world outside altogether, or only to exclude one's enemies (objects, to the Christian at least, quite reconcilable), I cannot say. But certainly, when one has passed under that lofty doorway, nearly seventy feet high, and threaded a winding passage, arched with much strength and beauty, and crossed by solid beams from which lamp-chains are suspended, and has put off his shoes from off his feet at the further end, one feels he is leaving everything worldly behind and is entering on a spot set apart and sealed. Sealed it certainly is, but to earth only ; for as one emerges into light again, one stands in a vast court entirely open to the sky. In the centre stands a large round basin-shaped fountain, roofed over by a cupola, supported on pillars. Here the worshipper goes through that rite of outward cleansing which, from Jewish times at least, has been inseparable from the thought of fellowship with God. All round the floor is polished marble, unsoiled by any dust from the street. On the north, south, and east sides are enormous square recesses, spanned by a single arch, the slightly raised floor of which is covered with strips of carpet, where the worshipper stands motionless, his face turned towards Mecca, then bends forward with his hands on his knees, then kneels, and finally prostrates himself with his forehead to the ground. The action is an impressive one, and the devotion seems far more deep and undistracted than that of similar devotees in Roman Catholic countries. The eastern recess is larger than the others ; most seem to pray in it. A high pulpit, with steep staircase at the back, and a stone table in the centre, the meaning of which I could not make out, were the only objects it contained. The whole reminded one of the Jewish and the Puritan modes of worship. So did the plain windows above, with their barred ornament, of which the pattern suggested, if it was not actually suggested by, strings of beads crossing each other. Even the high apertures in the wall, resembling niches and roofed in with an ornament like drooping flower-stems cut short, contained nothing. There was nothing on any hand to make the thought stop, or even to catch the eye, short of the infinite blue—no representation of the human form, far less the divine. The worshipper's own self was quite lost in the great spaces surrounding it, unobserved save of the omniscient heavens above. The sole decoration, and it was everywhere, on fountain, canopy, frieze and portal, was drawn from the world of the Unseen; it spoke of the spirit of man and the mouth of God. Words from the Koran in the old picturesque character—these were the images and the adornment. Silent or muttered petition from the individual's own lips to the Heartsearcher—that was all the ritual. A wild, fanatical rallying cry, ringing from the summit of these narrow stairs to the thronging thousands of the faithful, on some feast, or pilgrimage, or sudden outbreak —such, one could well fancy, would be the only sermon suitable to these four walls.

As in a lightning flash that scene brought before me the fierce 'Protestantism' of twelve centuries since, which burst like a whirlwind from the desert on the indolent, corrupt, idolatrous Christianity of those days, and dashed the altar with its bread-god from the choir, and the stone-goddess from her bracket in the aisle, and reared in their place, sometimes of their very substance, these gaunt tabernacles, whose architecture and outlines are all of the wilderness, and whose pavement is mingled, in terrible irony,—a mosaic of heathen and Christian marbles.

Through a massive door in the east screen, we reached another part of the building, a kind of square nave or tribune, where the founder's body lay. Like the Pharaohs, these Arab rulers made religion the handmaid of their fame. The mosque, like the pyramid, was a monument of royal magnificence and a reminder of kingly claims. In the walls of this second chamber there were again recesses, the faint horse-shoe arches of which (almost Norman in their character) were brought out in finely pieced marble. A curious wood-work, apparently of the broken-flower-stem pattern, filled the corners downwards from above.

Immediately on the outside of this tribune, *i.e.* in the south-east corner of the mosque, rises for close on 300 feet its one surviving minaret, a grand palm-stem in solid stone, with prayer balconies projecting over the same inverted moulding (as if the first droop of the feathery branches had formed the model) near the summit. It, with hundreds like it, though less lofty, we watched from the overhanging citadel an hour later, rising all through the city into the purple air like stately flowers from the thick-sown buildings of the city; and from one to another came the voice of the muezzin in rhythmic monotone summoning the faithful ere night fell to bethink them of the Almighty and betake themselves to Him in prayer. Sleepless sentinels, they seemed posted on the bristling ramparts of this religion of the sword, keeping watch against the enemy. Verily, if God's work could be done by an arm of flesh, then this people of the prophet must have accomplished it long ere now.

Killarney,
Sabbath Morning, October 9, 1897.

It is the loveliest, most peaceful of Sabbath mornings, the mist has cleared away, and lake, woods, mountains, skies, all stand revealed—a scene of wondrous beauty. We are just going to church. It is a quarter to eleven with us, but 11.15 with thee; and I think of thee going with Freeland and Maida about the paths and under the trees of dear Bonskeid—Greta too, the pearl, in her white shell, somewhere in a nook of the boudoir, or nestling in thine arms. God bless my four darlings on earth, and help us to praise him to-day on earth, as our Robin is doing up in heaven.

2 p.m.—It is still Paradise—sunshine in full flood upon the lake, and on the mountains luminous blue and green.

We worshipped in the noble and beautiful church of Ireland, built by the people in the last ten years. They have learned liberality with freedom. Like all the Protestant churches we have seen, it is perfectly simple, yet not bare—the communion table standing in its ancient shape and place, unadorned except by the words, "Behold the Lamb of God, which taketh away the sin of the world." The congregation was fairly large, earnest and reverent—members of the leading households in the neighbourhood (Kenmares and Herberts), a few townspeople, and several visitors, some ten soldiers with their lieutenant, and an officer of constabulary.

The service was expressively and deliberately said ; the prayers of the litany, especially those for 'unity, peace and concord,' heartily responded to ; the psalms (xliv.-vi.) seemed as if chosen for to-day—cries to the true King to come and rule over a perplexed and troubled people ; and the sermon, from the text in Joel ii., "Rend your hearts, and not your garments," a weighty and wise appeal to individual and united prayer in view of the present condition of 'our country.' "Other means," said the preacher, "are difficult to use ; we can all use this greatest and best of means—hard to manage—prayer."

We came away, thankful to have been united with those who were seeking the true peace of Ireland in such a fashion. One is not surprised to learn, as the constabulary told us, that here in Kerry there is little or no religious animosity. Mr. Wynne, the English rector, is revered and beloved of all.

6 p.m.—After a quiet hour, Mr. Bain and I went out (3.30) to the lake side and sat on a seat perched on the ruins of an old castle, now the landing place, while he read aloud a bit of the life (strange life-story) of one of the Indians in the 'Wild West.' Then, the north-eastern air growing chilly, we put our books and wraps inside (into the house), and skirted the lake westward. Soon we found ourselves in the grounds of Muckross Abbey, an old seat of the Herberts, open to visitors. We wandered on for about a mile, amid the loveliest wildness, reminding one at every step of Milton's mazy wildernesses or Spenser's enchanted forests. Every sort of tree grows there in profusion, from common ash and beech and chestnut, to Norfolk pine and yew and cedar and deodar, and over everything runs the densest tangle of overgrowth, ivies and that wavy red berry with the thorned ivy leaf, and a wonderful silky-tufted creeper of a silvery lilac grey. Laurustine, rhododendron, hart's-tongue and every kind of

fern flourish luxuriantly; and every now and then the
great mountains come and look down at you, like strength
rejoicing over beauty. We turned in by the ruins of the
Abbey, hardly more than unroofed, and like a grand
rockery filled with every kind of moss and fern and growing tree. The little square cloisters hold a huge trunk,
of which the branches almost cover in the enclosure. All
round it and within are the resting places of Killarney
people.

Now the great hills are changing from deep purple to
steel black, and the lake is a mirror of polished metal.

I gave a Gospel of Matthew to a maid here to-day,
saying it told about our Lord Jesus Christ and His mother:
" Does it tell about the Blessed Virgin," she (my friend)
returned with such an eager delighted look. I showed
her the passages where Mary was mentioned, and she
took it, well pleased ; nowhere do they refuse the Gospels
if they are given with a kindly word and in the right way.

Our old carman from Mitchelstown to Fermoy yesterday
was a most interesting and amusing character. He told us
if we only read the 'glories of Mary,' we should either
believe in her altogether or disbelieve altogether. He
thought the humble and ignorant should not have the
Bible for fear they should explain it amiss, and so have

U

the condemnation of adding by wrong interpretation or
taking away by want of understanding. We did not
argue, but I tried to tell him what the effect of reading
Christ's own words for ourselves was—how it made us
try to do better. To this he responded—"Ah, that's
it, we often hear but we don't do." He regretted greatly
having lost a life of Christ he once had, so I gave him
the Apostle John's, whose figure he knew in the church,
and told him what a friend of the Blessed Virgin's John
was, and marked John iii. 16; and he took it with
pleasure. How it condemns one to see the devotion with
which they hold to the form of faith which has been
delivered to them, and the small and often misshapen
fragment of it allowed them. What it does for their lives!
If one does not contradict their way of it, but simply
repeats instead the New Testament way, they seem wonderfully reasonable and ready to receive it.

Now, goodnight to the three darlings,—Freeland, Maida,
and Margaret.

5.30 p.m. Monday.—This has been a day of days; six
or seven hours in the open air, under a lovely sky, and in
every manner of conveyance—wagonette, one's own legs,
and boat, round thirty miles of the loveliest scenery
in all creation. "Shure and this was the last county

made in all Ireland, ay, and in all the world," said
an old guide, "and everything that was left over from
the rest was thrown into it—that's how you have a bit
of everything." And so it is—rich grove, green pasture,
flowing stream; birds wild and tame; vast mountains,
wild glens, dashing torrents; everything. I yield to no
man in praise of Athole, but Killarney is Athole and
Badenoch both in one. It is Argyleshire and Perthshire
in one, Loch Katrine planted in Loch Awe. Our companions were from New Zealand, South Africa, and
Lancashire; and we had a guide a great character—Sir
John he is called—prince of talkers, singers and buglers.

The two sweet messages of Friday and Saturday met
us on the way at the Post Office. I think the Lord put
it into Freeland's heart to send the pictures; for I had
just got them when we began to meet children who asked
for something, and I gave a dozen of them away, and they
were so pleased.

MISCELLANEOUS.

MISCELLANEOUS.

Friday Night, August 30, 1878.

STRANGELY enough, the last long talks I had at college with —— were about the Atonement (he was reading Dale—a good book, but not that of a theologian); then when I was telling you about some glimpses I had been getting in a practical way from talking with a man in trouble, you said, I think, you wished you knew more about it. Then the two nights in ——, Mr. —— and I talked nothing else—he stating the old hard way of it (such as I, at least, never heard), and I trying to meet him with a more excellent way—the whole thing ending in smoke. Then —— came, also talking of it, who preaches the doctrine far the most (of any of us) and knows it quite the least.

Last of all, after devouring Dorner all summer and creeping in at corners from the Person to the Work, I had the matter much laid upon me these past weeks, and

on Sabbath last resolved to try and have a message about
it. I had to fill Pitlochry twice. In the morning I
preached on the knowledge of God before and after Christ,
from the texts, "Thou art a God that hidest Thyself"
and "He could not be hid." But it was cold, dry, intellectual, and moral; scarcely beyond the prophet-part of
Christ's ministry, and altogether unsatisfactory. The afternoon I spent with —— in the garden at Donavourd.
There our talk all turned on the same theme. I found
he had just got Dale; but was longing for light, and
feeling, as we all do, that we want a centre for our
theology, so long as we have not got the Atonement
into position; that we want not only to place the
undivided image of Christ (His Person) before men's eyes;
but must feel where the point of contact for them is in
it; what it was that He *did* for men. We were asking for
it all afternoon.

In the evening very tremblingly, half thinking I had
done wrong, I took for my text, "Behold the Lamb of
God which taketh away the sin of the world." I had
these divisions: the surroundings and circumstances of the
speaker, the sight which he saw, and certain finger-points
towards that sight. The first part I had carefully prepared, and seemed to get in (and bring the people in with

me) to the spot where John was standing at the time. But more I had not prepared, for further I knew not. But just at that moment it broke upon me the thing that he saw ; and I saw it for myself, and cared not whether the people saw it or no, and yet showed it them as I saw it. I did not seem to speak ; but One spoke for me, and the words came and went, and only the sight remained. I will not tell you what I said, for I cannot tell you what I saw ; and it was more a picture than a truth, more a seeing than a believing. Any way since then I have had no doubt of the thing ; the formulæ of it we have known since our childhood—the power and the presence of it not till now. I don't desire to rest in any past sight of it—the words of last Sabbath are already old, but the thing is not. I am resolved to go through the New Testament looking for this one thing, and have already begun. —— came in afterwards, and we both felt that God had been hearing our prayer. I walked half the way home with —— (of whom I have seen a good deal) who has been nearer this, I believe, at times than any of us, and who talked me clear upon it. He too has been longing for a fuller view.

Do you see what a great and marvellous thing God has been doing for us—making us all feel our need of

this thing; and, indeed, to speak of one's making out so
long to do without it, brings more of utter humiliation
than even of thankfulness.

Murthly Castle, Murthly,
Perthshire, May 31, 1879, 5 p.m.

Jeanne and I arrived here at 12 to-day. At once
Sir Douglas had Jeanne forth to show her some of his
pet pines, and Miss Fraser (Lady Stewart's sister) took
me up and down some of the grassy green walks. The
place is the perfection of beauty ; two castles—an old and
a new (the old inhabited, the new a lonely stone shell
dropped in the bosom of a wood), in the former of which,
a curious, contradictory building of all ages, I am writing this.   . . Down from the side of the castle runs
an avenue of yews, ending in the old and new chapels
(the former now the mortuary and serving as the vestry),
and, parallel to it, another avenue of very black yews entirely over-arching, down which no one ever goes, except
when they carry the master down it to rest with his
dead. Beyond this is a terrace of deodars with rhododendrons below and grassy turf between ; everywhere there is
the same endless avenue of green grass, shorn to the roots,

mossy to the look and velvet to the step. Further along is an avenue of Douglas pines, giants with great spreading fans, shot at the tips just now with something like gold, and rustled-through by wild doves or rushed-under by rabbits no bigger than your little hand. All the avenues end in a great one which goes by the river, walled in at first by yews, but then opening out as it skirts an immense field, dotted over by ample trees and backed by a belt of wood in every conceivable shade of green. Round the park you wind by this unwearying avenue of soft green grass and ascend a slope where the broad branches of the *pinus nobilis* hang over you, and at their feet is an outburst of colour beyond compare. It is the rose-red rhododendrons in full bloom, blushing out amid the green, as if lavish of their too great loveliness, and yet pressing back against the pines, as if ashamed of their beauty. With these are blood beeches, where the sap is stealing up in all stages of strength, from a faint suspicion of orange through which the fibres shine, to fine tints of claret and deep imperial purple; beeches beside them of the common kind with a light veil of emerald hanging upon them, scarcely enough to conceal the loves of the pigeons or the sports of the squirrels; birches, the glory of the Highlands, with a mere mist of yellowish green shaken through the airy branches, making you afraid that the next breath of air will brush it off again; oaks ashamed of being later than ashes, and reddening up in a hasty russet, and ashes afraid of being much behind oaks and sallying forth in taper slips, almost too tender and slim; Scotch firs, holding up what spring this year has given them like lighted candles on the end of their long, spiny boughs; there is nothing like it in the whole range of language; there is something in the end of Isaiah lv.: "The mountains and the hills shall break forth before you into singing, and all the trees of the field shall clap their hands."

After a little of this, we came in to luncheon in an old-fashioned, lofty-roofed room, where you seemed afraid to speak above your breath, and were severely criticized by the old ancestry upon the walls, who had got beyond the deadening and debasing influences of eating and drinking. Then Jeanne and I got leave to trot away by ourselves, along by the river, where lilies of the valley grow, and joined the others in the rhododendron avenue, and drove with them to have the finest view of the castles from the high terrace. It was wonderful to see the world of woods, everywhere of every colour, and yet all one with the spirit of spring; to see those Highland hills that give us our narrowness and our gloominess and rudeness—aye, and our constancy, our inspiration, and our faith; to feel my own heart rise up with the uprising of them, and "beckon to them" (ἀσπάζειν), as the saints of Heb. xi. did to the distant promises, and be drawn by them forth from all its earthliness, fickleness, and meanness to their eternal loftiness and immutability and nearness to heaven; to greet the gates of the Highlands, Birnam Hill and its fellows, and feel that round the shoulder and up the strath lay the land of my fathers, my own dear land.

10.30 p.m.—I have just left Sir Douglas in the drawing-room to come and read over again Heb. xii. 20-25. What an intimate connection between εἰρήνη and καταρτίσαι; only in peace and at leisure, as it were, can the great Artificer perfect His work; only in peace does perfection come; action perfected is near passing into peace. "Thus saith Jehovah, Creator of the Life's fruit, Peace, peace (*i.e.* perfect peace) to him that is afar off and to him that is near." And, again: "Thou wilt keep him in peace, peace, whose mind is stayed on Thee, because he trusteth in Thee." Then, how very wondrous to think He will work in us, if we let Him have His way with us, something εὐάρεστον ἐνώπιον αὐτοῦ, something for His eyes to linger on and for His lips to say: This is very good.

Springland, June 4, 1879.

I have just been to grandmamma. On a little table
at her bedside lay a great, glossy-backed, brown book,
with faded gilt edges. She gave it me. It was her
mother's, Miss Oliphant of Gask, eldest daughter of the
house, and elder sister of Carolina Oliphant, Aunt Nairne.
Her mother, you know, married Dr. Stewart of Bonskeid,
and grandmamma was their only child. '. Her mother
brought this Gask Bible away with her on her marriage,
and out of it and the Book of Common Prayer bound up
with it, she taught her child, Margaret Stewart of Bonskeid, reading every day the Psalms, and every Sabbath
the Service, so that grandmamma was reared in the English
church (a strict Episcopalian), and in those daily lessons
from this book she learned first the marvellous acquaintance with Scripture which she has. She never loved the
Episcopal Church, and after her marriage and conversion
joined the Presbyterian Church and 'came out' at the
Disruption in 1843 into the Free Church.

I must tell you something about Springland. It is a
lovely little place, a mile up the Tay from the town of
Perth, with beautiful, simple grounds, and a tower built on
the river (the mark for boat races) overlooking the Inch,
where the battle in the "Fair Maid" was fought; in that

tower the 'schöne Magd' herself, my mother, as the towns-
folk fondly talked of her, taught for years of unconscious
waiting a little school of children, while my father was
building up his business and a stainless name in Manchester. Such a funny mixture it is—to come of high
chivalry, poetry, Jacobitism and Episcopacy, hard work,
strong sense, Lancashire cotton and Presbyterianism—such
is some of what has gone to the making of me. And
from this door the *mutterlich-gesinnte* herself (for she had
brought up a whole army of brave boys, managed a high-
spirited mother, and been submissive to a strict, resolute-
minded father) was married away thirty years since, to
begin a life of suffering and deliverance, of succouring
others and succour sent from God, only second to grandmamma's. I feel almost 'to inherit' too rich 'a blessing.'
There have been clouds gathering in every quarter of my
heaven for a hundred years, since my great grandmother,
Marjory Oliphant Stewart, began to lead an invalid's life
in a little house in town here, and retired every day at
noon for an hour to pray for her place of Bonskeid, for
her child Margaret Stewart, and for *everyone who should
ever come of her house* or come into it.

I want to tell you about Bothwell. I had half-an-hour's wait in the College Station, Glasgow, where my father used to sit as a student in his red gown, and where Adam Smith, the economist, and Reid and Hutcheson, the philosophers, and Sir D. Sandford, a great Grecian, lived and taught (now turned into a railway station). At 6.27 p.m. I got out of this into the Bothwell train, and at 6.55 was welcomed by Mr. Moody and his two boys, one of whom seized my probationer's bag and marched off with it in triumph. I felt quite at home from the first and did so all through. A short walk brought us to 'Benvue,' a little red house climbed all over with green, and looking over the Vale of Clyde to Ben Lomond. So in a moment or two I was kneeling in my own room.

After tea a walk was proposed, and I was sent off in search of Bothwell beauties under the guidance of the two boys. It was a quiet, sombre evening, but the gorgeousness of the green, relieved by the pretty red stone of the buildings, made colour enough to shame the clouded sun. I drew as near the boys as I could, and we rattled on about books and railways, coal-pits and country life, and all the round of garrulous Gespräch that boys' talk will ramble into when it is let run whither it will. And so we came to the valley of the Clyde, a deep still river sunk in a bed of green, with high banks clothed in summer or rather second spring. Over it ran a light and airy-looking bridge. Could this be Bothwell Brig, the darkest spot of Covenanting days? That was surely a narrow, high, impassable place. But the boys took me down the 'brae' to the 'borne's side' and let me into the secret. There underneath the new building one could make out the old arches cleverly let into the later structure. This, then, was the old 'Bothwell Brig'; here was a bit of history. Below us stretched a lovely flat green field, called in Scotland a 'haugh,' and the farm on it, which gave his name to the murderer of the good Regent Murray. Down the river a bit lies Bothwell Castle, a beautiful ruin, ringing with the memory of Mary's unhappy husband. Opposite is an old priory. Up the river, again, is a fragment of Roman aqueduct. So one's history had to hop about and fly like a bird from tree to tree. But most of all to me were the beautiful banks themselves, with that strange story of the Scottish woman and her song in Arabic, told me by the Pfarrer at Tübingen. Through my head the words went ringing, "O Bothwell Bank, thou bloomest fair." So we wandered on, wondering

x

at the May flower out so late, and at the exuberant foliage, broken here and there by the sharp points of a coal-pit chimney, signs of labour and the stern work of life. Then we turned up through a steep gully to a green hill-top, crowned by the old Parish Church, an ancient bit of building from before Reformation times, some fifty years since restored to a large cruciform with buttresses and roof of stone. A light, square tower rises from the centre. I made a stand with my boys to try and take the thing in. Home we came by the Free Church, a pretty red stone thing with two towers, I think, and a slender spire. The manse was just over the way. Coming in, we had a quiet talk in the long light, and then I had prayers, singing our psalm 'O hätte ich Flügel.' The children sang delightfully.

Yesterday, Sabbath morning, at 11.15 Mr. Moody took me to the vestry, where the beadle shortly found me, and, to my surprise, proffered the right hand of fellowship (in encouragement, no doubt, to the poor probationer). Next came the precentor and persuaded me to change "Ye servants of the Lord" to "My God and Father, while I stray," which he said was a favourite; which I did. Then I had a good time alone, and then the beadle came and robed me, and, after he had taken the Bible in, came back, and I followed him to the foot of the pulpit stair, where he left

me to take my way up a funny spiral stair to a little round
pulpit. Then I think I was helped to forget nearly everything except that many were praying for me. The church
was pretty well filled, the singing was good and helped
me much, especially "Thy will be done" and "Oh! for
a heart."

Ross's Rooms,
Dundee, August 2, 1879.

When I came back here at 5, I had a great welcome
from Ross, whom I found writing his sermon in his study.
We dined and teaed together and had the old student talk,
deepened by the deepening experience of his ministry. This
is the end of his first year as an ordained minister, and it has
been a time of much learning. He says " personal influence
is the chief part of a minister's work."

Then we had a walk such as comes once a summer, when
the world is still and the sun has time to set slowly and all
the land lays aside its labour and thinks only of rest and
peace. We rose above the town, over the blue haze of smoke
beautiful in the evening air, and saw the stretch of river widen
as we rose. Then we came into a public park and climbed
and gazed.

The whole earth every way undulated in light and
shade, mist-wreathed and sun-smitten, cloud-shadowed and
light-pierced. Sometimes the trees against the sky seemed
carved ebony ; sometimes, standing out in the fields,
wrought ivory. Then the sun slid down and wrought a
new wonder at every step, forcing the land to deliver up
its entire riches of outline and colour. Here it drew
purple out of the hills, there chased a mist down every
glen, now it laid the fields level with gold, now heaped
up the mountains in heights and ridges of iron. Then
the earth suddenly leapt up, lit with the sun's own glories,
fired with its own thought, and caught the sun in an
exultation of desire and hid it in her breast ; and so the
triumph of the earth ended. For when the earth caught
the sun, she darkened instantly. But then heaven began
and gave a glory for everyone of earth's, and all the
wonder was gone through in sky scenery, as late in the
land. New strata, every instant, of cloud were caught and
elevated in a golden moment and tost aside for some new
thing to toy with—fleeces of snow, flakes of crimson,
swan feathers turned flamingo's. The whole air changed
like a dove's breast when the sun passes over it. In the
west there was first a furnace of pure fire, then bits of
amber, vermilion, and Indian red fell into it and remained

burning as the furnace flame went out. Meantime the long flats of water were flecked with the faint reflex of these glories, dappled with blots of unsympathetic sand.

Monday, Aug. 4, 1879, 9.30 a.m.

Now, let me tell of yesterday. Breakfasted at 9, and then read and prayed together. We had had a good time before turning-in the evening before. At 9.30 I lay down and got up my sermon till 10.30, when I had prayer. At 10.40 Ross took me round to show me the church, while he went on to preach for a friend. I enjoyed the service, though not in first-rate bodily form; and it is always an effort to speak to a somewhat small congregation in summer time, when sleep and sultriness are in the field before you.

At 2.15 I went to church again, and found a larger congregation and less sleep. I greatly enjoyed the devotional exercises — praise, prayer, and reading — but the sermon was again an effort. Ross enjoyed it, but I felt humbled, and yet I was not unhappy. Going home, I met a New College man from Leipsic, who promised to visit us in the evening. Ross and I dined at 4.30, then rested an hour and talked on our wants and our work: it was a very good time.

At 6 came two of the elders from Cupar to tea; they were kind, honest men, but it was not easy. Then at 7 Ross and I went to his little mission meeting, which was very delightful. We both spoke a little on " He that is unjust," etc.—on how our actions fix our character, how we are making our eternity to-day, and how that sentence is being already pronounced ; but how Christ can break that fearful chain of consequences ; how He breaks the power of inbred sin ; how He gives the new heart, and destroys the works of the devil, in those who believe on Him.

Then I walked with Ross on his way to see an old elder of his church who is dying, and returned to meet our friend from Leipsic. Then for one and a half hours we had the rare treat of a college talk on Germany, on professors and books, men and events ; on the *Durchgängig-kcit* of German students ; of the views one gets of the lie of the theological land there ; of the religious life ; of the moral and social state of the country; of what it needs just now. Then we spoke of ourselves ; of the dear New College, which has our warmest devotion, as it holds some of our most delightful memories ; of his feelings and responsibilities as a "4th year's man," and of mine as near my ministry.

Then Ross came, and we supped together, not without merriment over some reminiscences, but with the deeper gladness of friends who have crossed each other's path, and wished one another God-speed.

Then from 11-12 Ross and I talked on, still of our work and our wants, of how much was opening to us, and more was yet to open ; and chiefly of our need of a deeper sense of sin and of the presence and help of God's Spirit. We read Rev. i. and prayed.

About Cupar, I felt from the heart I could pray to the God whose never-failing Providence orders all things in heaven and earth, that He would put away from us all hurtful things and give us those things which are profitable to us, through Jesus Christ our Lord.

I did not tell, did I, how when the sunset on Saturday night was near its height, we were standing on the slope of a fair green hill to the west of Dundee, away from the smoke and the din, with a stretch of land filled with dust of amber and wreaths of golden gloom ? It is the cemetery of the place, not a crowded city of graves like most of ours, but, as they have in America, a large and beautiful bit of country dedicate to death. As we returned, the moon rose up out of a cloud, the "silver sickle" of Wilt-shire become a "golden shield" in Fife, immense as it

emerged from earth and held half of heaven, not ashamed
to face the other half, though that was pearls and roses,
roses and pearls unspeakable. One yellow band, not
ruffled even to the roughness of rich silk, joined us and
it across the broad estuary. It was like the golden ray
that Giotto and his fellows saw and we so seldom see,
that we think their sight was less, not more, than ours.
Have you ever seen how sunsets and moon-rises rival
each other? But then they are brother and sister, are
they not, under one roof, and their combats of beauty
are most beautiful.

Springland, September 8, 1879.

Before the colour is quite off to-day, let me try and tell
you how it was when I went first to visit Gask.

I have been back in my school and college days, walking along a Roman road, back in my childhood with the
'Auld Hoose' on the Earn, back in my poet's life with
Lady Nairne, back in history with the Jacobites, back to
everything that has helped me in the outer world from
rich solemn music to bright sunshine and flowers.

At nine this morning, Jeanne and I changed the Highland
for the Crieff line at Perth, and soon were going leisurely

enough up the rich valley of the Almond, clothed with green. It runs westward at right angles to the Tay, under the shadow of the first ridge of the Grampians, and into the heart of the Trossachs at the further end. At 10 we left the train, getting out at a small roadside station called Balgowan and struck south and climbed the hill. A sign-post by the wayside said "Gask," so we went on without question. It was wonderful how, as we rose, to north and west rose the blue rim of glorious mountains, laid like a tiara about the land, whose locks were yellow corn and brown barley. We passed a miniature pine forest, then a real "selva selvaggia," where broad-fanned spruce were weighted with the flakes of sunlight, and slim, solemn Scotch firs were glancing, like veins of flesh colour in the deep darkness of the wood. Over the sky went clouds, and after them came sunset, shivering them gloriously, then clouds again, bright spots in heaven, fair shadows upon earth. The south wind came up in our faces, as we climbed to the top of the hill, and then sank or was sucked into the breast of a forest, when we were on the summit. And then a sight, and then a memory. The sight—a straight line of highway shot along the very ridge of the hill, cleaving the firwood, and going on, like a messenger in haste. It was broad and level as one's palm,

with a ditch dug on either side, and then a dyke of earth
and stones, so old that aged trees took its cope for firm
ground. The memory—a thunder of legionaries along this
Roman highway, a thought of the order, the wisdom, the
immense purpose, the indomitable energy of old Rome.
Jeanne and I turned eastward along it, till, with our map,
we found an entrance to an open field, descried a mound
in it, and jumping the fence, stood in the centre of a
veritable "statio" or post, for changing horses and so
on, to keep up communication between the camps. There
was the "agger," the rampart; "the vallum," the ditch;
the "pons," the bridge; and we thought we could hear
the clatter of a cohort up the "stratum" or street, and
the picket in the "statio" hail their leader with a "Quid
novi adfers?"—What's the news? Then we went back
and found the Gask gate and entered, and found ourselves descending already into Strathearn, lying like an
open leaf at our feet, one stretch of fertile valley, veined
with ripening grain.   An instant's turning showed us
the masterly eye of the Roman, for the road we had just
left rose against the horizon, tipping the very crown of
the hill, and commanding at a glance all Glen Almond
north to the Grampians, and all Strathearn south to the
Ochils.

But we were on other ground now, and sacred to other
memories. Here, we said, had Lady Nairne walked and
ridden, and loved and sung, till Strathearn, that made
Caroline Oliphant so beautiful and such a poet, was made
by her more lovely and lyric still. We walked down the
avenue and, turning to the right, came through a thicket
of unannouncing trees, and were upon the gravel before a
large, brown country house, eighty years old, generally in
the Grecian style, flanked by porticoes and fronted by
steps, with two geraniums, like rosy cheeks on either side
the door, and fascinating glances down endless avenues of
green, opening every way just enough to tell you that at
the end of them were water, sunshine, and green fields.
Shortly, we were in the drawing-room, cool with drawn
blinds, the faint green of the walls broken by family faces
—Raeburns and Watson-Gordons. A piano, rich reading-
stand, and centre-table, with old and choice books, were
what I noticed ; only you felt there were flowers at the
window and on the table among the books. A little table
near the fire made you think it was a friend of Christ
lived here, from the names and papers and the general
appearance. In a little a side door opened, and in the
room was (not came) a widow lady, neat as a picture in
black and white, about the prime of life, with a face

remarkable for its look of pleased good nature, its constant liveliness, yet its placid calm. An ordinary face, elevated by having its conversation in heaven. First, there was a welcome in manner, words and countenance, passing immediately out of that region, for we were friends from the heart instantly. We talked of common interests, and went back to the past, where our friendships were, and stayed there for a while. It was a quarter past eleven as we arrived, and at the half hour, when the good lady thought us rested from our walk, she left us to look at family records and pictures of the place, and reappeared instantly in hat and umbrella and soft velvet coat, with a bunch of keys, entries to the sweetest batch of secrets I ever saw.

We were moving over the gravel and down by a lawn, the sunlight moving over us and streaming among the grass as the leaves gave it entrance. Down the hill we moved, treading on ground soft with dead leaves of recollection and fresh with the latest grass of this grassiest of summers, till the view was stopt by a low outline of ruin, irregular with ivy, which scarcely allowed inlet to the sharpest sunbeams to pierce it into shape. That is the "Auld Hoose," she said, as you might say it of an old friend. "There, look!" We looked. And sight veiled

herself with memory, as memory at this moment would
fain veil herself with tears. Just the south wall stands,
one mass of ivy, wrapt up in unutterable associations. We
stept through it, as men say they step through ghosts,
who were men once upon the earth, but are now no more,
and came out upon other things. For here memory had
sat down and spread out her lap, and lo! it was filled
with flowers. We crossed by the flower beds, as you go
by happy children, happy, but not disturbing them, and
stood under a glorious hedge of plane and yew at the spot
where Caroline's pencil took the picture that opens "Lays
of Strathearn" nigh a century ago. There was the outline
—indistinct, but the same—a low-roofed, sloping, "dear
wee house," with a balcony of wood before and a tower
at one end; the "auld pear tree" leaning its age sorrowfully against the ruin still. We turned under the shade,
"sheltered by the sombre-eyed yew," and soon were at the
site of the old church, screened from the house by plane
and chestnut. It was removed many years ago, and now
in its place stands a brown stone chapel, beautiful with
high walls, Saxon windows, and stone slates, built by James
Oliphant (Lady Nairne's only brother's second son), the
last heir male and his bride, Henrietta Graeme, in 1845.
It was Henrietta herself who guided us, (for her husband

went from her two years later, and she weeps, some foolish people say worships, him still) and she unfolded for this the first of her shining bunch of keys, used every day. It is a lovely little chapel, erected for the English rite, with oaken pews, pulpit, reading desk, and communion table. They were English Episcopalians, though, when the Scots Episcopals had become so high that they would not connect themselves with them, she and her husband went to the Parish (Presbyterian) Church. On his death, the Lord touched her heart, and she attended to the things which were spoken by a faithful servant of Christ, and joined the Free Church. There is no further Episcopal service there; only a meeting, like our own, for the poor people in the evening. We went reverently forward to where, on the left side of the aisle, was written in brass on the floor, "Caroline, Baroness Nairne. Died, Oct. 27, 1845. Buried here, Nov. 4." In the whispering summer, in the loveliest fold of earth's lap, lies the form of the sweetest woman-singer God has given to Scotland. Across the aisle and before the rails, lies James Oliphant himself. We spoke low and long, though words were few, about them; the wind was saying *requiescat* round and round the place. We knew the lady's ancient love of music and her old gift of song, and, as she pointed to a lovely little oaken organ in a deep alcove, the story rose to me of how the people said that often at night they saw a light in the chapel and that, if you went near enough, you heard the solemn boom of the instrument, and knew the lady was alone with herself, her Lord, and her dead. I was afraid to ask anything, but she said: Would we hear it? I said: "If we dare ask it, it would be such a delight." So she only said, "But we want more light," and went and closed the western door by which we had entered, and opened two broad leaves opposite the organ, letting in the summer and the south and the sound of rustlings and flutterings innumerable, and the sight of streaming sunshine and branches beating with brilliance. Then she ascended into the organ seat and sat down.

Jeanne sat in one of the oaken pews, I moved to the doorway and stood between the opened leaves, betwixt the strange coolness and quietness within and the stranger movement and warmth without, and then the organ began. It was a quiet note at first, but full and grand, as of chords preluding. Then there stole through the little chapel a melody wondrous sweet. It was a child's hymn, and a voice, soft and simple as a child's, sang "I am so glad that our Father in heaven." My heart was filled with prayer. Then Jeanne was called up into the little alcove and soon with fingers trembling at her first attempt to touch an organ, but voice that trembled nothing, she sang, and I prayed, "Nearer, my God, to Thee." Then she sang the "Lost Sheep" and I joined from the doorway. Then we all drew near and united together in a song, "I am coming, Lord." Then I asked for one of Lady Nairne's and sang the "Land of the Leal"—Jacobites to the Lord Jesus, everyone of us three as our fathers were all one hundred years ago. For to them, too, as to us, and to us, too, as to them, "the king is over the water," and we keep our heart's best place for an absent one. Then the organ was closed, and we communed together, speaking of her who joined these twin loyalties in a chain of golden song, and of the comfort that comes from music, and of the blessing of solitude. "I come into another country here," said the lady, "but before we leave, will Robert lead us in prayer?" She pointed to the pulpit, and I went and lifted off the white coverings and kneeled down, and they kneeled in the last pew. Then we thanked God for the ties of family that drew us together there, and for the past, but more for the present, for these closer bonds that bind us to our Father, our Head, our King. We prayed for all our household, and joined our prayers with the Church throughout Scotland, asking for fine weather, were it the

Lord's will. So we worshipped, and, as we went to the door, Mrs. Oliphant stopped and pressed my hand.

Then we went forth, feeling no strangeness, into the sunshine and the myriad-motioned green. By vista and view, by terrace and lawn, she led us, drinking draughts of the goodness of the Lord. We went reverently up to the "Old Dial"—"The old dial" of the dear song—and saw it reared once again from 'weeds and grass.' Then we turned to the edge of the plantation and looked up and down. The strath stretched away for miles, faltering from under our feet in folds of beauty, quartered by sunlight and shade.

Then we strolled along the southern terrace at Gask, skirting a great bank of laurels between us and the river, and a beautiful, useful garden with a rustic fence. This led us to the other corner of the grounds, whence we looked south and west up the Earn Valley over to Orchill, her old home; Auchterarder, famous in the Church struggle of 1833-43; Aberuthven, where the Lords Ruthven (you remember the Ruthven raid) live. Here the view was surpassing. A wall of mist, transparent to the sunlight moved down the valley, concealing and revealing everything. The serried clouds sent all the sunlight down in shafts of gold, and the first faint colour on the corn sent it back again. Then we turned at right angles up the

Y

west terrace, past immemorial chestnuts and fragrance-
laden limes; everywhere an avenue, a vista, or over-arch
of green—green above, green under, green around—all a
wonder in the chequered light and shade. Round the
back of the house we stept, and, "Will you see the dairy?"
the lady said. We assenting, she led the way to the pretty,
low, brown stone building—all in the one style her husband
had loved and planned with home-stone from the estate—
whose cupola had made us wonder as we saw it through
the trees on approaching the house. Every bit of gravel
seemed in its own place, and it seemed natural that it
should be so; for art was only labour in love, and toil in
triumph, at such a place, except where summer's second
gift of green in this astonishing year had defied the
following of gardener's hoe or woodman's hatchet, and crept
up or thrust itself forward in sheer abundance. Another
of the bright keys came out and we were in a large open
chamber with tiled floor, venetians in the door panels, and
in the cupola, from which the only light came, losing its
heat by the contrivance. Round the room were shelves
of spotless wood, and on them large liberal bowls in their
simple chocolate and olive, full of milk and cream that
lent an odour to the air. Behind the bowls the walls
were polished earthenware, Dutch tiles, porcelain—her father's

gift, sent from that country of cows and Cuyp's pastoral pieces—from Holland. We praised them all, and were only kept from tasting by being warned of an early dinner. Then all was locked again, and we went and sat in the parlour of the place, where visitors rest and resume their journeyings. We rested and resumed. Then came the makers of the milk to be inspected themselves, great happy-looking kine, in a clean, bright cowhouse, filled with their "soöte brethe," as Chaucer says, and inviting praise and pattings. You could go round by their heads and gaze into their great, mutely-luminous eyes and understand what βοῶπις meant. Then came the scalding-house and the cheese-loft, and everything neat and trim. After that we were led to the stables, for the lady is fond of driving. We saw two sturdy Norse "hestas"—ponies—as comfortable as everything in this land of plenty, very unlike their brethren of the trace in Norway, also asking for strokes and compliments. So we went in about 1.30 to the great cool hall; like all Greek houses this one had its αὐλα, paved with pavement of the place, and surrounded by a semi-circular wall with niches. We were taken to two rooms, up broad stairs, and to 'landings,' all of bare stone with strips of τάπης, and lighted by a cupola covered with canvas, making for coolness in the air and mildness in the light. My room was Aunt Nairne's sitting-room in the two years when she closed her life here under the roof of her brother Laurence's second son, James, and his young wife, Henrietta Graeme, of Orchill, our hostess. Here they brought her in 1843, and in 1845 she died in the next room. There is a sketch of her in a book below, stolen one night as she sat with her fingers ever full. She was very like what our noble grandmother is now; the same hooked nose, large countenance, and high spirit, utterly subdued to Christ. I knelt down, prayed, and wrote one line to thee, and then went down. I took Mrs. Oliphant across the hall, from the drawing-room to the other wing, where, in a coolness like sun-pierced sea-water—for the walls were green, light green, and all the blinds were down—the tables were spread. A great hydrangea filled the centre of it. We sat down and the meal was made less earthly than meals usually are; for was there not the wall there to talk to, and to talk to us. Behind Mrs. Oliphant were her father, Graeme of Orchill, and her brother-in-law, Laurence Oliphant, in full Highland dress. Then there was Laurence, her husband's and this Laurence's father, a 'lovely' man, brother of Lady Nairne, and Mrs. Stewart of Bonskeid (the lady who prayed for us), and Mrs. Steuart of Dalguise, and Mrs. Keith of Ravelstone, who, in full length, filled, with her husband, the foot of the room. This Laurence was there with his father, the good Laurence, Lady Nairne's father and his father again, who was out in the 1815 with his son, and lost health, lands, and name for it. Then there was Miss Robertson of Ardblair, Laurence's (Lady Nairne's brother) wife, mother of seven lovely daughters, the youngest of whom was Caroline the younger, poetess and dweller at Gask, and one of whom, Margaret, *made* her English husband, Mr. Kington, Kington-Oliphant, a son of whom is the heir to the place. On the window side was Lord Nairne, a grand old gentleman in old age, and at the other corner, Aunt Nairne herself, with her proud aquiline in eye and nose, pressing her only child, Lord William (who was buried the night mamma arrived to be with her at Brussels) of six to her side. In the centre lay this same child, a dreamy boy of ten ; over the door, an original of Robert R., the Bruce himself, whose daughter married Sir Walter Oliphant, the direct male ancestor of our great grandmother, May (Marjory) Oliphant of Gask, Mrs. Stewart of Bonskeid. Over the fireplace, is a splendid piece by Frank Grant, James Blair Oliphant, her husband, riding a favourite mare near a ford where he was nearly swept away by the Earn. All the other pictures in the room, except the Oldbues, were Watson Gordon's. So we had a picture-

went out very happily through the evening air, from the Earn Valley to the Almond and took the train home. People from all parts were gathering in at the general station, Perth, for the Conference. We went out to Springland. There we found papa, mamma, and Margaret, all well, and above all, "the noblest Stewart of them all," grandmamma.

Grandmamma was full of a wonder that had happened. She has had her house full for weeks of work-people—plumbers, masons, slaters. Last week they left the house completely *raccommodée*, beautiful and clean. It is an old haunt of swallows and they have to be driven every year out of the porch, or Springland would be one big nest. However, when the work was done, they came about the house in flocks, screaming and flying and settling on it, and nestling around it and "loving" it. And when they were not allowed the porch, they went to the coalhouse and nested and brought out a second brood, till, last Sabbath, the roof was black with them; they clustered on the fresh gilded vane and chattered to it and to one another. They cannot feed the young ones fast enough, to get them fit for flying by the end of the month, and they keep up a continual fluttering and practise the little creatures for flight. So saying and fluttering her hands like one of

themselves, grandmamma told us the whole story at the
tea-table and went out of the room, and I heard her singing to herself, and the song was "Swallow, fly high."

'Εμβλέψατε εἰς τὰ πετεινὰ τοῦ οὐρανοῦ : are we looking up
to them, who feel what weak-winged things we are in the
nest where we have dwelt, and fear the new journey and
the short time to prepare. Οὐχ ἡμεῖς μᾶλλον διαφέρετε αὐτῶν ;
will He take care that those little black, woolly things get
so many worms before they have to go; will He see to it
that they have their full number of bites (He counts them,
be sure) before their time comes; will He provide that
these bits of soft down become strong and regular and curved
for flight, before the frost comes ; and will He not feed us
against our flying time ; is there not grain in His granary
enough to satisfy us. As thy day so shall thy strength
be ; let us take what the Lord sends us and rest in the
strength of what He has already sent. Did He not know
what was before us when He appointed us our food, and
if He sees we want more, will He not send a hunger to
our hearts, His angel to waken us again, saying :—"Arise
and eat, because the journey is too great for thee." And
we shall go in the strength of that meat just so many
days as He sees to be before us when He sends us food.

Rossie Priory,
11 p.m., September 13, 1879.

My chapter to-night tells us that all the grace we have is meted out to us of Christ's free gift. Is not this consecration, then? that it shall all be given to the furnishing-forth of holy lives both in us and in others, given to the work of service, given to rear the church, which is His body. If the strength He gives us be measured by these objects, to how simple and single a thing it reduces life. To live is to make better saints both of ourselves and of others; to work only in our own place and all for others; to be growing members of Christ's growing body. To us, then, to live is Christ; Christ in us—the making of saints, Christ in others—the work of servants, Christ in all—the building of the temple of His body, wherein as saints we serve, wherein as servants we are sanctified.

Good-night; yes, night is good, and all is good, with knowing that the thing which joins our spirits—the ἑνότης τοῦ πνεύματος—is a band of *peace—συνδεσμός εἰρήνης.* Peace unites as nothing does. The sound of its name is the snapping of a clasp. For when a Greek said εἰρήνη, he knew it came from εἴρω, to join. But no Grecian lips were our teachers when we heard, as we hear to-night, One stand in the midst and breathe on us, Εἰρήνη ὑμῖν.

I am just going to rest after reading our verses. The end of all His gifts to us is the "measure of the age of the fulness of Christ." That is the true date in Heaven's calendar of our marriage-day, the ἡλικία τοῦ πληρώματος τοῦ Χριστοῦ. To be filled with Christ—with the grace He gives for any event—is to be of full age for that event. The seasons of our lives are brought round by the supplies of His grace. If the day be a wedding-day, it will be wedding strength He will give. If His wise purposes call Him to a friend's marriage, He will be there with a marriage miracle. He will be there, and where He is they have plenty of wine and love. He crushed the clusters of human wedded love into the sacramental cup, wherein His bride drinks eternal union with her Lord. And so He bids us love each other as "He loved the Church and gave Himself for it."

Oh, can we fear to lose anything of the hallowed simplicities of childhood, when He draws us images, makes us promises, gives us precepts such as these? It is only the νηπιότης, the childishness, He bids us lose—ἵνα μηκέτι ὦμεν ν ή π ι ο ι, νη-έπος, you know; (aye, He has a new language for us, then, in the life before us)—κλυδωνιζόμενοι. To think that we may be free from all the stammering, the uncertainty, the wavering of infancy, *and grow up together now and for ever unto Him* at all points, unto Him who is our common Head ; and, united in Him, start off again, from Him, to grow compact and fitted together to build each other up in love. That is what Paul says of the union of believers in Christ, and therefore of the vine. He says we grow together in two ways, first up into Him as our Head (εἰς αὐτὸν), and then down from Him (ἐξ οὗ) into each other, helping so to build each other up.

And the way of all this wonderful union seems to come to me to-night as my consecration-command, 'Αληθεύε ἐν ἀγάπῃ : Be true, be loving. Let the tongue be truth, and the lips be love.

At Inchture I got out, about 5.15, and found a dog-cart waiting. We drove across the strath, and then into a pretty village. Another pretty village, and then came the avenue, deep with trees, and lively with rabbits skipping everywhere over the green sward. Lord Kinnaird has a very soft heart to such creatures, and they take advantage of it. After a long drive, the trees opened, and, at the end of a straight stretch of road, out of a frame of fresh green trees, came the Priory, a beautiful bit of brown stone with open porch in front, and surmounted by a spire. A wing of stone came out to the left as we drove up, matched by

another, beyond the body of the building. We were led
into a great corridor—the cloisters running from end to
end of the main house, itself antique and a museum of
antiquities, old statues from Italy along the sides and in
niches, whole floors of mosaic, from an old Roman villa,
let into the walls, inscriptions, altars, bas-reliefs, monuments
—things that are classics even of an age and country that
was all classical. The floor was polished stone. We went
into the drawing-room, rich with old pictures, some the
first efforts of Frank Grant (portraits of the Lord Grand-
father and Lady Grandmother of the house, the former of
whom was a devout antiquarian and lover of the land, and
buyer of the best books). There were flowers and statues
in the room, an Achilles' head, monster-size and in marble,
and, to match, some R.C. saint's—heathen both, but the
former more noble and pure. It was as if you should
lay our Iliad by the Acta Sanctorum. Then came afternoon tea, the old Lord joined us, fresh from driving to
some far away corner of the estate, full of friendliness and
pats on the back for me. Miss Kinnaird asked if I was
too tired to walk, and I, who want to know all lovely
things, went with her. It is so much easier to be with
Christians. The house had the *Heimathsathem* to me from
the first. There are no introductions, ceremonies, pre-

liminaries, where all are Christ's people. The world has this feeling, they say : τοὺς ἰδίους ἀγαπᾷ. But we love Christians, not because they belong to ourselves first, but as part of our Master's dear possessions.

We went by terraces and green slopes, fringed with a rare forestry, peeped into gardens bright with earth's blushes, and down avenues dark with the strong children of the wood, and looked over them and beyond to where the Carse lay like Achilles' shield, with all the scenes real and acted out in full upon it,—here a cornfield, there a farm, yonder a forest, further on a hamlet—all rounded, like the Homeric earth, with the silver rim where sea and river join—the real ὠκεανός, half ocean and half stream.

Then we turned, and swept round the house, and into the wild wood beyond. Here nature was at her best, and thrust a white arm of silver waterfall through the thick drapery and rough rock-ornament of the wood. We watched it gathering the waifs of sunlight to one sparkling sheaf, leaving the sombre pines the sadder for that theft. Then we broke from this—the Rossie Glen—and out into the open, and ascended the steep hill to their cousins' (the Ogilvies') farm, and turned and took in the view. You fancy Achilles' shield grown from the round Greek target to the long oval of old Rome—the clypeus they called it — and bossed about the edges with the blue Cyanean hills (that wondrous colour, κύανος, that comes every evening on all my Highland hills, but never came yet into Crusius or Bekker; and how should it come into a scratchy letter, written in a third-class carriage, with seven others besides the writer, all of them more or less amused at his extemporized desk and his efforts to keep steady).

For, far up the strath, as far as the eye went, went the fair Carse of Gowrie, sung by Lady Nairne, and down the strath, where the eye stopped, it saw Dundee beginning, one solitary stalk outstanding in the evening light, the advance guard of labour.

We turned and came back, telling people of the meetings on the morrow, and giving and getting good words from the workpeople on their way home. Then there was dinner, and drawing-room talk and worship, and at tea we parted, I to my room to rest and study. At 9 yesterday morning was worship, and we read Eph. v., then breakfast, and after a little quiet time (at 10.45) the old Lord took my arm and I piloted him up the lovely Baledgarny Glen, with sunlight at the top, thick trees, and at the bottom a brawling stream. At last we came out upon the uplands, and breathed the northern air, and

looked on the valley asleep in the sunshine, and joined
the knots of worshippers making for the little village of
Aberfoyle. I preached in the little Free Church, full to
the door, with sunshine everywhere in it. We came down
the glen another way with the south-west wind washing
up in our faces and in the golden face of the ripened
grain. 3.30-4.30, I spoke to the household (in the picture
gallery) joined by the tenants (in the conservatory); at 5.30
I joined Mr. Kinnaird and his sisters on their way to the
evangelistic service in the Parish Church of Inchture. I did
not know the meeting was to be there when I was asked
to speak at Rossie, but I had no doubt in my own mind,
as it had so happened, that I ought to do it. It was my
first time of speaking in an Established Church. The
knocking of the Lord Jesus never seemed so real and near
to me as it did last night. The people were hushed, and
I felt God's hand had been with us. We walked home
through the avenue, speaking about books about Christ.

Mooranbank,
Brechin, N.B., February 8, 1881.

Thanks for your card. Hugh knows all about 'Conscience,' they 'deaded' it in his year at College. The
creature hadn't recovered twelve months later, when I

came that way; some fellows did fetch it a poke with their umbrellas, but, like a stuffed animal in a museum, it didn't even cheep. The ticket was on it, I remember, but that was all.

But, joking apart, I don't even remember the references to the subject: all Kant is ringing with it of course, and Bp. Butler in his two sermons. Then there is Trendelenburg's Platonic theory of the uprising of the soul against itself (Repub. IV. is it?), than which I don't know anything better has been said on the subject. You find that in Lorimer's book on law. But there's more about it in the 'Ode' ('blank instincts before which this mortal nature doth tremble like a guilty thing surprised') and in Lady Macbeth and such like, than in half the philosophies. It was Carlyle's gospel: 'there's a better man in you, and you had better obey him, or be eternally lost.' That was his truth, and he stuck to it.

Conscience, I believe, comes to about this: it's the sense that you've something within you to reckon with now (and, if you like, somebody, both now and afterwards). It's the soul coming into direct relations with itself—its higher self—and Him who gave it.

z

Eden's Room,
Auckland Castle, April 28, 1882.

I suppose it is the curfew which has just rung, for my watch says 8 o'clock, and I feel as if I were at home, and indeed should be quite content were my wife and wee one only with me. For I think every true Bethel —every house of God, or of a Godly man—feels like home, however different the outward form of the life be. And, indeed, the form here seems to me quite a secondary thing, and quite separable from the reality. The stone and lime of it is different to ours—the choir-stalls and the palace-chapel—but the songs are the same, and the hearts are one. So I felt at the practising to-night. But to say so is to run on to the end of my story.

At Darlington I crossed from station to station, as we did eighteen months ago. Here there was a dog-cart waiting, with a big St. Bernard, I believe, in attendance on it. But before we had fairly driven off up came Eden, so we walked home together.

Why should I tell thee of the walk down the 'long, unlovely street,' the escape from the square through the archway to the great castle, with its square masses and little ornament, except where the chapel takes hold of the heavy Tudor and lifts it heavenward—not a bad likeness in stone of the Bishop himself? Why should I tell thee what thou knowest? It was good to have been here with thee, it felt safe ground and hardly strange. The absence of any lady was another appropriate element in the experience. One does not know what kind of creature could have sat by the Bishop's side and not have seemed inappropriate, or detracting, or unworthy in some way.

A cup of tea waited in the small drawing-room. A man, Bampton I think, Eden left beside me and ran off to his choir practice. We had some good words on personal influence as the crowning part of a Christian's and consequently of a minister's life and how hard (as the crown always is) of attainment. I said it was like humility, it escaped if you pursued it directly. The most that could be done in the way of cultivating it, was to remove and cut off what interfered with it—pride, hypocrisy, unreality, and harshness of every sort. Easy to say, and very hard to do. But it was good to hear a man begin his overture by taking a deep string.

Then we joined the little party in the chapel. Some six little boys on either side sat in the stalls, Eden just beyond at the harmonium, the men in residence in the back seats. This happens, not every day, but every second, when the psalms and hymns for morning and evening prayers are gone over. I sang tenor, with Eden's brother, I think; they call Eden 'the Dean.' The singing was sweet and real, though we were a little rough. I forgot to say that the Bishop had come in while we were having tea. He received me so warmly, and trotted out and in so simply. There is an air almost of wistfulness, a dumb kind of devotion in his face, that gives you an impression of the most downright honesty. You know the way a New-foundland or a setter looks at you when it wants to show you it loves you. Well, it is not unlike that. I think the cherub with the face of an ox which Ezekiel saw cannot have been far from the Bishop's. Just as Mozley or Westcott make one think of the one with the eagle, and Rainy or J. H. Wilson of the lion, and Livingstone or Dr. Stewart or Mr. Stalker of the *man*. After chapel we went into the tea-room, Dr. Lightfoot showing the way with such a womanly grace. The table was ample, and the table talk easy to a degree. The talk was about the book "John Inglesant," which everybody had been reading but myself. The Bishop's words were always worth taking to-day. Such a *judgment* it is. He always speaks with a pair of balances in his hand, like Justice, only he is not blind-folded like her. And yet he looks about after speaking like a child, as if to see whether he has not made a mistake.

"I know the plot" said one man. "There is plenty of plotting in it, but little plot," rejoined the Bishop, evidently without any sense that he was using the language of repartee. "A curious condition of mind to be in," he went on to remark, "to be scrupulous about honour and to have no regard for the truth." He spoke, too, of the contrast between the contented life of a country gentleman and these sudden stirrings of spirit which came to John Inglesant. "I wonder," he asked, "whether such a state of mind ever existed to any extent in those days." I thought of saying that it was a common enough type of character in our own day, and that the writer had probably carried it thither out of his own time. "But," added Dr. Lightfoot, "I imagine the description of Roman society is perfectly correct." Somebody quoted a lecture of Seeley's on Pope Leo the Atheist *versus* Luther the Dogmatist. "That is putting it very strongly," rejoined the Bishop; "Leo was a sceptic rather." These are just a few crumbs. Meantime, remarks on tennis, offers and acceptances of 'grilled chicken,' 'cocoa,' 'toast,' and college stories flew about. It was not brilliant, but it was very bright. Dr. Lightfoot asked after Cults and Pitlochry, and smiled upon us all.

10.45.—The evening worship was very uniting. The servants came in, and we sang the psalms and hymns, and Dr. Lightfoot and a chaplain read and prayed (from the new version and the prayer book) in his own voice and with his own devout, simple soul uttering itself in all. His after talk in the drawing-room was even more charming. You know how a mastiff will lie down (out of sheer love for the canine race) and let a crowd of small dogs jump and tumble over him, and put them off, and egg them on with great pawings and immense 'laps' of his broad tongue. Even so did Dr. Lightfoot.

Since then Eden and some of the men have come in from the Boys' Institute, where they have spent the evening attempting to solve the impossible—how to command the wild, wicked young life of Bishop Auckland.

It is good for me to be in the midst of so much informal earnestness and Christian manliness.

Auckland Castle,
Bishop Auckland, April 29, 1882.

I write at an open window of the little drawing-room here. I have so often longed you could have moved about with me through these rooms and among these men; for it is, I think, altogether the best glimpse you can get of the English Church both outside and in. Everything that adds honour to her name is here. There is a good tradition in the diocese. The bishops have not seldom been men of piety and power. Butler's memory alone is enough to ennoble any place in any Church; and the history of Auckland Castle both before and after his time is not out of sympathy with the thoughts you have when you hear his name. They are thoughts, are they not, of honest bravery in theology, of a great man doing battle by himself in a quiet corner, until the Church at length awoke and found he had won her victory.

Then I suppose it is not taking her past out of the hands of time, to say that Butler's seat is now filled by his nearest successor; a man as great in his work and in his day, as his great namesake (for they both are written 'Joseph Dunelm'). I know not if there be any better test of true lastingness in any man who is yet living, than when, knowing his written works, one is able to compare them with his person, and to say that these correspond. The same judgment which you admire in Dr. Lightfoot's commentaries meets you in his conversation. He seems, like Justice in her statues, always to give his sentences, holding meantime a pair of other scales. Indeed, the analogy might be extended. Justice is but badly described in stone as being blind-folded in her decisions. But there is in the bishop a strong cast of eye which enables him, when he speaks, to address himself to nobody in particular; although, immediately after speaking, he turns on you a glance that conveys an impression of the most absolute impartiality.

It has been an old custom here for a number of students to reside with the bishop. The practice is, I believe, a relic of that order of things in which almost all our pre-Reformation Universities arose; the habit, I mean, of having a school attached to the church (though *that* of course by itself is as old as the synagogue), and of having a separate body of clergy appointed to teach. There is, or was, such a foundation of teaching canons in connection with the parish church of this place. The remains of a college still exist behind the castle. Some bishop, who was as much knight as minister, turned these into stables. As it is, Dr. Lightfoot has some six or seven young men in residence with him. They come here from Oxford and Cambridge for a year before ordination. Some have taken their degree in arts; others (according to the later custom, which allows one to occupy his undergraduate course entirely with divinity — an arrangement

which saves theology at the sacrifice of general culture)
others, I say, are bachelors in divinity. They have an
ordered life in the castle. Breakfast is at 7.45, and is followed by prayers in the chapel at 8.15. Then one of the
chaplains lectures to the men from 9-10. For instance,
this morning a Mr. Southwell has been saying some
things upon the genius of Hebrew poetry, previous to
reading the first forty psalms, which is a subject of examination for Orders. Then follows an interval of two
hours which is filled with reading, directed (by the chaplain) to the foregoing lecture. Another lecture comes from
12-1. To-day my friend, Eden, will take introduction to
the 1st Epistle of Peter, if his economic duties (for he is
purser, caterer, steward, and I know not what all, to his
chief) allow him any time. The bishop is to lecture
shortly on principles of textual criticism. We dine at
one. The afternoon is taken up with district visiting.
Each man has a little plot of ground to work in the
agricultural and mining country round. One evening a
week is, I think, given by each to a cottage reading.
Other nights these men help my friend in evening classes
and recreations at an institute for lads in the town.

This, you will think, is a long, but I assure you it is a
needful, interlude between telling you how beautiful a

thing the bishop's household life is, and saying in so many words wherein its beauty lies.

He calls these lads (and I can imagine worse things than to feel myself, for the nonce, one of them) his family, and they treat him as frank, ingenuous English gentlemen's sons would treat their father. He is accessible to their difficulties and their doubts, if they have any; but, a thing more remarkable, he is open to all their kittenhood of mirth and fun. To hear him alone with them is to feel you are on the edge of a circle, which tempts you almost to stand on tiptoe and look over and wish you were inside. It is a searching trial of true homeliness, to observe how it comports itself when there are strangers present. But I assert my coming in has not bated one jot of all this family joy. Last evening after prayers, they were poking fun at the bishop. One man was asked how he was getting on with Hebrew. The fellow boldly turned the weapon round by inquiring whether his lordship was prepared to teach him. Dr. Lightfoot was gently demurring, when somebody else burst in, as if with a child's impatience and fear of some older uncompleted promise: "No, not before we have had these lectures on botany." Then, assuming the air of someone to whom that study was even as his necessary food, he went on to report his observations, taken daily on his walks to and from the district, of two *interesting weeds*. It sounded like a clever parody upon Darwin and his climbing plants trained up the bed-post.

I have written all this in order to show—if it is within the power of words to show a thing which lies more in the feeling of the whole, than in any enumeration, however complete, of the details—how happy an example one has here of the spirit and the action of the English Church. Within, you have a home and a beehive both in one ; without, everything is plain, and simple, and strenuous. The bishop preaches such sermons as the one I sent you. His chaplains teach, and visit, and preach. The students are an earnest and healthy set of men. Nothing is allowed in the castle which speaks of pomp or pretension. You go down morning and evening to prayers in the chapel ; I suppose it is about the finest palace chapel in Britain. A simple service is held. The bishop and a chaplain read the lessons and lead the prayers. Another chaplain has trained a choir of boys from the neighbouring town. Behind these choristers sit the students ; the bishop and servants (eight I counted) are in the back seats. One or two from the outside also seem to attend. The psalms and hymns are simply but sweetly sung. So anxious is

Dr. Lightfoot that nothing should lie unused, nothing rest
in an empty name, that I believe he is fitting up the
chapel with seats, so as to have a service every Sabbath.
Much of what I have seen here, the earnestness and
the manliness of the men, the order of the household,
the thoroughness of the instruction, the devoutness of
prayers, the sweetness of the singing, the beauty, the
learning, the goodness, the simplicity make me hang my
head for shame both as a man and as a minister; for my
whole heart consents to these things that they are right.

And yet something within me always rises and says:
Thou hast a better portion in the North than all these
things if thou only knewest it. Thy God, thy father's
God, hath wrought nobler things in Scotland than any
that are here. I know not altogether what it is, unless it
be the feeling that there is nothing in our existing
Scottish Church that one cannot find in Scripture, and
that there is nothing in our history that does not speak
of conscience and of independence. I come to no bit of
Revelation which is not illustrated or exemplified somewhere in our worship and our faith; but I also find no
demand made on integrity, or truth, or courage, or self-
sacrifice which has not been answered, and thrice answered,
by the lives of our ministers and our people. The former

part of this grand claim can be urged, perhaps with equal force, by England. It is in the latter part that Scotland's glory lies. To have welcomed truth—that is England's honour as it is ours. But to have rejected all that is untrue, Scotland has done that for me; would God that I might do it now for her. I mean, that all which separates us from the Church of England—the civil supremacy in matters spiritual, the several orders, and the exclusive succession through them (for to the system of permanent bishops, merely considered as one of several alternatives offered by providence I have no objection), the cross in baptism, the bowing at the name of Christ, the kneeling at the communion (though *this* I think less than *that*)— all this seems to me an embodiment of the fatal weakness, which, while it welcomes the truth, will not also dismiss the untrue. We are much blamed in Scotland for preaching a gospel of denials and practising a religion of 'thou-shalt-nots.' Of course, there is a negation that never comes to belief or love; but there is also a negation which says, This I believe and love, but this and no more. To do that, I must abstain from doing this.

These thoughts have come to me to-day, since hearing the bishop's beautiful prayer added (by his own hand and heart, I believe) to the morning service. He asked the

Lord of the Universal Church mercifully to direct those who were now charged with the choice of a chief minister for this county of Northumberland, that they might appoint one who could set forward God's work in the district and further the salvation of all men. That was for the new bishop of Newcastle, a see to which Dr. Lightfoot has parted with a considerable part of his living.

But I thought of one man, my countryman, who just 300 years ago refused this very place (for Newcastle was to be divided then too) because he did not think he ought to serve in a church which admitted the royal supremacy.

What surprises me in Knox's life is the sure-footed way in which he took up his ground on all these questions, so that we have for centuries been but 'following the footing of his feete.' No doubt he had the advantage of the Genevan and German successes and the English failures before and in his time. But I imagine Knox owes his originality (after his genius and his other studies) most to his possession and command of Scripture truth on every point. I think we ought to go back more to that *fons fontium* for everything than we do. Our system of giving the prominence to preaching is all in favour of that. We want more exposition—continuous and comparative exposition—of whole tracts of Scripture. It is wonderful how

Knox always seemed to be lecturing on something which he could fling at the head of any evil that arose, or on the top of which he could stand and blow a blast to rally his friends. For instance, I find him in the book of Haggai when the first reformed parliament is sitting, in Matthew when he began the reformation in St. Andrews. It is indeed a 'living' word, were it only for the command it gives you over the life of your time.

Auckland Castle, May 1, 1882.

I think my last letter ended on Friday night after service in the little chapel at half-past nine. True family worship it was.

At 12 this forenoon I came up to the students' room and took notes of an oral lecture of Eden's on 1st Peter. It was a discussion of the ἐν Βαβυλῶνι ch. v., based on the Bishop's notes. At 1 we dined, and at 1.30 ran for the train to Durham, whither Eden had invited me to go with him for the afternoon.

Thou knowest—dost thou not?—the steep, picturesque little town that lies on the wooded Wear, the old and thronging bridge, the climb to the castle—as precipitous, we said, as the ascent to Killiecrankie—the cottage, the old gateway, the open square, a retreat (like the Wartburg) from the busy town, with dean's, canon's, archdeacon's houses about. First we went through the cloisters and cathedral to the castle where the college now is. We explored the rooms of the 'Union,' saw the dining-hall and the pictures, and the places of state just vacated by the judges on circuit. Eden showed me with a kind of rapture the rooms where the Bishop's party first resided on coming to Durham. The tapestries and carvings were very fine.

But by far the finest remained. About three we went into the cathedral. An enthusiastic but sensible verger, Eden's friend, showed us over it; and we joined in his praises as he passed from point to point of the history and the building. Cuthbert's legend came first; we heard it standing over his tomb. The old apse-end of his Norman Church was traced out to us; the transformation of that into the ground plan of the place, which began in Early English; the transition thence into the 'decorated' and 'perpendicular' styles; the gradual growth of the whole and the peculiarity of each part; the tombs of famous bishops, and the pained face in stone of the last temporal lord Van Mildert; all this and more we heard before the 3.45 service began. We sat in the choir-stalls and saw Canon Greenwell sitting opposite us. The air was cool, the scene solemn, the worshippers reverent, the prayers beautiful. But I could not help feeling out of sympathy with the service. The chanting of the psalms I could join in and enjoy ; but the chanting of the prayers ("Christ have mercy upon us" for instance) seemed to me unreal and unedifying in a high degree. The anthem too was, like Nazianzen's lyre in E.B.B., 'out of reach.' Perhaps it is a defect of harmony in me. But I could not find these parts of the worship correspond to any part of my spiritual nature. I like a service best in which everybody can join. I have a horror of having the thing done for me. But much I have seen here makes me feel how we must give more attention to worship with us in the North. I still think, however, that the Reformers were right when they wished never to have any worship that was apart from exhortation.

After the service (about 5) it rained heavily. We sought refuge in Canon Tristram's, whose house is, like himself, a treasury of birds and beasts. From the canonry we descended into an archdeacon's, whom we found full of emptiness, new paint, and house ' flitting.' From thence a hand-gallop brought us through the drenching rain to the station.

Before tea (at 7) I had a little talk with a man, Gore-Brown, who has been in the army for a year, just to see how

2 A

things are there, that he may know to work among men.
In the evening I sat in the drawing-room reading the newspapers.

Then some words with Eden followed in his den ; then
prayers ; a talk with him again in his 'den' about our work.
He is a truly lovable and lovely soul, seeking truth and
hating hypocrisy.

Yesterday morning the bishop and his men all went to
early communion in a neighbouring church. I rested till 8,
and then joined them at 8.30 in the chapel. After breakfast I went with Dr. Lightfoot and Mr. Eden to one of the
town's churches, where we had a simple easy service, and an
earnest popular sermon from the words, "Whence then
cometh wisdom?" The preacher showed us how even in
Job's day the devout heart felt through and behind all the
phenomena of nature, and the explanations of these offered
by men, and reached to an Eternal Power before which it
bowed, and to which it trusted for a life beyond. It was
beautiful to see the chief minister worshipping among his
people, and going in and out before them like a true ποίμην
λάως.

Both sermons were *extempore*. It was beautiful to see the
supper table in the evening with Dr. Lightfoot. All his
ministers and curates and students gathered about it, after

the day's work was done. The evening worship was full of solemnity. You felt the influence of good men being all about you. "Verily God is in this place."

Im Zug n. Brechin, November 26, 1880.

On your advice we went to hear Cook. He is indeed a man, a 'Gottgesandter Mann.' It was, by all accounts, his finest appearance—gathering up the threads of past evenings, gathering, too, the enthusiasm. He spoke on God in Conscience—(1) On the evidence in Conscience of a Law; (2) on the evidence in this Law of a Person; (3) on the relation of these two facts to the Christian Revelation. All night he was travelling along the level undeviating roads of Kantianism, flying along them, so that it "winded" one to follow—you only caught a mile-stone now and then—saluting and acknowledging the parallel path of science so far as it came, but in the end breaking off with a magnificent fresh effort and far away beyond it, and reaching out hands of Reason to grasp the very goals of Faith. Another thing was his wealth of reference, not, as in Farrar, of loaded and elaborate reading, but merely a familiar and passing nod given to each of the great witness-faces that smiled upon his progress from their heights of serene attainment—Euripides, Bacon, Shakespeare, Kant, Rothe, Müller, Mrs. Browning, Carlyle, Tennyson. His own bits of poetry were splendid, brief photographic illustrations of his theme, especially that beginning, " Duty done 's the soul's fireside, Blest who keeps that ingle wide." Altogether it was an assurance, a stimulus, an inspiration.

His lines were clear (what he fights for is *clearness* first, not *truth*—" was klar ist, wahr ist"—one for me, you say), especially his riding of the marches between the judgment accompanying conscience (which may be fallible, so far as it falls *outside* the person's will and comes into the court of prudence and imprudence in respect of external ends) and conscience as an *intuitive act itself*, which cannot fail, being the *soul's immediate perception of right and wrong in its own choices or intention*. I never heard such a combination of philosophical firmness with popular freedom— *e.g.* in explaining what an intuition was, viz., the perception of that which you cannot imagine away, he gave a most telling description of Kant's illustration in the case of the intuition of space, by pointing to a corner of the roof and asking 'you to try to bring down that part of space so as not to leave space still where you took it from.

But his κεφαλαίωσις about getting God ever present in any act of conscience was the masterpiece.

He asserted God (by previous demonstration) _One._ Therefore, wherever God acts, there Father, Son and Spirit are—
not pantheistically, as immanent, but theistically, as trans-
cendent. Then he laid on the table before him, like any
master of experiment, one critical case, the bit of live,
beating conscience laid open and exposed in the men of
Israel at Pentecost. What means this cutting to the heart?
Peter asserts, and all philosophy and theology approves,
that it was the coming of Him who as God the Son
promised—" A little while and I am coming to you "; of
Him who, as God the Spirit, that day came and proved
Himself present by the immediate demonstration of conscience. Wasn't it beautiful?

These are but the "hearing of the ears." I wish you
could have seen it, and thank you many times for sending
me to see.

Monday, May 1, 1882.

I have just come in from visiting an old Saxon church,
in the midst of a mining village, where Christian service
has been carried on for well over a thousand years. My
holiday is drawing to an end, but it is already full of
κτήματα and of ἐπιθυμίαι (in the good sense). North Berwick

lies behind me as a bright accomplishment. I think it was in many ways the best meeting we have had. It was very good to get you among us again. I think you were much helped to make us happy, and to move our thoughts to higher things. We remember your sorrow—*our* sorrow —though not with words. I have just read Calvin's words to Knox about this very matter. "Viduitas tua," he says, "mihi ut debet tristis et acerba est." In a letter to a friend he says, what we say: " Fratrem nostrum, etsi non parum doleo suavissima uxore fuisse privatum, gaudeo tamen ejus morte non ita fuisse afflictum, quin strenue operam suam Christo et ecclesiae impendat."

Velumis, mi fratre, operam ad huc majorem impendas.

Cults, March 7, 1883.

Thanks for your very clear, full, and satisfying account of dear Grandmama's death. I was looking very eagerly for it, thinking there might be last words and other precious things; for memory has suddenly become jealous of the least fragment of her treasures. But the reality was beautiful beyond all poetry. The close was worthy of the career; that is high praise, great glory to God. He is 'the best poet' and we are His ποίημα. . . . So often the last days bring strange surroundings. Sad changes come within, and there is hurry and excitement and whispering without; but here the Lord had it all arranged for and over before He let any one, except those to whom it was no secret, know. " Nothing is here for tears" (I have been singing),

> " Nothing to wail
> Or knock the breast, . . . nothing but well and fair
> And what may quiet us in a death so noble."

And what more touching, even to tears, than the grand and reverent woman, the ripe saint, become again at last the little child laying its tired head down with one sharp cry on the bed, which turned out to be the breast of Jesus. How even He must have thrilled to have her at last, to have her all to Himself, who was His already here so wholly.

"Precious in the sight of the Lord is the death of His saints"; for He has them to His heart's content.

Saturday, 2.15 p.m.

I am waiting on the station at Inverramsay for the Turriff train. I have had a pleasant journey thus far, clear north-west wind blowing into the carriage off fields of 'tedded' hay and bearded barley. Harlaw Castle, where Provost Davidson and his stubborn Aberdonians fell stemming the tide of Highland invasion in 1411, is peeping out on the right from a cluster of firs, while Don and Ury come down from the heights of Bennachie with the same old song they did that grim summer day, to meet and mingle at Inverurie. My companions have been an honest E.C. layman, with whom I talked of the church's future, and gave him Nelson's Bill; a lieutenant of the Salvation army—gentle in sex and English in speech, who received Dr. Saphir's "Christ and the Scriptures" gladly; an old lady and a young mother with a baby, two 'labourer' lads with a bit of a bagpipe, and a little girl!

Now I am comfortably packed in a 'Turra' carriage, among sundry of Johnny Gibb's good simple country folk —a lame old gentleman, who might have kept a school at the 'Walls' in his day; two or three old wives with baskets and flowers; a young lady bound for 'Fyvie,' and two little girls. The train we left has just disappeared along the foot of Bennachie towards Insch, while we are speeding seaward. We have three-quarters of an hour or so of this gently undulating land, over which one can still hear the 'trundle' of Johnny's cart, and the trot of Johnny's pony, before reaching 'Turra.' At Aberdeen I had just three-quarters of an hour. So after leaving the note at the tailor's I took the tramcar up Union Street to the top and called on Mrs. ——. It was one of those visits that make one happier to have paid them ; she spoke so quietly but surely of having found Christ at some meetings in the Music Hall after Mr. Moody's visit seven or eight years ago. "No special one it was," she said, "but just going to and from them all." "I wish there were the like of them often ; but those who never attend such don't seem ever to care about these things. You don't hear it in some of the churches." It made one feel the wish to make the glad sound audible every time one opened one's mouth.

Rothie-Norman, 2.40.—We have another passenger, and a boy eating dulse in the carriage now. He has a bit of Johnny about him, and the good lady opposite might be Sir Simon's henwife ; she has been giving an account of a thunderstorm she was in, which reminded me of that garrulous individual.

Now there are bits of ' knolls' with pine trees growing upon them and a little ragged heather, and fields with hay set up in sheaf to save the seed. This is Fyvie.

It is curious how individual localities are. One could almost have told that this corner of Aberdeenshire had produced 'Johnny Gibb' from the spicy character of the conversation.

Das Huhnweib versucht in diesem Augenblick meinen Brief zu lesen, so muss ich acht nehmen. The afternoon is lovely. The Lord God is a Sun, as Henry says, and David said before him.

He is a Shield too, our Shield, who keeps us for each other while we are away.

Edinburgh, January 22, 1884.

I have just come in from Professor Butcher's junior lecture, to which Condie took me at 9. It was a great refreshment and stimulus. He had the explanatory style to perfection. The first half-hour was a dictation upon the difference between the use of οὐ and μή with substantives, participles and adjectives. He drew the thing out of these backward, awkward Scotch pupils, with beautiful courtesy and helpfulness. His illustrations from the parallel uses of Latin were exquisite. The second half-hour was half a page of Plato's "Laches," about Socrates' *maieutic* art (I think), which was simply a further lesson in phrases, only given the analytic instead of the synthetic way. His method is the English tutorial, with perhaps a little overrefinement of expression, but for the purpose, and considering the stage of his scholars, perhaps the best possible. 'White Cross' papers were being given at the door, as the class came out.

I had a long talk with K. upon his book (translation of Schopenhauer—the Pessimist—kind of modern Buddhist), and upon his own views. He gave me some hints about how one needs to preach the goodness of the Unseen, not as a future after death, but as a present possession—something above us which may be in us *now*. That, of course, is just what Jesus has been saying for two thousand years: "he that hath faith *hath* eternal life"; "everyone which seeth Me and believeth on Me *hath* everlasting life." One must not preach the hereafter only, especially to those who feel (like the young) the livingness, and greatness, and earnestness of the *now*. But neither must one forget that other word, so often repeated after those I have quoted: "and I will raise him up at the last day." For aged, for outworn, for laden souls, for dying and bereaved, ay and for children lately come from the other land, *that also is God's truth*. And even to us, 'in the midtime' (especially if "nel mezzo" means still for us as for Dante some "selva selvaggia" of doubt, and temptation, and sin) it is sometimes said: Young man, see thou live in full face of that 'after'; see thou turn

thine eyes that way, even if it be thou see but a horizon
line, whose light is borrowed from things quite over the
edge and out of thy seeing.

I walked with him to Hugh's rooms. He wants a book
to put before men, especially working men, how wealth is
not the thing to work for: to supply the motives which
will bring the ideal and avert the perils which Political
Economy is able to teach, but is quite unable to deal with.

Prince of Wales Hotel, Grasmere,
May 5, 1885, 10 a.m.

. . . When I ran up the old-fashioned, continuous-
corded roller-blind at a quarter to 9 this morning a lovely
picture was framed in its place. Before the simple, neat
hotel garden a daisied lawn, with two half-tidy flower
beds, an araucaria and two or three weeping ashes ; then
over a belt of straw-coloured reeds—of which you could
almost catch the rustle through the crisp morning air—a
breath of Grasmere lake, with all the strange 'far-away-
ness' water always brings, partly from its hidden depths,
partly from the reflection of heaven ; a green island-
knoll beyond it, and behind, a breadth of mountain-side
big enough to fill the eye but not to weary or overbear

it, with two delightful, quiet English 'chalets' crowned by woods and resting on green meadows. Someone says the scenery here is just the right size—it has just enough of everything, and I think it is true. . . .

5 p.m.—We sauntered through the village this morning and into the little village church, where there is a tablet to Wordsworth, beautifully worded by Keble, and telling how he was a poet and a champion of the poor and simple 'by the special gift and calling of God.' The High Church fittings did not fall in with the homely old building. But outside in the churchyard all was harmony. Here under the church shadow and looking to the mountains he so loved is the poet's grave. He lies among his people, the plain grass marked by an unadorned slab which only bears the name and year of his departing. A flat stone on another tomb prepared before his death tells how it was his wish to lie near his 'kindred' in the humble hope of a blessed resurrection with them in Christ. No fitter monument could have been found to our noble Christian poet and man of the people. The hills around and the whole country seem to make the grandest of Westminsters. Hartley Coleridge rests behind.

We trudged on, off the high road, by a brawling stream, then up a grassy hillside, in the hollow of which the

water rushed and plunged with creamy whiteness. 'Sour-
milk gill' seemed rather a poor name for it. At the foot
of crags behind we reached a lonely mountain tarn and
felt another of the charms which water lends an English
landscape. Thence we turned and came back across a
ridge which showed us numbers of lovely sheets of water
with valleys well-cultivated and well-peopled, and the
dim blue lines of Cumberland hills behind.

In the train,
Plymouth, March 3, 1886, 2.15 p.m.

Dadda has had a comfortable journey hitherto. The
wind has been cold, but his warm greatcoat and rug have
kept him from feeling it, and the bright sunshine on
everything has spoken to him of gladness. A few green
ears pushing through the rough brown earth, like good
dogged Britons determined not to be beaten, are all there
is to tell that spring is coming.

He had a good talk with a Cornish miner coming up to
Truro. He had worked for thirteen years at a town called
Calumet, on Lake Superior, in a copper mine, where they
never got up in time to see the sunlight except on Saturday afternoon and Sabbath, and where the snow lay six

feet deep in winter. He had once been a drunkard, but for six years an abstainer, and had one boy of eleven at home who he hoped would never work underground. On parting, he said "I wish you all that's good," or something like that. It seemed an earnest of God's blessing on this journey. Now I am with other two. Bath, 6 p.m.—Since Exeter I was left with one of them. We had a good time. He was on his way to London to be appointed to a mine in the Transvaal. When asked if he was a Christian, he said sadly—"No, but he had once been." Six years of seeking first the world and its gains in Mexico had lost him his peace. It was very hard to make him realise that God's forgiveness was there for the taking more fully than ever. But as we prayed a great softening came, and he said he could trust again. He asked for my address, and promised to write to me. God heard Freeland's prayer that God would not only "take care of father, but bless him."

Hotel Continental, Ajaccio, Corsica,
January 20, 1887.

Your letter of Saturday reached us this afternoon. We took it out and read it on a big granite boulder under the olives, and it seemed to carry us right into the shaded room where you were sitting beside that dear, noble presence just entering into rest. Thank you very much for giving us such a glimpse of that solemn, blessed scene; what more could we have desired for him than the abundant entrance' which was being ministered even as you wrote. What struck me most in the last days we were with him was the wonderful meekness which was given him. He asked so gently for his cap to be put on, or the clothes to be moved, and received little services so gratefully. It was like the trait of an old child-nature coming out again, after the struggle with the world was past and over. The thirty-seventh Psalm has often, and long since spoken to me of papa. As I looked at him, I seemed to hear one say: "The steps of a good man are ordered by the Lord; and He delighteth in his way. . . . The law of his God is in his heart: none of his steps shall slide. . . . Wait on the Lord, and keep His way, and He shall exalt thee to inherit the land." And now the Psalm is finished: "Mark the perfect man, and behold the upright: for the end of that man is peace"; or rather, he is gone to finish it above. And we may hear his voice among the rest, saying for us, who are still in the struggle, as well as for himself, for whom it is ended: "The salvation of the righteous is of the Lord; He is their strength in the time of trouble. And the Lord shall help them and deliver them; He shall deliver them and save them, because they trust in Him" (Psalm xxxvii. 11, 23, 31, 34, 37, 39, 40).

Oh, how reverently, how heartily, he will join in that cry we used to hear him read on Sabbath evening when anyone dear or noble had been taken away: "Salvation to our God which sitteth upon the throne, and unto the Lamb" (Rev. vii. 10); and, however sore our hearts may be, yet how heartily can we join with him in it now, and how earnestly must we seek to live for the day when we may again sit around one table and join in one Psalm.

We think often of you in the crowded duties and calls of this week, and shall be with you in spirit all Saturday. May you be kept from all harm of body and all distress of mind. Do give yourself good meals and long nights, and remember papa's advice about how the former should be taken. I find myself saying over that funny string of imperatives he used to give us, like a grace during meat, at the *table d'hôte*.

[To Robert Browning's sister on her brother's death.]

Bonskeid, December 21, 1889.

Although we have never met, and although I only
saw your brother as a boy, I think that for his sake you
will allow me to write and tell you how a little circle of
friendly hearts he drew around him in this Highland valley
eighteen years ago, and has held in growing, though un-
uttered veneration ever since, has been with you during
these first days of a deep sorrow, and is with you still.
For him

      " Nothing is here for tears,"

but how much for you. May the strong consolations with
which he comforted many be yours now to the full.

My wife and I were up in the little glen where he lived
during the summer of 1871, this afternoon. It was beautiful
to hear his praises from those simple peasant people, whom
greatness in the face and in the soul seems to reach and
touch at first hand.

The good woman who waited upon him has an especially
clear and bright recollection of your brother. " He was the
pleasantest gentleman she had ever to do with"; and " he
was so happy ; he was always happy." " ' God bless you,' he

said on one occasion "; "and," she added, "there was always a blessing into that old gentleman" (the Gaelic way of putting it). How true it was she little knew.

If ever you should be able, or feel drawn to visit Glen-fincastle, be very sure of a friendly, dare I say a tender, welcome to our home.

We live at a house perched on the hill just above the cottage where he stayed. It is a quiet place, and the inmates quiet people, except for the voices of mountain-winds and falling waters and merry children.

You will not reply to this now, or think about it afterwards, unless the thought pleases you ; but whenever you come to see us, you will find us always,—Two grateful friends.

Fincastle,
Pitlochrie, N.B., 20th June, 1890.

How glad the Huntly call has made me. Of all places on earth I should have wished you to be in (next to Aden or Lovedale, which we both, I think, sorrowfully have been forbidden), there is none more dear to me, or more good for any friend of mine with 'grit' in him, than Aberdeenshire. And the heart of Christian Aberdeenshire has long been Huntly.

I shall never forget one Fast Day, the only one, I spent there in the manse and church and town. Everything that happened in these days was 'dinted with a silver pencil,' but Fast and Communion Days were 'graved in gold.'

The quiet hours of preparation in rooms where the Principal had passed his waiting time; the solemn rows of solid, God-fearing town and country folk; the silence in God's house; the pleasant converse round the manse table (Dr. Blackie was there, I remember); the grave counsels (about my first case of discipline) from the minister and his guest over the study fire; and, above all, the walk 'round about Zion' (for it was all Zion to me); the peep of the Castle towers, where the last Duchess held her court spiritual; the site of the meeting house which bred George Macdonald and Legge and other worthies; the R.C. Chapel, now (prosit omen) a carpenter's shop, in which Mr. M'Cheyne preached and took part in his first and only 'act of intrusion,' and where the mother of one of my church members was bidden by him go back and bend down for the first time over the cradle of her first born, and give herself and her child to the Good Shepherd, and did so; the farm (or other place of meeting) on the hill in which Dr. Whyte held the 'hinds' and other children of the soil in the strong grasp of his masculine divinity; all that and more remains with me, and shall remain, while I am with myself.

But why should I tell it to one who will drink where I sipped, and walk up and down many a long furrow over many a long field where I only scattered a handful of seed? God bless you, going, such an one, to such a place. God bless you and her who is (please God and a watchful husband!) to spend many a happy day with you in it all. These quiet-living Aberdonians leave a lately-wedded pair something to themselves! May you share it richly.

Fincastle,
Pitlochrie, N.B., 5th September, 1890.

Friends are utter 'beggars'; but they have sometimes to be sad recusants to their friend's request.

The truth is, my little pittance of not absolute inability for the month you mention is already signed away, on an old understanding to our common friend of Queene for October 11. The week following Wilberforce 'descends' on Edinburgh for an anti-opium crusade, and I must work for that whatever comes.

You know, perhaps, that on the very day my wife and I locked the manse door at Cults, and were once again homeless under my father's roof, he received his first distinct summons to bid us all good-bye. And during these days, as his life-long before, he bequeathed to me, forbidden a regular profession, the care of China, as a first charge upon all I should have to give of time, strength, means to the good cause. That is why I am taking up, *manu vel remissâ genibus(?)que solutis*, this quarrel with the opium dealers, who are ourselves.

Pardon such a long story; but a friend has a right to hear, and to inflict, a reason for small inconsistences.

God bless you : He is blessing you : and help you to hold His blessing with a hand trembling for very thankfulness.

The first few months of things—of wedding to one's people, or one's bride—settles much. Well taken, it is not easily lost ; ill, it is not easily regained. But you know that, I trust, and will act upon it better than,—Yours most hopefully.

P.S.—I try to remember you on Sabbaths : preach the Cross.

The conference has been as happy and uniting as it was last year. The idea is a true one, for it bears fruit.

I do want to come to Huntly one day, for your sake and China's. It used to be a missionary stronghold : *teste* Legge !

I have re-opened this letter to say that one of our China

missionaries, John Watson, a man full of faith and of the
Holy Ghost, is at present at "Whitestone Cottage, Banchory
Devenick, Aberdeen." *He* could fill your pulpit and your
people's hearts (D.G.) with fire on the subject of the
heathen's need one day you were away, if you are able to
ask him. Forgive me for making the suggestion.

11 Belgrave Place,
Edinburgh, Sabbath, October 5, 1890,

I am still kept in the house by a tedious cold, which is
now however, I hope, beginning to take leave.

Convalescence is in some ways the most trying stage
of sickness. And for two reasons, I think. The full
effect of the disease—fever, or whatever it is—is not felt
while the strain lasts. It is only when the struggle
between the forces of life and its enemy is over that the
full gravity of it is realized. And, besides, the return of
life to its old ascendancy is generally by gradual steps and
slow. So is it, too, in the spiritual experience. It is not
conversion, but what follows conversion, that tests the
virtue of the new man in Christ Jesus. During the excitement, so to speak, of the crisis—of the decision which
means ultimate victory—there is a certain exhilaration and,
to borrow a figure from the body, a heightened tempera-

ture of the soul. But when the tension begins to slacken,
then it is that lassitude sets in, and the soldier who waxed
valiant in fight grows faint when the fight is over. Also,
the flow of the spirit's tide is, like the flow of the ocean's,
wavering and wearisome to the eye that watches long for
it. The prize that seemed all gold, and altogether worth
the winning in the long-run, gleams but little in the
thousand steps towards it, and is sore, sickening sore, to
win. We pray for grace to withstand the temptations of
the world, the flesh, and the devil. But there are two
worlds, the favouring and the frowning one; and two
fleshes, the flattering and the enfeebling; and two devils,
the angel of light and the roaring lion. And whether of
the two is the one we ought to pray against and fight
against the more, I know not. The Holy Spirit and the
particular occasion must instruct us. Society and solitude,
health and disease, the temple and the wilderness, have
each their usual and wonted temptations. But the enemies
of God and of His saints keep no faith with their
opponents : they acknowledge no rules of warfare. Therefore is there safety, not in the multitude of counsels, but
in this one precept of the only Victor—"Watch," He said,
"and pray," that ye may not *begin* to go into temptation.
"The Spirit, indeed," *i.e.* the new man who hath in him

the Spirit, "is willing; but the flesh," *i.e.* the old man, which hath both the world and the devil in him, "is weak." "Watch," that is, set a guard entirely over thyself, look well to thyself, and "Pray," that is, "look away from thyself entirely to Me thy Captain."

The foregoing is a meditation I had with myself in the forenoon when the others were at church.

11 Belgrave Place,
Edinburgh, November 29, 1890.

Your letter was very good to get. You did right to leave the flock and go to the house of mourning. Everything that cuts *across* the seeming continuity of the life of sight, and shows us life in its true dimensions—which are directly contrary and opposite to those of *time*—helps to reinforce the life of faith, which is all the real life we ever have and never lose. Browning makes the raised Lazarus look continually at his life *across* and not *along.* But, ah, it strains the vision.

I am thirty-six years old to-day, one year over '*il mezzo del cammin.*' And already, even while the clock is striking, another eager year is hurrying on.

This has been an eventful week in the life of our nation—a great political crisis, an immensely greater moral one. We have lived an era since last Sabbath. God be magnified, who only doeth wonderful works. Is not His word like a fire and a hammer?

How silently and unforeseen the mightiest steps in a nation's upward course (or downward) are taken. Last spring revolt against the publican; this autumn's rising against the debauchee—all the work of an hour.

I am with you heart and soul for pressing Christ's gospel of purity into the code of our public life and law, far beyond any recognition it has yet attained.

Glad to hear of any prospect of early closing in our great towns. We must nibble as well as gape in the temperance as in every department of the one good cause. I confess that I gape a good deal.

CHILDREN.

CHILDREN.

Hotel Continental,
Ajaccio, Corsica, Tuesday, January 25, 1887.

DEAR SONNIE (that is what Mother called you just now),
We got Nurse's letter after lunch to-day, and when
the two little browny-green leaves came out we said,
" These are from Freeland," and so they were. Thank you
very much for them. We send you a fern and a little bit
of heath.

We were so glad that you sent a wreath of white
heather to George Square. Grandmother wrote and told
us to-day that when she saw it in her room she was made
glad. The last time I saw her with white heather was at
Elm Grove on Mother and Father's wedding-day.

We have got a new room to live in now, on the third
floor. One window looks to the hills, and one to the sea.
There are many fishes caught here, and such funny ones.
We saw them in the market yesterday, in the fishwives'
baskets. Some were a bright steel-blue, and some gold

Train from York to London,
Dec. 22, 1888.

FREELAND, my boy,

Here is a "good joy,"

  And the end of a fifty days' sorrow;

For mother and I think of Gastard and cry:

  " We'll be there the day after to-morrow."

Freeland, my boy,

We shall bring you a toy,

  And Maidie, and dear little Miss Ma. S.;

But you mustn't expect to get them direct,

  Toys come the day after—that's Christmas.

Freeland, my boy,

Sailors say, "Ship ahoy!"

  When they're coming in sight of each other;

So Freeland, our boy, and two maids sweet and coy,

"Ship ahoy!" from your father and mother.

[*To Maida.*]

Train from Paris to Aix
(called " Aches ") les (" lay ") Bains (" Bang "),
Saturday, March 30, 1889, 10.30 a.m.

Mother, Aunt Minnie, and Father slept last night at Paris, in two beautiful rooms on the second flat of the Hotel du Louvre, Paris, where the Kings of France used to hunt the wild dogs called 'Loups,' that is, 'wolves,' when there were woods there ; now there is a large, broad street, of which the hotel forms one whole block, nearly as long as grandmamma's side of George Square. We were wakened by the rolling of the carts in the street, and ringing of the tinkling little bells which many of the carthorses carry on their harness.

We had for breakfast these dear little, round, white rolls and delightful butter, which the French people make so nicely, and fried fish and tea. Then we drove in a cab, with two brave, little horses, along the river Seine a long way to the Lyons railway station, and got into a large, first-class carriage, where a gentleman and lady and two nice boys and another lady, their companion, got in after us.

At first we ran along by the river Seine, where the water is green and smooth. The land is beautifully kept by

2 C

the peasants. It is drier than England, but they water it by canals from the river. The trees are small, but they trim them carefully. Every little spare twig is cut off and bound into bundles with others, to burn. When the trees are cut down, the bigger branches and the stems are burned a little, and so made into charcoal, which is used in the French fireplaces instead of coal. We saw a man pruning the vines (nurse will tell you what that means). A vine is just a poor little bush, like a gooseberry bush or a currant bush at the bottom, but not at the top. Every year the top branches are cut off or pruned (when the grapes have been pulled), and then in the spring-time the old root puts out new branches, which are nailed against a wall or over a wooden frame, or even twisted round a tree, and when autumn comes bear more grapes than the old branches would have done if they had not been pruned. When the new branches begin to grow, you can hardly tell which is the vine root and which are the vine branches. Perhaps nurse can tell you what Jesus says (John xv. 5) about vines, and why He calls Himself "The Vine" and says that we are His branches.

11.30.—Now we are in another county of France, called Yonne ("Yon") from a beautiful river which is running beside the railway. We have seen two oxen drawing a cart with a piece of wood tied across their necks, which is called a "yoke" because it joins them together. Jesus says that He wishes to put His yoke upon us, that means that He wishes to come close beside us and wants us to walk close beside Him. Now we have seen four oxen in one cart, two and two.

Father and mother are happy about their three dear little ones; they often think of them and know that they are being well cared for.

To-night father and mother will be near the borders of France at a place called Aix (that means, in old French, "Waters," because there are waters there that make people well when they drink them or bathe in them). On Monday they expect to be in Italy.

From FATHER.

Kiss Margaret, if she wants a kiss, and do you and Free-land say, each to yourselves, " Mother and Father love me."

Hôtel de l'Europe, Aix,
Sabbath Evening, 31st March, 1889.
6 o'clock.

DEAREST SONNIE,

Mother and I are sitting in a bright room, with doors and windows newly painted white and newly-washed muslin curtains. The walls are covered with a pretty white paper of leaves and roses against a shining gold ground; the floor, with a carpet of leaves and flowers on a cream-coloured ground. Everything is fresh and clean. Outside the two windows, which are made to open, runs a balcony, where you can walk or sit and see the view.

It is a beautiful view. Over the hotel garden and the roofs of the houses there is a long brown hill, the slopes of which are planted with vines. Many of the vines are trained on elm trees, and the earth underneath is sown with wheat or grass, so that two crops grow on the same piece of ground. Behind the hill rises a great mountain, 1000 feet higher than Ben Nevis, called " Cat's Tooth."

This morning we all slept very late, for we were very tired ; we had been travelling from 8 yesterday morning till 11 at night. We read our Bibles in the house, and then took our books out with us to the open air. There was no service in the English or Scotch church, as the visitors have not arrived yet. We are nearly the first who have come. We think no one had been in our rooms this season before. But the kind people had lighted a nice fire of beech logs in them.

We climbed up two lovely hills above the town until we could see all the houses lying at our feet. Then a most beautiful lake, called the Lac de Bourget, came in sight. Its waters were a lovely dark blue, in which the shadows of a large house and of the rocks along the lake side were clearly seen. All round and round us were great mountains, streaked with snow and dotted with dark fir trees, which climbed, like soldiers, far up the heights. Wreaths of mist, like white breath, hung upon the topmost peaks, hiding them sometimes quite away from us. Then the strong sun came out and cleared them away. It felt as hot as in summer.

Sweet, pale primroses were peeping here and there from among the dead leaves and stones on the hillside, and a bright, little blue flower, something like a tiny hyacinth, stood up here and there. There were brambles too, with their pretty leaves and sharp prickles, and junipers with berries purple and green.

Father said aloud some of the beautiful Scotch Psalms (such as Psalm xxxvi. 5-9), which tell about such things as we were seeing.

This afternoon we had tea in our room, just at the same time as our three dear little ones would be having theirs with nurse and Sarah in their nursery at Nairn. Mother made tea, and Aunt Minnie and she 'cleared away' and 'washed up.'

9 at night.—Now we have had dinner, and are soon going to bed. To-morrow we shall go through the Mont Cenis tunnel to Italy.

With dear love to you all from

FATHER.

Florence (that means Flower town),
Hôtel Paoli, Lung' Arno, April 6, 1889, 2 p.m.

MY DEAR GIRLIE,

We came here last night in the train from a place called Siena. Siena is a most beautiful town; it is all built on the top of a hill, or rather two or three hills. The streets are covered with great flat stones like a pavement; and they go uphill and downhill, like the roads at Bonskeid. They are very narrow, just broad enough for two little carriages to pass, and no more. There is a beautiful big church on the top of the town, built with black stones and white turn about, and a very high tower with a sweet-sounding bell, which goes 'ding-dong' at one o'clock, two o'clock, and so on. Then there is a market-place with a very pretty fountain in the middle, all built round with white stones cut into the shapes of Bible pictures. There are a great many dear little children in the town, with merry black eyes, who laughed and chattered about us when we walked past. They had never seen a long white ulster like daddy's before, and thought it a good joke.

Father and mother and Aunt Minnie went to see the house where a good lady lived long, long ago. She was called Catherine. She had a little room all to herself, where she used to pray, and a beautiful prayer she used to say was written on one of the walls of it. Here is a bit of it:— "My dear Lord Jesus, help me now in all that I do for Thee; Christ, Thou lovest me, Christ, thou lovest me; come into my heart, and make me love and fear Thee!" Then, when she had prayed, she went and helped her father and mother, her brothers and sisters in the house; and when they did not need her, she took breakfast and dinner to poor people who had none, and nursed people who were very ill, and made people who were quarrelling friends again; and every evening, when her work was done, she went up to a church on a hill behind her fathers house, and told the Lord what she had done for Him, and asked Him to help her to do more.

Was she not a sweet lady? How daddy would be delighted if his dear girlie was like that (and little Meg too)!

Outside our windows runs the river Arno, a greeny colour, with a fine walk on each side of it. There is a hill opposite covered with trees, and houses on the top.

Please thank Freeland for his two nice letters—one to father and one to mother—and say to Meg she is a dear little girl.

From your loving father, who loves to hear that Maida thinks of him sometimes.

                                        Train (Express)
                        Chiusi (called " Kee-oosy ") back to
                                Florence, Saturday, April 20, 1889.

DEAR SONNIE,

Mother and Father and Aunt Minnie went a long drive (15 miles—as far as from Dunkeld to Perth) on Thursday to see a famous town (about half the size of Perth) called Assisi ("Asseasy"). We drove down the hill on which Perugia stands (1700 or 1800 feet above the level of the sea), and then across a fruitful plain, where corn and vines were growing. We went over the river Tiber (which runs on to Rome) by a very steep bridge, like the one at Tummel Bridge, then over another stream, and so up the side of a mountain called Subasio. There is a great cluster of houses above you, with high walls and brown tiles very like the colour of the mountain. That is Assisi. The horses stopt at an hotel called Subasio, after the mountain, I suppose. There we got out and left our wraps. We walked a little further up the hill and saw a big church, three stories high. In the lowest story of all is buried a good man, Francis of Assisi, who lived there about 700 years ago. In his days the church of Christ was very unlike what Christ said it was to be: it was very rich, and the ministers were idle and fond of pleasure. Francis heard what Christ said to His apostles about being poor, and not having many spare clothes or houses or lands. He gave up all he had in order to be like what Jesus was. He did not take the money he might have had from his father; he wore only *one* coarse cloak and no shoes. He eat just what people offered him. Then he went about and preached everywhere, and got other men like himself to do the same. He did not know very much about the Bible, and did not understand all that he heard out of it; but what he knew, he tried to *do* himself, and tried to get others to do. He was very patient and gentle, and kind to everyone and everything. He made friends with birds and hares and rabbits, and is even said to have tamed a wolf. You will read his life, I hope, when you are older.

In the second church there are pictures of the three promises Francis made : to be poor, to have no wife, to do whatever God or God's servants bade him. God does not want us to make such promises, unless He Himself puts it into our heart, and He does not tell us to try and get our friends to make them. After Francis died, his friends, who were called 'Franciscans,' got idle again, and the monasteries, or monks' houses, became as bad as the ministers' houses ; and so God sent Martin Luther to 're-form' (that is, change the form of) His Church, and make it more like what the Church of the New Testament is like. John Knox was the Reformer of Scotland.

In the church that is highest of all, we saw pictures of many wonderful things which Francis is said to have done. Some of these things I do not think he ever did : for they are not things God tells us to pray for. But some were just wonderful answers to prayer, and such things happen to God's children still.

Coming home, we saw some curious tombs, called ' Etruscan,' cut in the rock, with stone images of the people who lived long, long ago, in the days of old Rome.

Yesterday was Good Friday, which many Christians keep in memory of Christ's dying on the Cross. We went to service in a little room at the bottom of the hotel. An

English church minister preached beautifully from Jeremiah's Lamentations, ch. i., v. 12. He told us how Francis tried to follow Jesus, and bade us do so too. We sang, "Oh come and mourn with me awhile."

This morning we were up at 6.30, and at 8.30 two brave, black horses, harnessed in a large carriage, trotted off with us for a 30 miles' drive, right west across country. We passed many fine old castles and churches (with houses round them) perched on tops of hills, and rounded a most lovely lake called "Trasimene," where a mighty soldier, from Carthage in North Africa, beat the soldiers of Rome. At Chiusi we had some nice soup, and now (3 p.m.) we have passed dear old Florence again, and are going to climb up through the Apennines (in tunnels) and so get to Bologna (for Sabbath) at 6.25.

P.S.

Hôtel Brun,
Bologna, Sabbath Evening, April 21.

This morning father and mother were at the Communion in the Free Italian church, and this afternon at the English church in this hotel.

Love to Maida and Margaret, and kind remembrances to nurse and Sarah from

FATHER.

DEAR SONNIE,

Our train you will see is late through a breakdown which happened here to the 11.30 on its way north (we crossed at Dalguise); and as 'Cromartie' has gone off with a truck, I do not think we shall be in Perth much before twelve.

It is a warm day, though at Fincastle the air was cold. The hay in the first field (where we worked) is all put up in large cocks; they are working in the second field (to the west) now. The children—David, Katie and Willie—are helping them; Katie and Willie hope to see you on Tuesday night. You may, perhaps, come by the same train as the Principal and Mrs. Rainy; if so, you must point out the places to them as you drive up—Faskally, and Tighngiat, and the Pass, and Ben-y-Glo (from the Bridge), and the Falls Gate, and Lady Bath's Garden and Hill (the Falls Hill), and Coillebrochain, and Bonskeid, and the Well and Chapel, and Browning's House and his Walk, and anything else that you remember.

I am glad to have your text, and shall think of

you between six and seven at your service. It is a fine text.

I. The *Girdle*, Truth or Truthfulness. That means your grip of God's truth, and its grip of you—like a belt round your waist—which holds you up and keeps you together. Always love the truth, and speak it. The *new* man is the *true* man. Abhor lying.

II. The *Breastplate*, Righteousness. The uprightness of the man who is forgiven, and who knows it, and lives accordingly; looking God and man in the face. Be honest; do the truth ; owe no man anything.

III. The *shoes* (sandals), the Preparation of the Gospel of Peace. That means to be always ready to run Christ's errands. Blessed are the peacemakers.

IV. The *Helmet of Salvation*. To be saved, and to know it, is like a crown on your head. That is what a Christian is known by. He is a saved man, and carries his head high. His crest is the hope of salvation.

V. The *Shield*, Faith. Looking away from himself to the Unseen Defender. That keeps the Devil off.

VI. The *Sword*, God's Word, hung in the girdle of Truth.

VII. All—*Prayer*. That is calling on your Captain to keep you.

Love to all the Cousins, and Uncle Alick and Aunt Margaret. I hope the singing at the Church Rock will come off, and the Sabbath service too.

I think I shall buy 'Gipsy,' Mr. Craig's little dark brown horse. Kemp has tried her in harness, and she goes nicely. To-morrow we shall try her with one of the children and the leading rein.—Goodbye, old boy, from

FATHER.

Train, Edinburgh to London,
Feb. 25, 1891.
[After passing four months a prisoner
through illness.]

DEAR MISTRESS MEG,
I've eaten a leg
Of a chicken—and more ;
Some bread from a store,
Which mother had packed
In a box—that's a fact.

We are riding along
In a carriage so strong,
With three little rooms
Where nobody comes
Except only us six.

In the first there's no other,
But father and mother;
In the second are two—
Aunt Margaret and Hugh ;
In the third there are ladies,
—It is Sarah's and Maidie's.

Now I must not write more
Lest my head should get sore;
And if I've a sore head
Mother sends me to bed.
I just lie on the top,
Clothes and all, and then drop
Fast asleep, like my Meg,
Till I waken and beg
For my tea—which I sup
From a white China cup.

So goodbye for just now
To my dear Shaggy pow,
With seven kisses and hugs
For my queen of Pug-mugs,
And the rest (if you've any)
For my sweet little Gwenny.

From FADER-PADER.

BIOGRAPHICAL NOTICES.

2 D

BIOGRAPHICAL NOTICES.

FROM "THE FREE CHURCH MONTHLY," 1891,
WITH ADDITIONS.

ROBERT BARBOUR was born at Edinburgh on the 29th
November, 1854. His father, who died in 1887, was George
Freeland Barbour, Esq., of Bonskeid and Gryffe, loved by
his son's friends as a man of singular culture, piety, humour,
and liberality. His mother, who died in 1892, is known
throughout the Church by "The Way Home," and other
religious writings. She was a woman of great force of
character, who lived for her ideals—and she expected their
fulfilment from China to the Hebrides—with a thoroughness
of faith and a constancy of prayer very unusual in these days.
Consequently, to many she appeared eccentric. But those
who were intimate with her know that there have been few
women or men of greater shrewdness, humour, sympathy and
common kindliness. Through her mother, Mrs Sandeman, of
Perth, she came of a Celtic stock, the Stewarts of Athole, and
was a niece of the poetess, Lady Nairne. She had herself a

share of the poetic gift, more in her way of looking at things, perhaps, than in actual expression, and Robert derived from her both this and many of his other talents. Her brother, David Sandeman, went as a missionary to China and died there in the midst of his work. This gave her and her whole family that devotion to the China Mission, which has been one of their most beautiful characteristics. Four of the family survived childhood—Robert, two sisters (now married to Professor Simpson and Dr. Whyte), and Hugh, now in medical practice in Edinburgh. They grew up under such parents, and with these backgrounds to their education —Edinburgh, the Highlands, the Free Church, and the China Mission.

Robert went to school at the Collegiate Institution. The men who most influenced his boyhood were his father, his tutor, James Stalker, and Mr. Wilson of the Barclay Church : the Young Men's Society of which was also one of his training-grounds. At Edinburgh University he came at once to the front and achieved a very brilliant career. Ten class medals, the prize poem, essay prizes, a double-first degree in classics and philosophy ; in the debating societies a power of strong and ready speech ; an extra-ordinary capacity for hard and rapid work, the gift of a great imagination, a touch of genius on much that he thought and did—it was no wonder that to those of us who stood behind him nothing seemed beyond his reach. The usual sequence to such a career in Edinburgh at the time was Oxford, and he was tempted to go there; though, if no other reasons had been present, he believed too much in the sufficiency of the Scottish curriculum to have gone readily. But another claim was upon him. In early boyhood he had given himself to the Christian life, and ever since the hope of being a minister had grown upon him. From his letters this appears to have now become a passion—a passion which neither long study, nor the weariness of the ministry, nor the engagements for a time of another calling in life, nor ill-health, ever diminished in him. In his last illness he wrote much to one friend about the office of the preacher. ". . . I say most religiously, that if I had my ministry to begin again, I should try—not to study less—but to put myself, heart, soul, strength, AND MIND, more than ever I did into preaching. . . . I know—though I have had only five, and these five broken, years—the temptation to weary of the road. It is a strong temptation. But as the weight of the cross is heavy, so is the reward, both now and hereafter, heavy also. . . . I am now for four years a most interested and patient hearer of sermons, and the more I hear, the more I feel inclined to cry aloud : 'Covet to prophesy.' I have my own secret conflict going on, God knoweth, not since yesterday, upon this very point. Ever since I came into the world (36 years ago to-morrow) or rather came to know I was in it, I have had a drawing to one kind of work. Since I was called to the ministry that inclination has not left me. Whether God intends me by repeated intimations of bodily weakness to give myself to that other vocation, or—which I am as ready to accept, to surrender it and all effort beyond the daily burden—for a place in the ranks of those who do their little and suffer their little and so serve the grandest end—I do not know. I only speak of it to tell you how loud and imperative the οὐαὶ μοί εἰ μὴ εὐαγγελίζωμαι still sounds to me."

In 1875 Barbour entered the New College. In 1876 he took the summer session at the University of Tübingen, where Beck, Tholuck's real successor in Germany, was a great moral as well as intellectual influence ; and what Barbour got from Beck may be seen in an article he contributed on Beck's death to the *British and Foreign Evangelical Review.* His last session at the New College was full—perhaps, from what we now know, too full—of hard work. He won the medal of the Political Economy class at the

University, writing all the long fortnightly essays set by
Professor Hodgson ; he won the Cunningham Fellowship ;
he was a leader in the Theological Society ; he held classes
in continuation of Mr. Spiers's meetings for children ; he
was always helping some of us in our mission work ; and
in the spring he published a volume, " Jeroveam's Wife,
and other Poems." With the autumn came his marriage
to Charlotte Fowler ; their wedding journey through the
mission stations of South Africa occupied the winter and
spring of 1880. On this tour he came under another of
the great influences of his life—Dr. Stewart of Lovedale.
In December, 1880, he went as assistant to Mr. Fraser
of Brechin, and rejoiced, like all who have begun their
ministry there, in the field of work that is open, in the
sympathy that blesses it, and especially in the counsel
and example of his " bishop." In October, 1881, he was
ordained to the church of Cults, near Aberdeen. For
five years, broken by two absences in search of health, he
worked in Cults with all his own thoroughness and enthusiasm ; and then, in obedience to the doctors, he laid down
his charge, and went to reside at Bonskeid. There, and
afterwards on the neighbouring estate of Fincastle, which
he bought, he lived, while health and other work allowed
him, not only a good landlord and a most generous host,

but the pastor of all the countryside. Urged by his party to enter Parliament, he was true to the vision of his youth, and replied that highly as he honoured a political career, he held still higher the vocation of a Scottish minister. It is certain that deep in his heart lay the hope of return to some stated charge as soon as strength came back. Meantime he shepherded "his Glen"; preached occasionally in the little chapel and for friends ; prayed and laboured for China (he was Scottish chairman of both the Presbyterian China Mission and the Anti-Opium League); kept his friends in heart by his strong, faithful letters ; and dispensed his wealth with a liberality rare in one who came so young to great riches. He laboriously investigated every one of the numerous appeals which reached him from home and abroad; but it was like him to lay it on his friends to tell him of needy men and causes, who might be helped without having asked him themselves. Barbour also continued another characteristic work, apart from which it is impossible to remember him—his work on behalf of temperance. This had three sides. In his preaching he constantly strove to keep the public conscience informed and tender upon what he felt to be our greatest national sin. He also believed very strongly in total abstinence as a Christian's duty,—not simply for the purpose of testifying, but also as a practical means of lessening the evil—see his tract called: *Why are you not an Abstainer?* Most of all, however, he believed in personal help to the victims of drunken habits. His zeal never got the better of his love, as it does with so many teetotallers. But in the course of his short life he must have laid himself in the deepest compassion alongside a very large number of worsening or desperate cases, and by his own patience with them, and the faith which he infused into them that God's grace was all-sufficient, he became the means of lifting many of them back to sobriety and health.

In 1888 Robert Barbour undertook the duties of the Church History Chair in Glasgow during Dr. Lindsay's absence. What he achieved not only as a lecturer, but in his personal intercourse with the students, as a spiritual force, was told by their warm tribute when he left. But indeed he was always at his best with young men. The pressure of their life behind, along the well-known passages which he himself had traversed with so much hope and vigour, was a most cherished stimulus. In one of his letters he describes a visit to the New College, Edinburgh, in these inspiring words : " I enjoyed being in the old place. It was a good sight : though ' new faces, other names' rather made ' the days darken round one ' and the

years. I felt how it should make us spur on to feel the hot breath of others already behind. We are getting fast pushed into 'the foremost files of time.' I feel like Meriones when Eumelus came up on him in the chariot-race :

' πνοιῇ δ' Εὐμήλοιο μετάφρενον εὐρέε τ' ὤμω
θέρμετ'· ἐπ' αὐτῷ γὰρ κεφαλὰς καταθέντε πετέσθην ' :

or like Ajax with Odusseus after him,

' ἴχνια τύπτε πόδεσσι πάρος κόνιν ἀμφιχυθῆναι·
καὶ δ' ἄρα οἱ κεφαλῆς χε' αὐτμένα δῖος 'Οδυσσεύς.' "

A man who felt the reality and force of the life behind him in as vivid and sympathetic a way as that, could not fail to be a leader. In 1890 another call came to him to another Church History Chair in the United Presbyterian Hall. It was much on his heart to take this work, not only for its own sake, but as his effort towards the union of Scottish Presbyterianism, which was one of the great ideals of his life. God's will, however, was otherwise. An illness, which had been first apparent in the trouble he gave himself in the spring about a sad piece of pastoral work, reappeared with bad symptoms. The doctors put off his teaching till Christmas, then forbade it altogether. In February he was moved to the south of France, and later to Aix-les-Bains. Tended by his wife and some dear friends, he lingered there till the end of May, when he sank out of great weakness into sleep. He was very happy. "Thy rod and staff," he said, "especially Thy rod—they comfort me."

It is almost impossible to tell how much he was to his friends and the Church—how much he is, and will be always, to those whom he touched. There have been very few men of whom their friends had the right to hope such high things as we had of Robert Barbour when he entered public life. But that brilliant career at college, on which he rose to the full height of his great powers, is to-day not so bright in our memories as the subsequent years of declining health, quieter preaching, and the pastorate, painful and broken, at Cults, and in "the Glen." If he has failed to build any monument worthy of his intellectual strength, it is largely because he consecrated his powers to pastoral work; but so he has left us an heritage of character we could not have expected even from those earlier years. I shall always feel his purity the most. In college days we knew it as (in the words Milton uses of himself) "a certain reservedness of nature, an honest haughtiness and self-esteem, which kept me above those low descents of mind." But during his ministry it took an active and

forward shape, a yearning to do the right and win others
for the right, which is only possible with a heart and
imagination that cherish no secret sin. Not that Barbour's
was a nature which found it easy to be good; on the
contrary no man ever felt temptation more strongly, or
had a heavier sense of sin and of the awful difficulty of
doing the Father's will. One of his last messages for
young men was: "Teach them to pray for forgiveness." The
"woe is me if I preach not the gospel of Christ," which
throbs through so many of his later letters, flowed from
the same source. The Cross was to him in the most experimental way the centre of all religion, and the enthusiasm
at least of his later years was born at the foot of it. As
to his gift of oratory, he had a rich voice, and a command
both of language and information; he had a conscience
about form, and his style was always stately; but you
felt as he spoke that the power was rather due to his
intense spiritual earnestness. When some graceful speakers
are done, it is as if they had said, "I have spoken because
I can speak;" but with him, most graceful of all, it was
ever, "I believed, therefore I spake." As to his poetic
gift, I do not think that the poetry of his book comes
near the poetry of his life. He saw the ideal in everything; especially in common Christian work and in our

Scottish life, in both of which it is so difficult for ordinary hearts to rise above the commonplace. He saw the blush of the heart's blood through the meanest face, and had a way all his own of glorifying the humblest means of grace. There was one thing which I have felt, and many other men younger than himself have felt, on our first introduction to him. He not only treated us sympathetically, but spoke of our work, whether accomplished or lying still before us, in its ideal light; made us ashamed of our own low opinions of it, and sent us back to it with new conscience and new hope. He was a thorough Scot, with a love for his land, her history, and her songs, that was very beautiful. He knew Scottish life to the bone, Scottish history to the fountainhead; and it was delightful, in conversation about parish politics and every-day matters, to be surprised by his emphasis of the historical meaning and national virtue of some ordinary event or institution. His company was always stimulating. How can we ever forget his look as he swung down one of "the Glen" roads with his cheery shout of welcome. How can we ever forget his happy ways with children, his chivalry in debate, his courtesy with the poor and aged, his humour and occasional sarcasm, his singing of. a favourite Jacobite song: *Will ye no come back again?*

But the virtue and honour of his life lay in his faithfulness as a pastor. With the same devotion—which in boyish years overcame most unusual temptations to idleness and pride by toil as hard as if he had his bread to win—he sacrificed in later years even stronger ambitions to be the mere preacher and poet, and gave his strength to personal service and rescue work. He took extraordinary pains with individual cases. At Cults and in Aberdeen and by the Tummel, numbers bless God to-day for the truth and love with which his servant dealt with them, for his perseverance and generosity. He always had some poor soul anxiously on his heart before God, fulfilling thus the pastor's highest office of intercession; and I believe it was the way in which he prayed for all who were weak and in error in his flock and in his neighbourhood that kept him so free from gossip or the misuse of those strong gifts of scorn which were natural to his lofty spirit. It was sometimes easy to criticise an enthusiasm so utterly regardless of self as his was; but now that it is gone from us, it seems to his comrades to be one of their holiest duties to preserve its memory and example—to live more strenuously by that faith in Christ and His Cross which was its secret.

GEORGE ADAM SMITH.

PRINCIPAL RAINY IN FREE ST. GEORGE'S, EDINBURGH.

MANY of you know that I am here to-day in connection with a bereavement which has nearly touched your pastor's family, and which is very sorely felt by a wide circle of friends. And, I confess, the text came to me in connection with his life. Our friend had many advantages, providential and natural. He had gifts of mind that were exceptional ; his capacity for enthusiasm was high, and, unquestionably, the light of genius gave its irradiation to all his other qualities. But he found the condition and the consecration of all other worth in Christ ; and for many years trust in Christ, and obedience to Christ, was the central influence of his life. All right human ideals harmonize with a supreme regard to Christ, although not all Christians see this, and few make it fully apparent in their practice. But to our friend this agreement and subordination were revealed, and whatever struggles he may have had, the impression he made on others was always that of a man at harmony with himself, a man whose ruling maxims were

loftily Christian, and whose daily life embodied them with
rare force and clearness. We have known few, indeed, who
have been so conversant with noble and ideal views, and who
carried them with more vigour and simplicity down into the
detail of ordinary life. His Christian thinking and Christian
walking had the glow of poetry, and they had the loftiness
and fineness we associate with the idea of chivalry. In the
case of one so conversant with the ideal, and so open to
fine enthusiasms as he was, it is, perhaps, not unnatural to
ask one suspicious question—to ask, "Was all this genuine,
or was it, perhaps, as sometimes it is, only a vivid perception
of what life might be, a perception that dazzled and stirred
the mind without inspiring the character?" I have alluded
already to the answer to such a question which has practically
given the answer to any doubts like these. But I might find
another answer in another direction. When lofty ideals are
not simply and seriously reckoned with, but are played
with in a windy and unreal way, that is always accompanied
by self-inflation and self-adulation; but in our friend's case,
these elements of his thought and feeling led him to cherish
high thought, never of himself, but very often of other
people. When he saw in others what struck him as good,
then he was willing to believe his ideals were there realized,
and was ready to give love and honour and trust as freely

as he gave his money for work that appealed to him as right. There could hardly be a better proof of the purity and sincerity of the man. It is very well known how freely he gave money ; but it will be a great mistake to think that he allowed this to stand in the room of real and practical ministry to men as the servant of Christ. In the most practical ways, amid all the limitations of imperfect health, he was a helper and a succourer of many. There survive him many an impression on human hearts and histories which mere money could not make, and grateful memories which money could never buy. As a Christian scholar and thinker there was to be ascribed to him this— that he combined the points of view of various parties that are apt to misunderstand one another. He could sympathize with each, and also perceive the defectiveness or the bias of each ; of the more advanced as well as of the less. Indeed, he personally had taken possession of the points of view which are sometimes treated as irreconcilable ; they were together parts of his own experience. He could sympathize—he did sympathize—with the anxieties that would guard the interests of experimental, evangelical Christianity, as well as with the instincts that dictated intellectual independence and veracity. Men of various schools found it easy to trust him. It is a loss to us of

2 E

no common order that such a man should have been called away. Our hope had been that, in coming years, he would have become more and more a source of elevating and strengthening influence, especially among students and ministers. Gifts and qualities like those he united under the inspiration of a Christian life, so intense and so consistent, it might well be hoped would form a stimulating power, would kindle fresh enthusiasm, would help men to conceive higher standpoints of attainment and of service. It might have been so. He had great love for students, and delight in ministering to their mental and spiritual progress. But these thoughts of ours are broken off and baffled. I cannot suppose that, to those who had not opportunities of knowing him, any of the things that I can say, or that have been said, can carry a very definite image or make a very strong impression. They are but reminiscences, echoes faint and straggling, of a character and a life. But I may be allowed to say this at least, that it is long since any one has passed away who left on my mind, and many a mind besides, a stronger admonition as to the spirit in which life can be lived, and what it may attain to be even here, amid all the pedestrian necessities, the spiritual dimness, the inevitable temptations of this present world. It is something—it is much—to have lived so by the grace of God, that a man's memory shall always be a help and a stimulus to whatever is best, highest, least tainted, and least craven; to what is most believing, expectant, and aspiring in the soul, and always a rebuke to that which is lower and misleading. It is something—it is much—to have lived so that the remembrance of him shall always bring back to our minds the words of Paul:—" Finally, brethren, whatsoever things are true, whatsoever things are honest, whatsoever things are just, whatsoever things are pure, whatsoever things are lovely, whatsoever things are of good report; if there be any virtue, and if there be any praise, think on these things."

June 7, 1891.

AN IMPRESSION.

I HAD been three years at Edinburgh University before Robert Barbour came up from the Collegiate School. His reputation as a scholar, and a scholar who might turn out to be a genius, had preceded him. We older students were interested in the shy, pale-looking lad, of whom the younger men spoke with bated breath. I can recall his figure in those early days, as he moved quickly across the quadrangle, with an air of aloofness from the boisterousness of his class fellows, and with an intensity of grave expression which marked him out, to those who did not know him, as a youth too old for his years.

It was not till his last year at the University that I got to know him personally. By that time he had proved himself a brilliant classical scholar, and an accomplished essayist and poet. University men were proud of him, and asked each other whether another Browning had appeared amongst them. His work for the class of metaphysics—his essays and examination papers—passed through my hands as

University tutor. For months he lived and moved in the
atmosphere of the mysticism of German philosophy. One
of his essays, I remember, was as nearly unintelligible as a
piece of philosophical writing could be, but the darkness was
lit up by the luminous phrases, in the making of which he
was even then a master. I used to think in later days that
his studies in metaphysics were largely responsible for the
trouble it cost him to make his meaning perfectly clear to
the average hearer.

In his last years at the University he worked harder than
would have been good for a man of robust constitution.
Compared with the University, the New College was a place
of rest. And it was only there that men who knew him but
little discovered what an amount of riotous fun was possible
to the grave pallid prize-taker of the University. His jokes
at the dinner table came as a surprise to those whose chief
impression of him was derived from his intense speeches at
the Theological Society.

During one winter some eight or ten men—mostly New
College men—met in my rooms in St. Vincent Street to
read together Schleiermacher's *Christliche Glaube.* Most
of us had been students of philosophy, and were feeling
about for a theology which could be harmonized with our
philosophy. Schleiermacher's view of theology as the

scientific exposition of the Christian consciousness attracted us. Those Sunday afternoon readings were fruitful in discussion. I remember how Barbour used to put in a plea on behalf of traditional views which found few supporters. It was indeed one of the characteristic features of his New College life that he was far less affected by the newer fashions in theology than most of his contemporaries. His friends were amongst men of the newer school, but his sympathies were with the older views. To the end this continued to be his position, and to this may partly be attributed the confidence with which he was regarded by men of opposite schools of theological thinking.

At college, as in later life, he was less interested in the problems of theology than in the problems of the religious life. And one of the secrets of his influence over his college friends was the glow of spiritual fervour with which he recalled us to the practical interests involved in theological problems. He might make excursions into speculative regions, but it was not there he found himself at home. The evangelistic meeting was more congenial to him than the debating society.

I have a vivid recollection of one of his sermons—a sermon on the Prodigal Son—preached in my old church in Small's Wynd. It was just beautiful talk. With that strong, sweet voice of his, he described the father's welcome of his son with a pathos which forced tears from my eyes. The preacher unveiled for his hearers the very heart of the Godhead. That sermon taught me what preaching might be.

On the Sunday after his death I could not resist speaking of him to my congregation in Dundee. The words found their way into print, and I am glad to have the opportunity of recalling them here :—

" Many hopes were centred in Robert Barbour. He was a marked man at college—easily the first student of his time, and with the stamp of genius upon his work. Culture, eloquence, poetry, philosophy—these were the things University men associated with the name of Robert Barbour. But amid all the triumphs of his college days, and all his prospects of distinction, to those who knew the inner life of the reserved, contemplative student, what stood out most prominently was the consecration of his life to Christ, and to Christ's causes in the world. He was strongly urged to go to Oxford as the proper sphere for gifts like his. But he had a higher ambition—to do the work of a minister of Christ in the country he loved as a Christian patriot. He began his professional work as a country minister in Aberdeenshire. His influence and that of his wife were like the

dew of heaven upon the parish. He was the most cultured
man I have met in any of the Scottish churches, but all
that culture he laid upon the altar for his little congregation. The fidelity of his ministry was an inspiration to
many a minister in Aberdeenshire and beyond. His
sympathy with the individual members of his congregation
reminded one of the tenderness of the Apostle Paul. It
was a great wrench when he was compelled by illness to
tear himself away from his loved work.

"In the years that followed, when his health was partially
restored, he was fast growing to be one of the most in-
fluential Scotchmen of his day. The range of his interests
was extraordinarily wide. He was as interested in all the
affairs of the Scottish churches as if he had been an eccle-
siastical leader. He was as interested in politics as if he had
been a professional politician. He was as interested in the
administrative work of the county of Perth as if he had been
nothing but a county gentleman. He was an ardent advo-
cate of temperance reform, and threw his whole heart into
the movement for the suppression of the opium traffic in
India. He was in touch with foreign missions all over the
world, and himself paid the salaries of several missionaries.
He was as interested in literature and art as if he had been
a quiet Oxford scholar, and he was as interested in all

questions which affected the welfare of his fellow-men as if he had devoted his life to works of philanthropy. In Robert Barbour the Church of Christ had one of her noblest workers, and Scotland one of her ablest and most patriotic sons.

"Mr. Barbour's life was rich in outward activities, but what made him so lovable in the eyes of a singularly large circle of attached friends was the charm of his character. In his company one felt that a bit of the upper world had been let down at one's side. There was a spiritual glow about him which kindled the duller natures of his friends. He lived in an atmosphere of aspiration. He was baptised with fire. One notable feature in his character was the thoughtfulness of his kindness. He could not be happy unless he was doing kind things. It was more blessed for him to give than to receive. In the spending of his ample means it was the law of the kingdom of Christ he obeyed. If men of wealth followed his example in discharging the responsibilities of wealth, the social question would be in a fair way of solution.

"A man so richly gifted in head and heart is a great gift of God to the Church and to the nation. As it seems to our imperfect understanding of God's ways, the gift has been withdrawn all too soon. It was men like him we

needed in these days, and he has been taken from us just
when it was beginning to be known how great a gift God
had given to our country.   But he has left to young
Scotchmen and to young ministers a memory that is rich
in inspiration.

D. M. Ross.

FROM A LETTER.

FEW men have had such a chorus of praise as was given to Robert Barbour. The praise was deserved. Yet I am not sure that it was the best that could be said, and I am quite sure it was not what he would have liked. You will remember, none of us can forget, the day we buried him. It was fit and right to sing that psalm, for he would have joined in it, and the words he would have sung with deepest meaning are, "My soul He doth restore again." My chief impression of Robert Barbour is the change effected in him. I felt more and more in these later years that he had attained; but not without effort, agony, and bloody sweat. There was that crooked which God had to make straight. Every one knows how he strove to gain, and gained, simplicity and directness of speech, and how much need there was. In the same way he had, with pains, endeavoured to be business-like. As Blackie said, he was "a mixture of poetry and piety," and it was only conscientious effort which made him diligent in business. It was the same with the deeper, more bitter, more sacred, and happier things, of which one may not speak. But one Sunday, as we went home from Blair Athole, and were speaking of the sermon in which mention was made of those who stand at the door of the kingdom, turning the handle, but not entering, I remember the humility and sincerity with which he spoke of himself. "Without were fightings: within were fears." But in due time, in God's good time, he did arrive.

D. M.

A MEMORY.

OLD letters are so pathetic, and often so painful, that one rarely has courage to open them; but amongst a packet of these I have found a letter written from Bonskeid, August 8, 1874.

It was Sunday evening, and we had just returned from the chapel in the glen, where we had been listening to a sermon from Robert Barbour. The letter says :—

"We had a marvellous sermon, such a one as I have scarcely ever heard before, and it was strange and wonderful to see such a boy (for he cannot be more than 20) carrying his own father and mother, and their own people, so entirely out of themselves. The sermon was from the 8th verse, iii. Ephesians, and instead of the unsearchable riches of Christ, the more literal rendering of the word, untrackable, was given. The illustrations were taken from the mountains and the valleys round us."

Even now I can recall, as it were but yesterday, the hush and stillness of that lovely Sabbath evening, and the rapt attention of the little congregation who listened to this boy preacher, so entirely absorbed in his subject as to seem almost unconscious of our presence.

The sermon was more poetical than theological, and it closed with a quotation from *Aurora Leigh*, but it was the reality and fire of the preacher that impressed me so much. Probably there was a something crude and undefined about that early sermon, because, as far as I can remember, his mind was more full of the world of books, from which he was then, and had been, absorbing so much, than of the work he was to do later. When we met once again, five years afterwards, the thoughts and yearnings of those young days had crystallized into the definite purpose of a life-time. We made acquaintance first over our mutual liking for Matthew Arnold's " Rugby Chapel," and in recalling those days I remember a description of Erskine of Linlathen I have read : " There is a sort of high-wrought spirituality about him, without a shadow of affectation or singularity ; he never dwells for a moment on mere decencies or common-places, but proceeds naturally, and at once, to matters of thought and feeling."

Even at meal times he produced books like " Samuel Rutherford's Writings " from under the table, and instead of the prelude of conventional remarks, usual at such times, he tumbled headlong into the character of Cromwell, or the right translation of a Greek word, or the poetry of Clough. There was much of the boy about his unconventionality then, and his absorption in the world of thought and poetry in which he was living. It is strange, perhaps, to say it, but in looking back I seem to feel that one of the strongest influences Robert Barbour appeared to reflect, was that of the world of nature round him.

The inspiration of that beautiful world must have become a part of his life, for my remembrance of the eloquent speech he made on his wedding day in Wiltshire is that it was like "flashing lights" over the purple mountains and the Scottish moors.

One other point I must mention. A conversation about preserving deer revealed to me that even in those days Robert Barbour was a genuine Liberal. This practical side of his character surprised me a good deal at the time, as it seemed a 'side-light' not altogether in harmony with the intense absorption in more abstract things. It struck me also from the unselfishness it betrayed, because it is not very often that those whose lives have fallen to them in such 'pleasant places' *really* desire great changes that can only benefit the less fortunate.

The faculty of imaginative sympathy is a rare one, and

those who knew Robert Barbour in riper years say that it was one of his special gifts.

My one far-off memory of him is like the meeting with a sign-post directing the road along the difficult journey of life. Even then the sign-post pointed upward, towards the better day of which he told us in the lines he quoted at the end of his sermon that bright August Sabbath :—

> " He turned instinctively, where faint and far,
> Along the tingling desert of the sky,
> Beyond the circle of the conscious hills
> Were laid in jasper stone as clear as glass,
> The first foundations of that new, near day,
> Which should be builded out of heaven to God."

S. S.

SPOKEN IN THE CHAPEL IN THE GLEN THE
SUNDAY AFTER THE FUNERAL. (JUNE 7TH,
1891.)

(From the Notes of a hearer.)

THIS is not an occasion on which one can say much.
One cannot trust oneself to say much. Mrs. Barbour
telegraphed to you from France the text that follows the
hymn upon our card. Let me read it to you,—it shall be
our text to-night. ' Except a corn of wheat fall into the
ground and die, it abideth alone ; but if it die it bringeth
forth much fruit.'

A man's life is but a corn of wheat. A corn of wheat
is a very little thing, almost a common thing. There are
millions of them in our own little country-side. Some of
them have more in them than others have, but after all
they are only corns of wheat and what comes of them
depends less on what is in them, than on what they immerse themselves in and spend themselves in doing. One
of you boys might put one of these corns in your vest

2 F

pocket and carry it about for years; it would never be anything else, it would never help to nourish any one. Put it in your garden and a stalk will grow up bearing 30, 40, or 100 grains by next autumn. Put these in the garden and some thousands more will grow from them. Go on sowing these, and in twenty years all the carts in Perthshire would not contain a fraction of them. Where has it all come from? It was not in the corn. It was in God's earth, God's air, God's rain, God's sunshine. And all a *man* has to do is to put himself in proper conditions, to immerse himself in God, and he will bring forth much fruit.

The worst thing that can happen to anybody is to live alone. It's a very easy thing to shut oneself in, to fence oneself round, to become silent and unapproachable. You ask at a house in the village about a neighbour, and the woman tells you with an air of pride that she has no dealings with her neighbours; she does not know them. That woman is outside life, has no influence on the little world of her district, is not bringing forth fruit. The condition of bringing forth fruit is very serious. It is that we must die. Unless we die we abide alone. That is a law of nature. Look at the blossom on the trees. Soon you will see it all lying on the ground. Except the blossom fall and die the tree will bear no fruit. It is the same everywhere. Death is the preliminary to life. That is not really death : it is only a stage in life : it is all a birth—the birth into a larger and fuller life. All life is sustained by death. The dinner table at which we sat down to-day was full of dead things, dead corn in the bread, dead vegetables, dead animals. We are clothed with the dead—dead sheep, dead silk worm, dead cotton plant. All the things we handle and work with are the product of sacrifice. The miner goes down into the bowels of the earth and brings out coal and iron and gold and silver. These all are gained at the cost of health and industry and life. We have no happiness, no comfort, no life, unless some one or some thing has died. So we are surrounded by death.

Much more is all this true of a human life. To do any good it must die. When I say "must die," I do not mean that the body must die. That is the mere case or husk. The life inside must be slowly laid down for others before we can bring forth fruit. Now I need not tell you that our friend—more perhaps than any one else we knew —laid down his life for others. He even laid down his bodily life.

Perhaps you would like me to tell you first of his last

2 F 2

months; but there is very little to tell. You know how he went to Edinburgh to prepare for a course of lectures in winter; how the doctors told him not to go out; how his illness was at first stationary; then showed, in the chest, symptoms of the disease that carried him away; how before the cold winds of March came, the doctors told him that the only chance to prolong his life was to find summer in a strange country. You wondered, I daresay, why he went away from you. It was his only chance. If he had stayed at home he would have died sooner. The science of to-day tells us that the only treatment for trouble like this is to go where the air is warm and mild and dry. Within thirty-nine hours of where we are, is a country where there is summer in March. Even when I went there in April the summer was almost over. The roses were past and the geraniums fading. You will not grudge his being among strangers when you remember that he was able for a time to drive by the blue Mediterranean and enjoy the beautiful sunshine in that lovely invalid's land. But he grew weaker and weaker, and by the end of April when I got there he was no longer able to go out.

Then it grew too hot in Mentone, and the doctors said he must go to the east of France where he would get

strength, if strength was to be given. He was taken in a
saloon carriage to Aix-les-Bains, almost under the shadow
of the highest hill of Europe, Mont Blanc. The boys know
where that mountain is. There was a hill behind the hotel
from which you could see the eternal snow of Mont Blanc.
There he felt more comfortable for a time. Many friends
came to see him. Dr. Simpson and his wife were with
him at Mentone ; Dr. Barbour was with him there and
again at Aix. He was surrounded with every comfort.
God spared him a great deal of suffering. He had some
cough and a great deal of weakness, but I may say he
suffered little compared with what many do. If you ask
me, " Was his mind clear ?" I should say "Yes." But his
body was too weak to allow his mind to act. You might
say that before he left Mentone the curtain had dropped
on the active interests of his life. If you spoke to him,
he was able to talk about anything, but did not take the
initiative. God was gradually withdrawing him from the
things in which he used to take so keen an interest. He
was too weak to think or feel deeply, and none of us liked
to trouble him much. The state of weakness went on,
getting extreme. On Tuesday of last week we were summoned at two in the morning, thinking the end had come.
The company gathered round, his wife, Dr. and Mrs. Whyte,

Dr. Webster and the nurse, expecting every breath to be the last. But he rallied and was almost himself during the day. Early next morning at five he had another attack. It was when coming out of this that his wife, holding his hand, repeated the xxiii. Psalm. When she came to "Yea though I walk through the valley of the shadow of death," he said "Again," until she had repeated it many times. Then she went on to the assurance "Thy rod and Thy staff they comfort me,"—"Especially Thy rod," he whispered.

He did not speak much about his end. Perhaps he was too weak to think about it. One thing I have learned most clearly from his illness is how impossible it is for a man to make his peace with God on a dying bed. You will die suddenly as far as religion is concerned. As far as religion is concerned, ninety out of a hundred die suddenly. He was lying ill for weeks, but the body always asserted itself: only at intervals we saw into the sanctuary of his inner life. When I came in on that morning of which I have just spoken—his last on earth—he looked up and said "Near Heaven,"—these, and when he spoke the words about Psalm xxiii., were the only times he said anything to me on the subject. At night, at a quarter to ten we were summoned. It was again a weak turn—the last. For five minutes a struggle with the king of terrors, for not more than one minute painful. And then the end.

Next night the funeral began. When all was ready, men came at midnight to carry him from the sleeping hotel to the little French Protestant chapel. I shall never forget that scene. Day was just breaking when the coffin was laid there covered with flowers. Then a nightingale began to sing. It was like God sending a choir. There is no bird that sings so like an angel. Probably none of you have ever heard the nightingale sing. Four or five days before he told me that the nurse had awakened him to hear one: "It was not like a bird at all," he said, "it was like a flute or a bell, great bubbles of music going up to Heaven." What a poet our friend was! He talked as easily that way as you and I talk about the weather. Genius was in his blood.

Next day we travelled through France and the next night he lay on the deck of the Channel steamer by moonlight. Another Englishman had died at the same time and the two coffins lay on the deck side by side. So we came to London and you know the rest; how kind friends received him at Killiecrankie, the service in the house. . . .

What brought that crowd there? The merchant from London, the principals of two colleges, professors, lawyers, doctors and ministers by the dozen, proprietors, servants, apprentices, schoolboys, the great and the small,—why had they all come? Because he was rich? People do not go sixty miles to the funeral of a man because he is rich. Because they had been invited? Many came unasked. Because he was famous? His name was not much known beyond his native land. What brought them? It was because he was like his Master. It was because he went about doing good. It was because he dropped kind actions and gentle words into the lives of others. There were none of you who did not feel that you had in him a friend. You all knew for yourself, at first hand, the marvellous beauty of his character—its childlikeness, its unassumingness, meekness, courtesy, forbearingness, considerateness, gentleness, the trouble he took about small things. You knew there was not anything he would not have done for any one in this district. This is what is meant by falling into the ground and dying. It is not the being laid in the West Wood. It is the taking of long walks at night to help this and that one, and spending the time in your houses which might have been spent on himself.

He was a rich man during the last four years. Did he spend his money on himself? He died to it. It is a thousand times harder for a rich man to lay down his life and die for others than it is for a poor man. The danger of riches is that they make a man proud and worldly and fill his life with engrossing cares. These things never touched him. There was no class of men that Christ pitied more than the rich, because He knew how they were tempted. Mr. Barbour had so entirely overcome the temptation that we don't even think of him in connection with it.

Then there were his accomplishments, his learning for example. He was out of sight the ablest man of his time at college. None of his companions came within miles of him, for he had what none of them had, the sacred fire of genius. His accomplishments were endless. He was an orator. Physically few had a more musical voice than he had. You have heard him delivering his message. You know how he shot up at once into the higher air. It was easy for him to see into things above, while we have to drag our limbs with effort along the common earth.

Then you remember the accomplishments of music, of literature, of poetry,—though even poetry never came to him as a temptation. What is the poet's temptation? To be a dreamer. He was no dreamer, he was a worker. He walked these roads more than his study, he wrote on men's lives more than he ever wrote on paper.

We could least of all afford to lose him, because the quality of his life was such that the slightest touch of it influenced others. None who were with him for ever so short a time can forget the impression of saintliness, gentleness, loving-kindness, humbleness, which he made upon them. Why do I say these things to you who were his best friends? Partly to help your recollection, and partly because we see least clearly those who live nearest to us. Sometimes we do not see the beauty of a life which is lived very near our own till God proves it by taking it from us. Partly because his life was so natural and perfect that you had to look hard at it to characterise it. God gave him grace to complete his character from year to year and from day to day, as he gave up his own time and ease and means, and lavished them upon others. The hard thing is for us to take trouble, to put ourselves about, to go out when we are bodily weak, and do good to some one at personal discomfort. To do that is to be like Christ. Tried by that standard these glens testify that his life bore fruit. Where is the fruit? None can answer. Part of it is only yet in blade, for you remember it grows up "first the blade, then the ear, then the full corn in the ear." Partly because it will be seen in many lands, in thousands of homes and after many generations. Some has been sown in China, and the fruit will be found there. Some in India, and the fruit will be found there. Some in Africa, where he spoke so often to the natives. Some in America and Canada, and that will have to come up. And he has had part in all the philanthropic movements of the time. In some of them he was a leader, and that has to come up. Don't imagine that his life is at an end. His body is at an end, but all the potency of his life has yet to manifest itself.

Must I not ask myself and you, can we get no inspiration from these words? His voice we shall not hear again, but through that text he speaks to us. Maybe he has sown seeds in the hearts of some of you. Has that been watered and encouraged to grow? Was there any advice he gave you—suggestion I should say, for he was too modest to give advice—any pure impulse to perpetuate? Let us hear through him the voice of Him who was his inspiration. We may not be able to make much of it for a while, but let us begin and try. Mr. Barbour had to struggle a great deal for his goodness. I know privately that it was at the bayonet's point that he got some of his virtues and it is at the bayonet point that we must get some of ours. Let each brace himself to the task.

"Life is a leaf of paper white
Whereon each one of us may write
His word or two, and then comes night.
Greatly begin! Though thou hast time
But for a line, be that sublime,
Not failure, but low aim, is crime."

EXTRACT FROM LETTER, —— S. TO —— S.

"WE do need, as you say, Robert's enthusiasm, and do you
know, I think we'll have it more than if he had lived. There
is this feeling over us all, that we must take up the fire he
is not here to carry. It is so near us to say of the living,
'Ah! so and so is enthusiastic; we don't need to be,' and
to criticise him, till we are driven to the opposite extreme
of temper. But the dead man's sword lies without a hand,
and it *must not be left to lie;* his temper must be continued.
As he is not here to show it let us take it up. Oh! just
because Robert is gone, we must be more enthusiastic."

GLASGOW: PRINTED AT THE UNIVERSITY PRESS BY ROBERT MACLEHOSE.

www.ingramcontent.com/pod-product-compliance
Lightning Source LLC
Chambersburg PA
CBHW021842290326
41932CB00064B/361